The Complete Ninja Foodi Digital Air Fryer Oven Cookbook 2022

1000

Easy and Affordable Recipes for Smart
People to Master Your
Ninja Foodi Digital Oven

Michelle Skylar

1kg brisket — sear
PC 250 ml beef stock for 1 hr 20 min
AF 10 mins

CONTENTS

Snacks & Appetizer Recipes..31

Red Meat Recipes..43

Beef, Pork & Lamb Recipes..60

Poultry Recipes...65

Fish & Seafood Recipes

Vegetables & Sides Recipes

Dessert Recipes..121

INDEX...138

Introduction

Cooking food is becoming much easier with this digital air fryer oven. For roasting, baking, and air frying lovers, the Ninja Foodi digital air fryer oven is the ultimate oven to have. The Ninja Foodi Digital Air Fryer Oven is revolutionizing healthy cooking, and it is proved to be a beneficial device for anyone using it. You can use this oven for many purposes, such as cooking with the convenience and functionality of a air fryer, heating as a frying pan, and cooking like a convection oven.

The LCD screen on the air fryer oven makes it easy for both professional and novice chefs to use by displaying timers and instructions. Another excellent advantage is that it cooks food evenly thanks to its Digital Crisp Control Technology, which helps you precisely cook all types of food. The oven is ideal for air frying, roasting, baking, and broiling.

With each passing day and the advancement in innovation, there are many alternatives for an individual to appreciate food. Ninja Foodi Air Fryer Oven is perhaps the main machine for making an assortment of food. It reduces the amount of oil used, allowing people to enjoy healthier and lower-fat foods. For me, I really don't like to use too much oil when cooking. One of the principal benefits of the digital air fryer oven is that it readies the food in significantly less time, which means I don't need to wait too long to eat what I want when I'm hungry.

Cooking with the Ninja Foodi Air Fryer Oven

The Functions of the Ninja Foodi Air Fry Oven

The primary function of the Ninja Foodi Air Fry Oven is clear from its name that is air frying. Furthermore, it can also perform other cooking functions like air roasting, dehydrating, toasting, keeping the food warm, baking, and air broiling. Considering the smaller size of the Ninja Foodi Air Fry Oven, an entire chicken cannot be put inside the device. Overall, the device is very promising in its overall performance parameters. Moreover, the food cooked with the Ninja Foodi Air Fry Oven is very nutritious, with the perfect aroma and a delicious taste. The overall working of the functions of the Ninja Foodi Air Fry Oven is as follows:

1. Air Frying

The Ninja Foodi Air Fry Oven is capable of air frying 4 pounds of food at a time. The air frying mechanism of the Ninja Foodi Air Fry Oven is very capable and outstanding, which evenly air fries your food. It provides ultimate perfect crispiness to your food, and the taste is without a doubt outstanding from any traditionally air fried food.

2. Toasting

Toasting your bread with the Ninja Foodi Air Fry Oven is a perfect combo. You can put in 9 slices of the regular bread available in the markets and without any squishing involved at all. The toasting function of the Ninja Foodi Air Fry Oven is very efficient and toasts the bread evenly, giving your bread the ultimate brownness and texture. You can also go for toasting bagels by using the bagel settings in the Ninja Foodi Air Fry Oven. Moreover, the Ninja Foodi Air Fry Oven offers broth high and medium toasting settings, which can be used at your discretion.

3. Air Roasting

The Ninja Foodi Air Fry Oven leaves behind all the air roasting appliances launched by the Ninja Foodi. The Ninja Foodi Air Fry Oven is the perfect companion for your sheet pan dinner that includes veggies, spices, steaks or seafood, chicken, etc. The overall air roasting time of the Ninja Foodi Air Fry Oven is very. It can air roast approximately 3 pounds of ingredients in around 22 minutes precisely, which serves you a delicious sheet pan dinner of 4 servings. Without a doubt, the Ninja Foodi Air Fry Oven is the master in air roasting.

4. Air Baking

You can easily bake a cake or muffin in a considerably shallow pan in the Ninja Foodi Air Fry Oven. Moreover, smaller items like cookies can also be baled in the Ninja Foodi Air Fry Oven in a sheet pan. However, you certainly cannot pack an entire pan or the Bundt pan in the Ninja Foodi Air Fry Oven. The baking function of the Ninja Foodi Air Fry Oven is considerably better than the traditional baking appliances.

5. Air Broiling

The air broiling time of the Ninja Foodi Air Fry Oven is also considerably lesser. The average time to air broil a chicken breast in the Ninja Foodi Air Fry Oven is approximately 20 minutes. The steaks prepared with the Ninja Foodi Air Fry Oven will have the perfect texture and crisp, matching the quality of any regular air broiler. The Ninja Foodi Air Fry Oven provides you with the finest searing and an unmatched taste and aroma.

6. Dehydrating

The dehydrating function of the Ninja Foodi Air Fry Oven is also very remarkable. The device is considerably noiseless when performing the dehydration function. Furthermore, it perfectly dehydrates your food. The overall average time taken by the Ninja Foodi Air Fry Oven to properly dehydrate your food is around 10 hours. The mechanism of dehydration is directly related to the total time of dehydration. The more time you give, the more dehydrated your food will be.

7. Keep Warm

One of the most promising functions of the Ninja Foodi Air Fry Oven that it keeps your food on food-safe temperature for a considerably longer time. It is very beneficial as you don't have to reheat your food at all. The food is thoroughly preserved and perfectly warm with this function of the Ninja Foodi Air Fry Oven.

How to Operate the Ninja Foodi Air Fryer Oven

For the Air Fry, Air Roast, Air Broil, and Bake Functions:

- To start the cooking process, use the dial to select the function you want. The default time and temperature setting will display. The oven will also remember your last time and temperature that was used—great for favorite recipes so you don't have to reset every time.

- To adjust the time, press the TIME/SLICE button and use the dial to change it. Press the TIME/SLICE button again to set the time.

- To set the temperature, press the TEMP/DARKNESS button and turn the dial to your recipe's temperature. Press the TEMP/DARKNESS button again to set the temperature.

- Place your food on the sheet pan or in the Air Fry basket and slide the pan or basket in the oven. Press START/PAUSE to begin cooking.

For the Toast or Bagel Functions:

- To start the toasting process, use the dial to select the function you want. The default number of slices and darkness level will display, and the oven will remember your most recently used settings for maximum efficiency in the morning.

- Place your bread or bagels, cut-side up, on the rack. (You can also do this after setting the slices and darkness level.)

- To adjust the number of slices, press the TIME/SLICE button and use the dial to change it. Press the TIME/SLICE button again to set the number of slices.

- To adjust how dark you want your toast or bagels, press the TEMP/DARKNESS button and turn the dial to your desired level. Press the TEMP/DARKNESS button again to set the level.

- Press START/PAUSE to begin toasting.

Cooking Tips and Tricks

1. When using the bagel feature, organize bagels cut-side looking up on the wire rack.
2. Halfway through cooking, either flip elements for crispier outcomes or turn the air fryer container 180 degrees.
3. When utilizing a marinade that contains honey, sugar, and different other options, brush the marinade blend onto meat partially through cooking time to avoid burning.
4. When dehydrating and air frying, organize food in a layer to guarantee proper cooking and crispier impact.
5. Food cooks faster when using the Air Roast function. Therefore, if you are utilizing the customary oven plans, bring down the cooking time and temperature.
6. Unlike other air fryer ovens, the unit preheats rapidly, ensuring that you have arranged all fixings and prepared to cook before preheating the Ninja Foodi Air Fry Oven. When you had preheated the oven, the clock begins checking down. Essentially turn the dial to add additional time.

Go-To Tools and Accessories

Another advantage to cooking with the Ninja Foodi Air Fry Oven is that you won't need a cabinet full of equipment. For most of the recipes, you'll only need the sheet pan once you start cooking. A couple of the recipes use the Air Fry basket, and some of the Staples recipes use a baking pan. But that's it. No pots and pans, no skillets. You may want to order a second sheet pan from Ninja so you'll have a backup, but that's optional.

1. Timer: I find that an extra timer is really helpful for those times when I have to check a dish halfway through to turn or toss ingredients. That way, I can set the Ninja Foodi Air Fry Oven for the total time and not have to reset it.
2. Meat thermometer: When you start using a new appliance, you may find that your usual recipes don't cook at the same rate. It's best to be safe when it comes to cooking chicken thighs or pork chops and check their internal temperature during cooking.
3. Oil mister/sprayer: I call for cooking oil spray in some recipes, and while you can use a store-bought spray, I know that some cooks prefer to use their own oil in a spray bottle.
4. Prep tools: For prep, you'll need a cutting board and knives, and a few bowls—small ones for sauces, larger ones for mixing ingredients. Other necessary tools include whisks and spoons for stirring and spatulas and tongs for moving food around. Of course, you'll need sturdy, thick pot holders or oven mitts for getting the hot sheet pan out of the oven.

Safety Tips

To ensure you are safe while cooking and the oven will keep going long, here are some significant hints you need to consider.

1.   Material Paper and Foil

Sometimes cooking can make everything messy, especially when using sauces. Maybe everything will fall on the oven or stick to the crumb tray. It is smarter to line your air fryer basket or sheet pan with foil or material for simple eliminating once the dish is cooked. Notwithstanding, ensure that what you put on top is adequately substantial to hold down the paper and not fly around when the hot air begins to course.

2.   Leave Enough Space Around the Ninja Foodi Air Fry Oven

Since hot air needs to circle to keep food fresh, you should settle your oven on a level surface while cooking. So don't push your oven against the divider while cooking. It will keep hot air from circling appropriately and may rather bounce back on you while you are working the oven.

3.   Remember Preheating

The Ninja Foodi Air Fry Oven requires just 60 seconds to preheat. So please don't skip it. The oven needs to have its appropriate warmth temperature before you push your food in there if you need to have its ideal advantage of cooking. Having the right wind stream and temperature level will guarantee that your food will have its fresh impact. Throwing your dish into the oven without preheating may not give you the ideal outcome you need.

4.   Try Not to Overload

You might need to cook your food quickly, yet if you need your food to come out flavorful and at its best appearance, don't attempt to lose your air fryer oven by overloading. Since the Ninja Air Fry Oven works by circling hot air, leaving no sufficient room for air to course won't leave you with the ideal impact on your cooking. An extraordinary cook shows restraint.

Breakfast Recipes

Chicken Egg Muffins

Servings: 12
Cooking Time: 15 Minutes
Ingredients:
- 10 eggs
- 1 tbsp parsley, chopped
- 1/2 tsp Italian seasoning
- 1 cup cooked chicken, chopped
- 1/4 tsp garlic powder
- Pepper
- Salt

Directions:
1. Place rack in the bottom position and close door. Select bake mode set the temperature to 400°F and set the timer to 15 minutes. Press the setting dial to preheat.
2. In a large bowl, whisk eggs with garlic powder, Italian seasoning, parsley, pepper, and salt.
3. Add remaining ingredients and stir well.
4. Pour egg mixture into the greased muffin pan.
5. Once the unit is preheated, open the door, and place the muffin pan onto the center of the rack, and close the door.
6. Serve and enjoy.

Banana Bread

Servings: 6
Cooking Time: 25 Minutes.
Ingredients:
- 4 medium bananas, peeled and sliced
- ¼ cup plain Greek yogurt
- 2 large eggs
- ½ ounce vanilla extract
- 10 ounces all-purpose flour
- ¾ cup sugar
- 3 ounces oat flour
- 1 teaspoon baking powder
- 1 teaspoon baking soda
- ¾ teaspoon kosher salt
- ¾ teaspoon ground cinnamon
- ½ teaspoon ground cloves
- ¼ teaspoon ground nutmeg
- ¾ cup coconut oil
- 1 cup toasted pecan

Directions:
1. Layer a 10.5-inch-by-5.5-inch loaf pan with a parchment sheet and keep it aside.
2. Mash the banana in a suitable bowl and add eggs, vanilla, and Greek yogurt, then mix well.
3. Cover this banana yogurt mixture and leave it for 30 minutes.
4. Meanwhile, mix cinnamon, flour, sugar, baking powder, oat flour, salt, baking soda, coconut oil, cloves, and nutmeg in a mixer.

5. Now slowly add banana mash mixture to the flour and continue mixing until smooth.
6. Fold in nuts and mix gently until evenly incorporated.
7. Spread this banana-nut batter in the prepared loaf pan.
8. Transfer the loaf pan on wire rack in Ninja Foodi Digital Air Fryer Oven and close the door.
9. Select "Bake" mode by rotating the dial.
10. Press the TIME/SLICES button and change the value to 25 minutes.
11. Press the TEMP/SHADE button and change the value to 350°F.
12. Press Start/Stop to begin cooking.
13. Slice and serve.

Cloud Eggs

Servings: 2
Cooking Time: 7 Minutes
Ingredients:
- 2 eggs, whites and yolks separated
- Pinch of salt
- Pinch of freshly ground black pepper

Directions:
1. In a bowl, add the egg white, salt, and black pepper and beat until stiff peaks form.
2. Line the SearPlate with parchment paper.
3. Carefully, make a pocket in the center of each egg white circle.
4. Press AIR OVEN MODE button of Ninja Foodi Digital Air Fryer Oven and turn the dial to select the "Broil" mode.
5. Press TIME/SLICES button and again turn the dial to set the cooking time to 7 minutes.
6. Press TEMP/SHADE button and again turn the dial to set low. To set the temperature, press the TEMP/SHADE button again.
7. When the unit beeps to show that it is preheated, open the oven door and insert the SearPlate in the oven.
8. Place 1 egg yolk into each egg white pocket after 5 minutes of cooking.
9. Press "Start/Stop" button to start.
10. When cooking time is completed, open the oven door and serve.

Basic Breakfast Bread

Servings: 4
Cooking Time: 15 Minutes
Ingredients:
- ⅞ cup whole-wheat flour
- ⅞ cup plain flour
- 1 ¾ ounces pumpkin seeds
- 1 teaspoon salt
- ½ of sachet instant yeast
- ½-1 cup lukewarm water

Directions:

1. In a bowl, mix the flours, pumpkin seeds, salt, and yeast and mix well.
2. Slowly, add the desired amount of water and mix until a soft dough ball forms. With your hands, knead the dough until smooth and elastic.
3. Place the dough ball into a bowl. With plastic wrap, cover the bowl and set it aside in a warm place for 30 minutes or until doubled in size.
4. Press the START/PAUSE button and turn on your Ninja Foodi Digital Air Fryer Oven and set temperatures to 350 °F for 18 minutes on the "AIR FRY" function.
5. Press the "START/PAUSE" button to start. Place the dough ball in a greased cake pan and brush the top of the dough with water.
6. When the unit beeps to show that it is preheated, open the door. Place the cake pan into the Air Crisp Basket and insert it in the oven.
7. When cooking time is completed, open the door and place the pan onto a wire rack for about 10-15 minutes.
8. Carefully invert the bread onto the wire rack to cool completely cool before slicing.
9. Cut the bread into desired-sized slices and serve.

Baked Breakfast Quiche

Servings: 6
Cooking Time: 55 Minutes
Ingredients:
- 8 eggs
- 1 cup sour cream
- 3/4 tbsp ranch seasoning
- 1 1/2 cups cheddar cheese, shredded
- 1 lb ground Italian sausage
- Pepper
- Salt

Directions:
1. Brown the ground sausage in a pan over medium heat. Drain well and set aside.
2. In a large bowl, whisk eggs with cream, ranch seasoning, pepper, and salt. Add sausage and cheese and stir well.
3. Pour egg mixture into the greased baking dish.
4. Select bake mode then set the temperature to 350°F and time for 55 minutes. Press start.
5. Once the Ninja Foodi Digital Air Fryer Oven is preheated then place the baking dish into the oven.
6. Slice and serve.

Hash Brown Egg Cups

Servings: 12
Cooking Time: 30 Minutes
Ingredients:
- 8 eggs
- 2 tbsp milk
- 1/4 tsp garlic powder
- 1 cup ham, cubed
- 1 1/2 cups cheddar cheese, grated
- 20 oz hash browns

- Pepper
- Salt

Directions:
1. Spray 12-cups muffin pan with cooking spray and set aside.
2. In a bowl, whisk eggs with milk, pepper, and salt. Add ham, cheese, and hash browns and stir to combine.
3. Pour egg mixture into the greased muffin pan.
4. Select bake then set the temperature to 350°F and time to 30 minutes. Press start.
5. Once the Ninja Foodi Digital Air Fryer Oven is preheated then place the muffin pan into the oven.
6. Serve and enjoy.

Breakfast Bars

Servings: 13 Bars
Cooking Time: 20 Minutes
Ingredients:
- 1 cup maple almond butter
- ¼ cup packed light brown sugar
- ¼ cup honey
- 2 eggs
- 1 teaspoon baking soda
- 2 teaspoons vanilla extract
- 1 cup mixed nuts of your choice
- 2 cups old-fashioned rolled oats
- 1 cup whole-wheat flour
- 1 cup semisweet chocolate chips

Directions:
1. Mix the almond butter, brown sugar, honey, eggs, and vanilla in a large bowl until thoroughly combined.
2. Meanwhile, in another container, combine well the oats, nuts, flour, and baking soda.
3. Combine the flour mixture and the egg mixture until well incorporated.
4. Add the chocolate chips and mix to combine.
5. Line the sheet pan with parchment paper. Spread the batter onto the pan and spread evenly with a spatula or knife.
6. Press the START/PAUSE button and turn on your Ninja Foodi Digital Air Fryer Oven and set temperatures to 325 °F for 20 minutes on the "BAKE" function.
7. Press START/PAUSE to begin preheating.
8. When the unit has preheated, place the sheet pan on the wire rack. Close the oven door to begin cooking.
9. Cooking is completed when the top sets and is golden brown.
10. Remove the pan from the oven and let cool completely.

Cheddar & Cream Omelet

Servings: 2
Cooking Time: 8 Minutes
Ingredients:
- 4 eggs
- ¼ cup cream
- 1 teaspoon fresh parsley, minced
- Salt and ground black pepper, as required

- ¼ cup Cheddar cheese, grated

Directions:

1. In a bowl, add the eggs, cream, parsley, salt, and black pepper and beat well.
2. Place the egg mixture into SearPlate.
3. Press AIR OVEN MODE button of Ninja Foodi Digital Air Fryer Oven and turn the dial to select "Air Fry" mode.
4. Press TIME/SLICES button and again turn the dial to set the cooking time to 8 minutes.
5. Now push TEMP/SHADE button and rotate the dial to set the temperature at 350 °F.
6. Press "Start/Stop" button to start.
7. When the unit beeps to show that it is preheated, open the oven door.
8. Insert the SearPlate in the oven.
9. After 4 minutes, sprinkle the omelet with cheese evenly.
10. When cooking time is completed, open the oven door and remove the SearPlate.
11. Cut the omelet into 2 portions and serve hot.

Healthy Spinach Egg Cups

Servings: 6
Cooking Time: 20 Minutes
Ingredients:

- 6 eggs
- 1/8 tsp onion powder
- 1/8 tsp garlic powder
- 1/3 cup feta cheese, crumbled
- 1 1/2 cups spinach, chopped
- Pepper
- Salt

Directions:

1. Spray 6-cups muffin pan with cooking spray and set aside.
2. Divide spinach and cheese evenly into each muffin cup.
3. In a bowl, whisk eggs with onion powder, pepper, garlic powder, and salt.
4. Pour egg mixture into each cup.
5. Select bake then set the temperature to 350°F and time to 20 minutes. Press start.
6. Once the Ninja Foodi Digital Air Fryer Oven is preheated then place the muffin pan into the oven.
7. Serve and enjoy.

Spinach Tater Tot Casserole

Servings: 8
Cooking Time: 40 Minutes
Ingredients:

- 8 eggs
- 15 oz tater tots
- 1 1/2 cups cheddar cheese, shredded
- 4 oz fresh spinach, cook until wilted
- 2/3 cup roasted red peppers, chopped
- Pepper
- Salt

Directions:

1. Arrange tater tots in a greased baking dish.
2. In a bowl, whisk eggs with pepper and salt. Stir in spinach and roasted peppers.
3. Pour egg mixture over tater tots and sprinkle with cheddar cheese.
4. Select bake mode then set the temperature to 350°F and time for 40 minutes. Press start.
5. Once the Ninja Foodi Digital Air Fryer Oven is preheated then place the baking dish into the oven.
6. Slice and serve.

Sausage Patties

Servings: 6
Cooking Time: 6 Minutes
Ingredients:

- 1 pound pork sausage patties
- Fennel seeds

Directions:

1. Prepare the sausage by slicing it into patties or using new patties, then flavor it with fennel seed or your favorite seasoning.
2. Arrange in air fry basket in a uniform layer.
3. Turn on your Ninja Foodi Digital Air Fryer Oven and rotate the knob to select "Broil".
4. Select the timer for 8 minutes and temperature to low.
5. Cook for another 4 minutes after carefully flipping the patties.
6. Serve.

Sausage Bake Omelet

Servings: 8
Cooking Time: 45 Minutes
Ingredients:

- 16 eggs
- 1 lb ground sausage
- 1 1/2 cups almond milk
- 1/2 cup salsa
- 1/4 tsp paprika
- 2 cups mozzarella cheese, shredded
- Pepper
- Salt

Directions:

1. Place rack in the bottom position and close door. Select bake mode set the temperature to 350°F and set the timer to 45 minutes. Press the setting dial to preheat.
2. Add sausage to a pan and cook until browned. Drain excess fat.
3. In a large bowl, whisk eggs and milk, paprika, pepper, and salt.
4. Stir in cheese, cooked sausage, and salsa.
5. Pour omelet mixture into the greased baking dish.
6. Once the unit is preheated, open the door, and place the baking dish onto the center of the rack and close the door.
7. Serve and enjoy.

Baked Breakfast Oatmeal

Servings: 8
Cooking Time: 30 Minutes
Ingredients:

- 2 eggs
- 3 cups rolled oats
- 1/4 cup butter, melted
- 1/2 cup maple syrup
- 1 1/2 cups almond milk
- 1 tsp ground cinnamon
- 1 tsp vanilla
- 1 1/2 tsp baking powder
- Pinch of salt

Directions:
1. Place rack in the bottom position and close door. Select bake mode set the temperature to 350°F and set the timer to 30 minutes. Press the setting dial to preheat.
2. In a bowl, whisk eggs with milk, cinnamon, butter, vanilla, baking powder, maple syrup, and salt.
3. Add oats and mix well.
4. Pour the mixture into the greased baking pan.
5. Once the unit is preheated, open the door, and place the baking pan onto the center of the rack, and close the door.
6. Serve and enjoy.

Savory Sausage & Beans Muffins

Servings: 6
Cooking Time: 20 Minutes
Ingredients:

- 4 eggs
- ½ cup cheddar cheese, shredded
- 3 tablespoons heavy cream
- 1 tablespoon tomato paste
- ¼ teaspoon salt
- Pinch of freshly ground black pepper
- Cooking spray
- 4 cooked breakfast sausage links, chopped
- 3 tablespoons baked beans

Directions:
1. Grease a 6-cup muffin pan.
2. In a bowl, add the eggs, cheddar cheese, heavy cream, tomato paste, salt and black pepper and beat until well combined.
3. Stir in the sausage pieces and beans.
4. Divide the mixture into prepared muffin cups evenly.
5. Press AIR OVEN MODE button of Ninja Foodi Digital Air Fryer Oven and turn the dial to select "Bake" mode.
6. Press TIME/SLICES button and again turn the dial to set the cooking time to 20 minutes.
7. Now push TEMP/SHADE button and rotate the dial to set the temperature at 350 °F.
8. Press "Start/Stop" button to start.
9. When the unit beeps to show that it is preheated, open the oven door.

10. Arrange the muffin pan over the wire rack and insert in the oven.
11. When cooking time is completed, open the oven door and place the muffin pan onto a wire rack to cool for 5 minutes before serving.

Bacon, Spinach & Egg Cups

Servings: 3
Cooking Time: 16 Minutes
Ingredients:

- 3 eggs
- 6 cooked bacon slices, chopped
- 2 cups fresh baby spinach
- ⅓ cup heavy cream
- 3 tablespoons Parmesan cheese, grated
- Salt and ground black pepper, as required

Directions:
1. Heat a nonstick skillet over medium-high heat and cook the bacon for about 5 minutes.
2. Add the spinach and cook for about 2-3 minutes.
3. Stir in the heavy cream and Parmesan cheese and cook for about 2-3 minutes.
4. Remove from the heat and set aside to cool slightly.
5. Grease 3 ramekins.
6. Crack 1 egg in each prepared ramekin and top with bacon mixture.
7. Press AIR OVEN MODE button of Ninja Foodi Digital Air Fryer Oven and turn the dial to select "Air Fry" mode.
8. Press TIME/SLICES button and again turn the dial to set the cooking time to 5 minutes.
9. Now push TEMP/SHADE button and rotate the dial to set the temperature at 350 °F.
10. Press "Start/Stop" button to start.
11. When the unit beeps to show that it is preheated, open the oven door and grease the air fry basket.
12. Arrange the ramekins into the wire rack and insert in the oven.
13. When cooking time is completed, open the oven door and sprinkle each ramekin with salt and black pepper.
14. Serve hot.

Breakfast Pizzas With Muffins

Servings: 3
Cooking Time: 6 Minutes
Ingredients:

- 6 eggs, cooked and scrambled
- 1 pound ground sausage
- ½ cup Colby jack cheese, shredded
- 3 egg muffins, sliced in half
- Olive oil spray

Directions:
1. Using olive oil cooking spray, spray the air fry basket.
2. Place each half in the basket.
3. Using a light layer of olive oil spray, lightly coat the English muffins and top with scrambled eggs and fried sausages.

4. Add cheese on top of each one.
5. Turn on your Ninja Foodi Digital Air Fryer Oven and rotate the knob to select "Bake".
6. Select the timer for 5 minutes and the temperature for 355 °F.
7. Serve hot.

Cheesy Chicken Omelet

Servings: 12
Cooking Time: 18 Minutes
Ingredients:
- 4 eggs
- ½ cup chicken breast, cooked diced
- 2 tbsp shredded cheese
- ½ tsp salt
- ¼ tsp pepper
- ¼ tsp granulated garlic
- ¼ tsp onion powder

Directions:
1. Grease 2 ramekins with olive oil and keep them aside.
2. Crack two eggs into each of the greased ramekins.
3. Drizzle seasonings and cheese into each ramekin.
4. Whisk well gently and stir in ¼ cup chicken to each ramekin.
5. Place the stuffed ramekins in the air fryer basket.
6. Return the fryer basket to the Ninja Foodi Digital Air Fryer Oven.
7. And cook on "AIR FRY" mode for 18 minutes at 330 °F.
8. Enjoy.

Sausage Cheese Frittata

Servings: 6
Cooking Time: 45 Minutes
Ingredients:
- 8 eggs
- 1 lb sausage
- 1 cup cottage cheese
- 2 tsp baking powder
- 1 cup milk
- 3 tomatoes, chopped
- 2 oz parmesan cheese, grated
- 6 oz cheddar cheese, grated
- Pepper
- Salt

Directions:
1. Brown the sausage in a pan and set aside.
2. In a bowl, whisk eggs with milk, baking powder, pepper, and salt.
3. Add sausage, cottage cheese, tomatoes, parmesan cheese, and cheddar cheese and stir well.
4. Pour egg mixture into the greased baking dish.
5. Select bake mode then set the temperature to 350°F and time for 45 minutes. Press start.
6. Once the Ninja Foodi Digital Air Fryer Oven is preheated then place the baking dish into the oven.
7. Slice and serve.

Healthy Oatmeal Muffins

Servings: 12
Cooking Time: 12 Minutes
Ingredients:
- 1 egg
- 1 cup old-fashioned oats
- 1 1/2 cups pears, diced
- 1 tsp vanilla
- 1/4 cup olive oil
- 1/2 cup brown sugar
- 1 tsp cardamom powder
- 1/2 tsp baking soda
- 1 tsp baking powder
- 1 cup whole wheat flour
- 1 cup milk
- 1/2 tsp salt

Directions:
1. Spray 12-cups muffin pan with cooking spray and set aside.
2. In a mixing bowl, add milk and oats and let it sit for 15 minutes.
3. In a separate bowl, mix flour, cardamom, baking soda, baking powder, sugar, and salt.
4. Add egg, vanilla, and oil into the oat and milk mixture and mix well.
5. Add flour mixture and mix until just combined. Add pears and fold well.
6. Spoon batter into the greased muffin pan.
7. Select bake then set the temperature to 400°F and time to 12 minutes. Press start.
8. Once the Ninja Foodi Digital Air Fryer Oven is preheated then place the muffin pan into the oven.
9. Serve and enjoy.

Sweet & Spiced Toasts

Servings: 3
Cooking Time: 4 Minutes
Ingredients:
- ¼ cup sugar
- ½ teaspoon ground cinnamon
- ⅛ teaspoon ground cloves
- ⅛ teaspoon ground ginger
- ½ teaspoons vanilla extract
- ¼ cup salted butter, softened
- 6 bread slices
- Pepper, as you need

Directions:
1. In a bowl, add the sugar, vanilla, cinnamon, pepper, and butter. Mix until smooth.
2. Spread the butter mixture evenly over each bread slice.
3. Press AIR OVEN MODE button of Ninja Foodi Digital Air Fryer Oven and turn the dial to select "Air Fry" mode.
4. Press TIME/SLICES button and again turn the dial to set the cooking time to 4 minutes.

5. Now push TEMP/SHADE button and rotate the dial to set the temperature at 400 °F.
6. Press "Start/Stop" button to start.
7. When the unit beeps to show that it is preheated, open the oven door and grease the air fry basket.
8. Place the bread slices into the prepared air fry basket, buttered-side up. and insert in the oven.
9. Flip the slices once halfway through.
10. When cooking time is completed, open the oven door and transfer the French toasts onto a platter.
11. Serve warm.

Apple Oat Muffins

Servings: 12
Cooking Time: 30 Minutes
Ingredients:
- 2 eggs
- 3 cups old-fashioned oats
- 1 1/4 cups apples, peel & dice
- 2 tsp baking powder
- 2 tbsp brown sugar
- 2 tsp vanilla
- 1/2 cup applesauce
- 1 cup milk
- 2 tsp cinnamon
- 1/4 tsp salt

Directions:
1. Place rack in the bottom position and close door. Select bake mode set the temperature to 350°F and set the timer to 30 minutes. Press the setting dial to preheat.
2. In a mixing bowl, mix together oats, brown sugar, cinnamon, baking powder, and salt and set aside.
3. In a large bowl, whisk eggs, applesauce, vanilla, and milk.
4. Add oat mixture into the egg mixture and stir until well combined. Add apples and stir well.
5. Spoon mixture into the greased muffin pan.
6. Once the unit is preheated, open the door, and place the muffin pan onto the center of the rack, and close the door.
7. Serve and enjoy.

Ham And Cheese Scones

Servings: 6
Cooking Time: 25 Minutes.
Ingredients:
- 2 cups all-purpose flour
- 1 tablespoon baking powder
- 2 teaspoons sugar
- 1 teaspoon kosher salt
- 2 tablespoons butter, cubed
- 1 cup ham, diced, cooked
- ¼ cup scallion, chopped
- 4 ounces cheddar cheese, shredded
- ¼ cup milk
- ¾ cup heavy cream

Directions:
1. Whisk baking powder with flour, sugar, salt, and butter in a mixing bowl.
2. Beat milk, cream, ham, scallion, and cheddar cheese in another bowl.
3. Stir in the flour-butter mixture and mix well until it forms a smooth dough.
4. Place this scones dough on a floured surface and spread it into a 7-inch round sheet.
5. Cut this dough sheet into 6 wedges of equal size.
6. Place these wedges in the SearPlate, lined with parchment paper.
7. Transfer the SearPlate to Ninja Foodi Digital Air Fryer Oven and close the door.
8. Select "Bake" mode by rotating the dial.
9. Press the TIME/SLICES button and change the value to 25 minutes.
10. Press the TEMP/SHADE button and change the value to 400 °F.
11. Press Start/Stop to begin cooking.
12. When baked, serve the scones.

Italian Frittata

Servings: 4
Cooking Time: 45 Minutes
Ingredients:
- 2 cups egg whites
- 1/4 cup fresh basil, sliced
- 1/2 tsp Italian seasoning
- 1/2 cup roasted red peppers, sliced
- 1/2 cup mozzarella cheese, shredded
- 1 cup ricotta cheese, crumbled
- Pepper
- Salt

Directions:
1. Place rack in the bottom position and close door. Select bake mode set the temperature to 375°F and set the timer to 45 minutes. Press the setting dial to preheat.
2. In a bowl, whisk egg whites with Italian seasoning, pepper, and salt.
3. Add remaining ingredients and stir well.
4. Pour egg mixture into the greased baking dish.
5. Once the unit is preheated, open the door, and place the baking dish onto the center of the rack, and close the door.
6. Slice and serve.

Breakfast Casserole

Servings: 12
Cooking Time: 55 Minutes
Ingredients:
- 12 eggs
- 16 oz ham, cubed
- 8 cups frozen hash browns
- 1 cup almond milk
- 8 oz mozzarella cheese, shredded
- 1/4 tsp garlic powder

- 1/2 tsp pepper
- 1 tsp salt

Directions:

1. Place rack in the bottom position and close door. Select bake mode set the temperature to 350°F and set the timer to 55 minutes. Press the setting dial to preheat.
2. In a bowl, mix together cheese, ham, and frozen potatoes and transfer them into the greased baking dish.
3. In a mixing bowl, whisk eggs with milk, pepper, and salt.
4. Pour egg mixture over cheese ham mixture.
5. Once the unit is preheated, open the door, and place the baking dish onto the center of the rack, and close the door.
6. Serve and enjoy.

Almond Soufflé

Servings: 4
Cooking Time: 23minutes

Ingredients:

- ½ cup all-purpose flour
- ½ cup butter
- 1-¼ cup almond milk
- ½ cup brown sugar
- 4 egg yolks
- 1 teaspoon vanilla extract
- ½ ounce of white sugar
- 1 teaspoon of cream of tartar
- Oil spray, for greasing

Directions:

1. Press the START/PAUSE button, turn on your Ninja Foodi Digital Air Fryer Oven, and set temperatures to 350 °F for 5 minutes.
2. Take a bowl and mix butter with flour. In a saucepan, pour milk and sugar and let it simmer over medium flame.
3. Add flour mixture to the milk.
4. Cook it for 6 minutes and then let it get cool.
5. Grease the soufflé dishes with oil spray.
6. In a large mixing bowl, whisk egg yolks, white sugar, vanilla extract, and cream of tartar, and Pour this mixture into a soufflé dish and top it with a flour milk mixture.
7. Put the soufflé dish in your Ninja Foodi Digital Air Fryer Oven and then BAKE it for 18 minutes.
8. Once done, serve and enjoy.

Ricotta Toasts With Salmon

Servings: 2
Cooking Time: 4 Minutes

Ingredients:

- 4 bread slices
- 1 garlic clove, minced
- 8 ounces ricotta cheese
- 1 teaspoon lemon zest
- Freshly ground black pepper, to taste
- 4 ounces smoked salmon

Directions:

1. In a food processor, add the garlic, ricotta, lemon zest and black pepper and pulse until smooth.
2. Spread ricotta mixture over each bread slices evenly.
3. Arrange the bread slices onto the SearPlate.
4. Press AIR OVEN MODE button of Ninja Foodi Digital Air Fryer Oven and turn the dial to select "Air Fry" mode.
5. Press TIME/SLICES button and again turn the dial to set the cooking time to 4 minutes.
6. Now push TEMP/SHADE button and rotate the dial to set the temperature at 355 °F.
7. Press "Start/Stop" button to start.
8. When the unit beeps to show that it is preheated, open the oven door and insert the SearPlate in oven.
9. When cooking time is completed, open the oven door and transfer the slices onto serving plates.
10. Top with salmon and serve.

Savory Parsley Soufflé

Servings: 2
Cooking Time: 8 Minutes

Ingredients:

- 2 tablespoons light cream
- 2 eggs
- 1 tablespoon fresh parsley, chopped
- 1 fresh red chili pepper, chopped
- Salt, as required

Directions:

1. Grease 2 soufflé dishes.
2. In a bowl, add all the ingredients and beat until well combined.
3. Divide the mixture into prepared soufflé dishes.
4. Press AIR OVEN MODE button of Ninja Foodi Digital Air Fryer Oven and turn the dial to select "Air Fry" mode.
5. Press TIME/SLICES button and again turn the dial to set the cooking time to 8 minutes.
6. Now push TEMP/SHADE button and rotate the dial to set the temperature at 390 °F.
7. Press "Start/Stop" button to start.
8. When the unit beeps to show that it is preheated, open the oven door and grease the SearPlate.
9. Arrange the soufflé dishes onto the SearPlate and insert in the oven.
10. When cooking time is completed, open the oven door and serve hot.

Pumpkin Muffins

Servings: 6
Cooking Time: 15 Minutes.

Ingredients:

- 1 cup pumpkin puree
- 2 cups oats
- ½ cup honey
- 2 medium eggs, beaten
- 1 teaspoon coconut butter
- 1 tablespoon cocoa nibs
- 1 tablespoon vanilla essence

- 1 teaspoon nutmeg

Directions:

1. Whisk all ingredients in a mixer until smooth.
2. Divide this pumpkin oat batter into a 12-cup muffin tray.
3. Transfer the tray onto a wire rack in Ninja Foodi Digital Air Fryer Oven and close the door.
4. Select "Air Fry" mode by rotating the dial.
5. Press the TIME/SLICES button and change the value to 15 minutes.
6. Press the TEMP/SHADE button and change the value to 360 °F.
7. Press Start/Stop to begin cooking.
8. Serve fresh.

Healthy Carrot Breakfast Bars

Servings: 16
Cooking Time: 30 Minutes

Ingredients:

- 1/2 cup whole wheat flour
- 1 tsp cinnamon
- 1 tsp baking soda
- 1 1/2 cups rolled oats
- 2 tbsp flaxseed meal
- 1 cup carrot, grated
- 1/4 cup maple syrup
- 1/4 cup mashed banana
- 1 tsp vanilla
- 1/2 cup almond butter
- 3/4 cup milk

Directions:

1. In a mixing bowl, whisk milk, butter, vanilla, mashed banana, maple syrup, carrot, and flaxseed meal.
2. Add oats, flour, cinnamon, and baking soda and mix until well combined.
3. Pour mixture into the greased baking pan.
4. Select bake mode then set the temperature to 350°F and time for 30 minutes. Press start.
5. Once the Ninja Foodi Digital Air Fryer Oven is preheated then place the baking pan into the oven.
6. Slice and serve.

Sweet Potato Breakfast Bake

Servings: 8
Cooking Time: 60 Minutes

Ingredients:

- 3 eggs
- 3/4 tsp cinnamon
- 1/4 cup coconut flour
- 1/4 cup raisins
- 1 mashed banana
- 1/3 cup maple syrup
- 2 sweet potatoes, peel & grated
- 1/4 tsp salt

Directions:

1. In a large bowl, add mashed banana, eggs, maple syrup, raisins, and sweet potatoes and mix well.
2. Add cinnamon, coconut flour, and salt and mix until well combined.
3. Pour mixture into the greased baking dish.
4. Select bake mode then set the temperature to 350°F and time for 60 minutes. Press start.
5. Once the Ninja Foodi Digital Air Fryer Oven is preheated then place the baking dish into the oven.
6. Slice and serve.

Baked Eggs

Servings: 4
Cooking Time: 12 Minutes

Ingredients:

- 1 cup marinara sauce, divided
- 1 tablespoon capers, drained and divided
- 8 eggs
- ¼ cup whipping cream, divided
- ¼ cup Parmesan cheese, shredded and divided
- Salt and ground black pepper, as required

Directions:

1. Grease 4 ramekins and set aside.
2. Divide the marinara sauce in the bottom of each prepared ramekin evenly and top with capers.
3. Carefully, crack 2 eggs over marinara sauce into each ramekin and top with cream, followed by the Parmesan cheese.
4. Sprinkle each ramekin with salt and black pepper.
5. Select the "BAKE" function of your Ninja Foodi Digital Air Fryer Oven by adjusting the temperature to 400 °F and set the time to 12 minutes.
6. Press the "START/PAUSE" button to start.
7. When the unit beeps to show that it is preheated, open the door. Arrange the ramekins over the wire rack and insert them in the oven.
8. When the unit beeps to show that cooking time is completed, press the "Power" button to stop cooking and open the door.
9. Serve warm.

Baked Veggie Quiche

Servings: 2
Cooking Time: 30 Minutes

Ingredients:

- 2 cups spinach, chopped
- 1 bell pepper, chopped
- 1 cup mushrooms, sliced
- 1 teaspoon olive oil
- 2 cups liquid egg substitute
- 4ounces mozzarella cheese, shredded
- ½ teaspoon garlic powder
- ½ teaspoon onion powder
- Salt and pepper

Directions:

1. Place your pan over medium heat and add oil. Heat the oil.
2. Add mushrooms and bell pepper into your pan Sauté until it becomes tender Remove the pan from heat. Let it cool.
3. Take a bowl and add egg substitute, spinach, cheese, onion powder, garlic powder, salt, and pepper.
4. Stir in mushrooms and bell pepper.
5. Pour into the greased muffin pan.
6. Place the wire rack inside your Ninja Foodi Digital Air Fryer Oven.
7. Preheat your Oven to 350 °F in "BAKE" mode.
8. Set the timer to 30 minutes. Let it preheat until you hear a beep.
9. Place the baking dish on a wire rack and close the oven door. Cook for 30 minutes.
10. Serve and enjoy!

Apple Pumpkin Breakfast Bake

Servings: 6
Cooking Time: 40 Minutes
Ingredients:
- 3 eggs
- 1/2 cup pecans, chopped
- 1 apple, peel & dice
- 1 tsp cinnamon
- 1 tsp pumpkin pie spice
- 1 banana, mashed
- 2/3 cup milk
- 1 cup pumpkin puree
- 1/4 tsp salt

Directions:
1. In a mixing bowl, whisk eggs, cinnamon, banana, pumpkin pie spice, milk, pumpkin puree, and salt until well combined.
2. Add apple and fold well. Pour mixture into the greased baking pan.
3. Sprinkle pecans on top.
4. Select bake mode then set the temperature to 350°F and time for 40 minutes. Press start.
5. Once the Ninja Foodi Digital Air Fryer Oven is preheated then place the baking pan into the oven.
6. Slice and serve.

Broiled Bacon

Servings: 6
Cooking Time: 10 Minutes
Ingredients:
- 1 pound bacon

Directions:
1. Evenly distribute the bacon in the air fry basket.
2. Turn on your Ninja Foodi Digital Air Fryer Oven and rotate the knob to select "Broil".
3. Select the unit for 5 minutes at low.
4. With tongs, remove the bacon and place it on a paper towel-lined dish.

5. Allow cooling before serving.

Carrot & Raisin Bread

Servings: 8
Cooking Time: 35 Minutes
Ingredients:
- 2 cups all-purpose flour
- 1½ teaspoons ground cinnamon
- 2 teaspoons baking soda
- ½ teaspoon salt
- 3 eggs
- ½ cup sunflower oil
- ½ cup applesauce
- ¼ cup honey
- ¼ cup plain yogurt
- 2 teaspoons vanilla essence
- 2½ cups carrots, peeled and shredded
- ½ cup raisins
- ½ cup walnuts

Directions:
1. Line the bottom of a greased SearPlate with parchment paper.
2. In a medium bowl, sift together the flour, baking soda, cinnamon, and salt.
3. In a large bowl, add the eggs, oil, applesauce, honey, and yogurt and with a hand-held mixer, mix on medium speed until well combined.
4. Add the eggs, one at a time and whisk well.
5. Add the vanilla and mix well.
6. Add the flour mixture and mix until just combined.
7. Fold in the carrots, raisins, and walnuts.
8. Place the mixture into a lightly greased baking pan.
9. With a piece of foil, cover the pan loosely.
10. Press AIR OVEN MODE button of Ninja Foodi Digital Air Fryer Oven and turn the dial to select the "Air Fry" mode.
11. Press TIME/SLICES button and again turn the dial to set the cooking time to 30 minutes.
12. Now push TEMP/SHADE button and rotate the dial to set the temperature at 350 °F.
13. Press "Start/Stop" button to start.
14. When the unit beeps to show that it is preheated, open the oven door.
15. Insert the SearPlate in the oven.
16. After 25 minutes of cooking, remove the foil.
17. When cooking time is completed, open the oven door. Remove the SearPlate from the oven and allow to cool for about 10 minutes.
18. Carefully invert the bread onto the wire rack to cool completely before slicing.
19. Cut the bread into desired-sized slices and serve.

Mushroom Frittata

Servings: 4
Cooking Time: 36 Minutes
Ingredients:

- 2 tablespoons olive oil
- 1 shallot, sliced thinly
- 2 garlic cloves, minced
- 4 cups white mushrooms, chopped
- 6 large eggs
- ¼ teaspoon red pepper flakes, crushed
- Salt and ground black pepper, as required
- ½ teaspoon fresh dill, minced
- ½ cup cream cheese, softened

Directions:

1. In a skillet, heat the oil over medium heat and cook the shallot, mushrooms, and garlic for about 5-6 minutes, stirring frequently.
2. Remove from the heat and transfer the mushroom mixture into a bowl.
3. In another bowl, add the eggs, red pepper flakes, salt and black peppers and beat well.
4. Add the mushroom mixture and stir to combine.
5. Place the egg mixture into a greased SearPlate and sprinkle with the dill.
6. Spread cream cheese over egg mixture evenly.
7. Press AIR OVEN MODE button of Ninja Foodi Digital Air Fryer Oven and turn the dial to select "Air Fry" mode.
8. Press TIME/SLICES button and again turn the dial to set the cooking time to 30 minutes.
9. Now push TEMP/SHADE button and rotate the dial to set the temperature at 330 °F.
10. Press "Start/Stop" button to start.
11. When the unit beeps to show that it is preheated, open the oven door.
12. Insert the SearPlate in the oven.
13. When cooking time is completed, open the oven door and place the SearPlate onto a wire rack for about 5 minutes
14. Cut into equal-sized wedges and serve.

Egg Sausage Bake

Servings: 8
Cooking Time: 35 Minutes
Ingredients:

- 12 eggs
- 1/2 tsp garlic powder
- 1/4 cup milk
- 1 bell pepper, diced
- 1 cup kale, chopped
- 1 cup spinach, chopped
- 1 lb breakfast sausage
- Pepper
- Salt

Directions:

1. Cook sausage in a pan over medium heat until browned.

2. Add kale, spinach, and bell pepper and saute for 3-5 minutes.
3. Pour sausage mixture into the greased baking dish.
4. In a bowl, whisk eggs with milk, garlic powder, pepper, and salt.
5. Pour egg mixture over sausage mixture.
6. Select bake mode then set the temperature to 375°F and time for 30 minutes. Press start.
7. Once the Ninja Foodi Digital Air Fryer Oven is preheated then place the baking dish into the oven.
8. Slice and serve.

Cinnamon Toast

Servings: 2
Cooking Time: 7 Minutes
Ingredients:

- 4 slices of whole wheat bread
- 4 tablespoons of salted butter, at room temperature
- 4 tablespoons of brown sugar, or to taste
- ½ teaspoon of cinnamon, ground
- ½ teaspoon of vanilla extract
- Pinch of salt

Directions:

1. In a bowl, mix butter with sugar, cinnamon, salt, and vanilla.
2. Spread this mixture equally over the bread slices.
3. Put the coated bread slices on a sheet pan and place them inside Ninja Foodi Digital Air Fryer Oven.
4. Select the "BAKE" function of your Ninja Foodi Digital Air Fryer Oven by adjusting the temperature to 400 °F and set the time to 7 minutes.
5. Press start so the preheating begins.
6. Remove it from Ninja Foodi Digital Air Fryer Oven and serve.

Breakfast Hash

Servings: 1
Cooking Time: 16 Minutes
Ingredients:

- 2 bacon slices, halved
- 2 small potatoes, chopped
- ¼ of tomato, chopped
- 1 egg
- 2 tablespoons cheddar cheese, shredded

Directions:

1. Arrange the bacon strips onto a double layer of tin foil.
2. Place the potatoes and tomato on top of the bacon.
3. Carefully crack the egg on top of the veggie mixture. With the tin foil, shape the mixture into a bowl.
4. Select the "AIR ROAST" function of your Ninja Foodi Digital Air Fryer Oven by adjusting the temperature to 350 °F and set the time to 20 minutes.
5. Press the "START/PAUSE" button to start.
6. When the unit beeps to show that it is preheated, open the door.

7. Carefully arrange the foil piece over the wire rack and insert it in the oven.

8. After 16 minutes of cooking, top the hash with cheese.

9. When the unit beeps to show that cooking time is completed, press the "Power" button to stop cooking and open the door.

10. Remove from oven and serve hot.

Breakfast Egg Bake

Servings: 6
Cooking Time: 45 Minutes

Ingredients:
- 10 eggs
- 5 bacon slices, cooked and chopped
- 3 cups baby spinach, cooked & chopped
- 2 tomatoes, chopped
- 2 tbsp parsley, chopped
- Pepper
- Salt

Directions:

1. Place rack in the bottom position and close door. Select bake mode set the temperature to 350°F and set the timer to 45 minutes. Press the setting dial to preheat.

2. In a mixing bowl, whisk eggs and pepper, and salt.

3. Add spinach, tomatoes, and parsley and stir well.

4. Pour egg mixture into the greased baking dish. Top with bacon.

5. Once the unit is preheated, open the door, and place the baking dish onto the center of the rack, and close the door.

6. Serve and enjoy.

Potato Bacon Casserole

Servings: 8
Cooking Time: 60 Minutes

Ingredients:
- 2 lbs hash brown potatoes, diced
- 1/4 cup butter, melted
- 1 tsp onion powder
- 1 1/2 tsp garlic powder
- 1 cup sour cream
- 2 cups cheddar cheese, shredded
- 25 oz cream of mushroom soup
- 5 oz bacon, cooked & chopped

Directions:

1. In a large mixing bowl, mix together hash brown potatoes, onion powder, garlic powder, sour cream, cheddar cheese, soup, and bacon until well combined.

2. Pour mixture into the greased baking dish. Drizzle with melted butter.

3. Select bake mode then set the temperature to 350°F and time for 60 minutes. Press start.

4. Once the Ninja Foodi Digital Air Fryer Oven is preheated then place the baking dish into the oven.

5. Slice and serve.

Date Bread

Servings: 10
Cooking Time: 22 Minutes

Ingredients:
- 2½ cups dates, pitted and chopped
- ¼ cup butter
- 1 cup hot water
- 1½ cups flour
- ½ cup brown sugar
- 1 teaspoon baking powder
- 1 teaspoon baking soda
- ½ teaspoon salt
- 1 egg

Directions:

1. In a large bowl, add the dates and butter and top with the hot water. Set aside for about 5 minutes.

2. In a separate bowl, mix the flour, brown sugar, baking powder, baking soda, and salt together.

3. In the same bowl of dates, add the flour mixture and egg and mix well.

4. Grease SearPlate.

5. Place the mixture into the prepared SearPlate.

6. Press AIR OVEN MODE button of Ninja Foodi Digital Air Fryer Oven and turn the dial to select "Air Fry" mode.

7. Press TIME/SLICES button and again turn the dial to set the cooking time to 22 minutes.

8. Now push TEMP/SHADE button and rotate the dial to set the temperature at 340 °F.

9. Press "Start/Stop" button to start.

10. When the unit beeps to show that it is preheated, open the oven door.

11. Insert the SearPlate in the oven.

12. When cooking time is completed, open the oven door and place the SearPlate onto a wire rack for about 10-15 minutes.

13. Carefully, invert the bread onto the wire rack to cool completely cool before slicing.

14. Cut the bread into desired sized slices and serve.

Banana & Walnut Bread

Servings: 10
Cooking Time: 25 Minutes

Ingredients:
- 1½ cups self-rising flour
- ¼ teaspoon bicarbonate of soda
- 5 tablespoons plus 1 teaspoon butter
- ⅔ cup plus ½ tablespoon caster sugar
- 2 medium eggs
- 3½ ounces walnuts, chopped
- 2 cups bananas, peeled and mashed

Directions:

1. In a bowl, mix the flour and bicarbonate of soda together.

2. In another bowl, add the butter and sugar and beat until pale and fluffy.

3. Add the eggs, one at a time, along with a little flour and mix well.
4. Stir in the remaining flour and walnuts.
5. Add the bananas and mix until well combined.
6. Grease the SearPlate.
7. Place the mixture into the prepared SearPlate.
8. Press AIR OVEN MODE button of Ninja Foodi Digital Air Fryer Oven and turn the dial to select the "Air Fry" mode.
9. Press TIME/SLICES button and again turn the dial to set the cooking time to 10 minutes.
10. Now push TEMP/SHADE button and rotate the dial to set the temperature at 355 °F.
11. Press "Start/Stop" button to start.
12. When the unit beeps to show that it is preheated, open the oven door.
13. Insert the SearPlate in the oven.
14. After 10 minutes of cooking, set the temperature at 340 °F for 15 minutes.
15. When cooking time is completed, open the oven door and remove the SearPlate to cool for about 10 minutes.
16. Carefully invert the bread onto the wire rack to cool completely before slicing.
17. Cut the bread into desired sized slices and serve.

Parmesan Eggs In Avocado Cups

Servings: 2
Cooking Time: 22 Minutes
Ingredients:

- 1 large ripe avocado, halved and pitted
- 2 eggs
- Salt and ground black pepper, as required
- 2 tablespoons Parmesan cheese, grated
- Pinch of cayenne pepper
- 1 teaspoon fresh chives, minced

Directions:
1. With a spoon, scoop out some of the flesh from the avocado halves to make a hole.
2. Arrange the avocado halves onto a baking pan.
3. Crack 1 egg into each avocado half and sprinkle with salt and black pepper.
4. Press AIR OVEN MODE button of Ninja Foodi Digital Air Fryer Oven and turn the dial to select "Air Fry" mode.
5. Press TIME/SLICES button and again turn the dial to set the cooking time to 22 minutes.
6. Now push TEMP/SHADE button and rotate the dial to set the temperature at 350 °F.
7. Press "Start/Stop" button to start.
8. When the unit beeps to show that it is preheated, open the oven door and grease the air fry basket.
9. Arrange the avocado halves into the air fry basket and insert in the oven.
10. After 12 minutes of cooking, sprinkle the top of avocado halves with Parmesan cheese.
11. When cooking time is completed, open the oven door and transfer the avocado halves onto a platter.

12. Sprinkle with cayenne pepper and serve hot with the garnishing of chives.

Savory French Toast

Servings: 2
Cooking Time: 5 Minutes
Ingredients:

- ¼ cup chickpea flour
- 3 tablespoons onion, finely chopped
- 2 teaspoons green chili, seeded and finely chopped
- ½ teaspoon red chili powder
- ¼ teaspoon ground turmeric
- ¼ teaspoon ground cumin
- Salt, to taste
- Water, as needed
- 4 bread slices

Directions:
1. Add all the ingredients except bread slices in a large bowl and mix until a thick mixture form.
2. With a spoon, spread the mixture over both sides of each bread slice.
3. Arrange the bread slices into the lightly greased SearPlate.
4. Press AIR OVEN MODE button of Ninja Foodi Digital Air Fryer Oven and turn the dial to select "Air Fry" mode.
5. Press TIME/SLICES button and again turn the dial to set the cooking time to 5 minutes.
6. Now push TEMP/SHADE button and rotate the dial to set the temperature at 390 °F.
7. Press "Start/Stop" button to start.
8. When the unit beeps to show that it is preheated, open the oven door and insert the SearPlate in oven.
9. Flip the bread slices once halfway through.
10. When cooking time is completed, open the oven door and serve warm.

Nutritious Vegetable Omelet

Servings: 4
Cooking Time: 40 Minutes
Ingredients:

- 2 eggs
- 5 egg whites
- 1/2 cup cheddar cheese, shredded
- 1/4 cup milk
- 1 cup spinach, chopped
- 1/2 cup bell pepper, diced
- 1/2 cup onion, diced
- Pepper
- Salt

Directions:
1. In a mixing bowl, whisk eggs, egg whites, milk, pepper and salt.
2. Add cheese, spinach, bell pepper, and onion and stir well.
3. Pour egg mixture into the greased baking dish.

4. Select bake mode then set the temperature to 350°F and time for 40 minutes. Press start.
5. Once the Ninja Foodi Digital Air Fryer Oven is preheated then place the baking dish into the oven.
6. Slice and serve.

Hash Browns

Servings: 2
Cooking Time: 5 Minutes
Ingredients:
- 4 hash brown patties
- Cooking oil spray

Directions:
1. Coat the air fry basket with your preferred cooking oil spray.
2. Place the hash brown patties in the oven in an even layer.
3. Spray them with your favorite cooking oil spray.
4. Turn on your Ninja Foodi Digital Air Fryer Oven and rotate the knob to select "Air Fry".
5. Select the timer for 5 minutes and the temperature for 390 °F.
6. Dish out and serve immediately.

Baked Greek Egg Muffins

Servings: 12
Cooking Time: 20 Minutes
Ingredients:
- 8 eggs
- 1/3 cup feta cheese, crumbled
- 1 cup spinach, chopped
- 1/2 cup sun-dried tomatoes, chopped
- 1/4 cup almond milk
- 4 basil leaves, chopped
- 1/2 onion, diced
- Pepper
- Salt

Directions:
1. Place rack in the bottom position and close door. Select bake mode set the temperature to 350°F and set the timer to 20 minutes. Press the setting dial to preheat.
2. In a bowl, whisk eggs with milk, pepper, and salt.
3. Add remaining ingredients and stir well.
4. Pour egg mixture into the greased muffin pan.
5. Once the unit is preheated, open the door, and place the muffin pan onto the center of the rack and close the door.
6. Serve and enjoy.

Mushrooms Frittata

Servings: 2
Cooking Time: 15 Minutes.
Ingredients:
- 1 cup egg whites
- 2 tablespoons skim milk
- 1/4 cup tomato, sliced
- 1/4 cup mushrooms, sliced
- 2 tablespoons fresh chives, chopped

- Black pepper, to taste

Directions:
1. Beat egg whites with mushrooms and the rest of the ingredients in a bowl.
2. Spread this egg white mixture in SearPlate.
3. Transfer the dish to Ninja Foodi Digital Air Fryer Oven and close the door.
4. Select "Air Fry" mode by rotating the dial.
5. Press the TIME/SLICES button and change the value to 15 minutes.
6. Press the TEMP/SHADE button and change the value to 320 °F.
7. Press Start/Stop to begin cooking.
8. When it beeps to signify it has preheated, insert the SearPlate into the oven. Close the oven door and let it cook.
9. Slice and serve warm.

Pancetta & Spinach Frittata

Servings: 2
Cooking Time: 16 Minutes
Ingredients:
- 1/4 cup pancetta
- 1/2 of tomato, cubed
- 1/4 cup fresh baby spinach
- 3 eggs
- Salt and ground black pepper, as required
- 1/4 cup Parmesan cheese, grated

Directions:
1. Heat a nonstick skillet over medium heat and cook the pancetta for about 5 minutes.
2. Add the tomato and spinach cook for about 2-3 minutes.
3. Remove from the heat and drain the grease from skillet.
4. Set aside to cool slightly.
5. Meanwhile, in a small bowl, add the eggs, salt and black pepper and beat well.
6. In the bottom of a greased SearPlate, place the pancetta mixture and top with the eggs, followed by the cheese.
7. Press AIR OVEN MODE button of Ninja Foodi Digital Air Fryer Oven and turn the dial to select "Air Fry" mode.
8. Press TIME/SLICES button and again turn the dial to set the cooking time to 8 minutes.
9. Now push TEMP/SHADE button and rotate the dial to set the temperature at 355 °F.
10. Press "Start/Stop" button to start.
11. When the unit beeps to show that it is preheated, open the oven door.
12. Insert the SearPlate in the oven.
13. When cooking time is completed, open the oven door and remove the SearPlate.
14. Cut into equal-sized wedges and serve.

Delicious Potato Casserole

Servings: 10
Cooking Time: 35 Minutes
Ingredients:

- 7 eggs
- 1/2 cup almond milk
- 1 onion, chopped & sautéed
- 8 oz cheddar cheese, grated
- 20 oz frozen hash browns, diced
- 1 lb sausage, cooked
- Pepper
- Salt

Directions:

1. Place rack in the bottom position and close door. Select bake mode set the temperature to 350°F and set the timer to 35 minutes. Press the setting dial to preheat.
2. In a mixing bowl, whisk eggs with milk, pepper, and salt.
3. Add remaining ingredients and mix well.
4. Pour egg mixture into the prepared casserole dish.
5. Once the unit is preheated, open the door, and place the casserole dish onto the center of the rack, and close the door.
6. Serve and enjoy.

Zucchini Ratatouille

Servings: 4
Cooking Time: 15 Minutes
Ingredients:

- ½ cup zucchini
- 1 yellow pepper
- 2 tomatoes
- 1 onion, peeled
- 1 garlic clove, crushed
- 2 teaspoons dried herbs
- Fresh ground black pepper
- 1 tablespoon olive oil

Directions:

1. Arrange a drip pan in the bottom of your Ninja Foodi Digital Air Fryer Oven cooking chamber.
2. Preheat your Oven to 392 °F in "AIR FRY" mode.
3. Cut zucchini, bell pepper, tomatoes, and onion into small cubes.
4. Take a bowl and mix in garlic, herbs, ½ teaspoon salt, season with pepper, stir in olive oil.
5. Place bowl in basket and slide into oven. Cook for 15 minutes, stir vegetables once when the "Turn Food" mode shows.
6. Stir well and enjoy it!

Moist Banana Bread

Servings: 12
Cooking Time: 55 Minutes
Ingredients:

- 2 eggs
- 3 ripe bananas
- 2 cups flour
- 1/4 tsp cinnamon
- 1 tsp baking soda
- 1 cup sugar
- 1 tsp vanilla
- 1 stick butter, melted
- 1/2 tsp salt

Directions:

1. Place rack in the bottom position and close door. Select bake mode set the temperature to 350°F and set the timer to 55 minutes. Press the setting dial to preheat.
2. Add bananas and butter to a mixing bowl and mash using a fork.
3. Add eggs and vanilla and stir until well combined.
4. In a separate bowl, mix together flour, baking soda, sugar, cinnamon, and salt,
5. Add flour mixture to the banana mixture and mix until just combined.
6. Pour batter into the greased loaf pan.
7. Once the unit is preheated, open the door, and place the loaf pan onto the center of the rack, and close the door.
8. Slice and serve.

Pepper Omelet

Servings: 2
Cooking Time: 10 Minutes
Ingredients:

- 1 teaspoon butter
- 1 small onion, sliced
- ½ of green bell pepper, seeded and chopped
- 4 eggs
- ¼ teaspoon milk
- Salt and ground black pepper, as required
- ¼ cup Cheddar cheese, grated

Directions:

1. In a skillet, melt the butter over medium heat and cook the onion and bell pepper for about 4-5 minutes.
2. Remove the skillet from heat and set it aside to cool slightly.
3. Meanwhile, add the eggs, milk, salt, and black pepper to a bowl and beat well. Add the cooked onion mixture and gently stir to combine.
4. Place the zucchini mixture into a small sheet pan.
5. Select the "AIR FRY" function of your Ninja Foodi Digital Air Fryer Oven by adjusting the temperature to 355 °F and set the time to 5 minutes.
6. Press the "START/PAUSE" button to start. When the unit beeps to show that it is preheated, open the door.
7. Arrange pan over the wire rack and insert in the oven when the unit beeps to show that cooking time is completed, press the "Power" button to stop cooking and open the door.
8. Cut the omelet into two portions and serve hot.

Egg In Hole

Servings: 1
Cooking Time: 10 Minutes
Ingredients:
- 1 piece toast
- 1 egg
- Salt and pepper, to taste

Directions:
1. Use nonstick cooking spray to spray SearPlate.
2. Place a piece of bread on the SearPlate.
3. Remove the bread by poking a hole in it with a cup or a cookie cutter.
4. Into the hole, crack the egg.
5. Turn on your Ninja Foodi Digital Air Fryer Oven and rotate the knob to select "Air Fry".
6. Select the timer for 6 minutes and the temperature for 330 °F.
7. When it beeps to signify it has preheated, insert the SearPlate in the oven.
8. Dish out and sprinkle with salt and pepper to serve.

Breakfast Potatoes

Servings: 4
Cooking Time: 35 Minutes
Ingredients:
- 5 cups potatoes, chopped
- 1/2 tsp old bay seasoning
- 1 tsp garlic powder
- 1 tsp paprika
- 2 tbsp olive oil
- 1 bell pepper, chopped
- 1 tsp garlic, minced
- 1 onion, diced
- 1 tsp sea salt

Directions:
1. Add potatoes and remaining ingredients into the large bowl and toss well.
2. Spread potatoes on a sheet pan.
3. Select bake then set the temperature to 400°F and time to 25 minutes. Press start.
4. Once the Ninja Foodi Digital Air Fryer Oven is preheated then place the sheet pan into the oven.
5. Stir potatoes and bake for 10 minutes more.
6. Serve and enjoy.

Tomato Spinach Muffins

Servings: 12
Cooking Time: 20 Minutes
Ingredients:
- 12 eggs
- 1 cup fresh spinach, chopped
- 1/2 tsp Italian seasoning
- 1 cup tomatoes, chopped
- 2 tbsp olives, sliced
- 4 tbsp water
- Pepper
- Salt

Directions:
1. Place rack in the bottom position and close door. Select bake mode set the temperature to 350°F and set the timer to 20 minutes. Press the setting dial to preheat.
2. In a mixing bowl, whisk eggs with water, Italian seasoning, pepper, and salt.
3. Add spinach, olives, and tomatoes and stir well.
4. Pour egg mixture into the greased muffin pan.
5. Once the unit is preheated, open the door, and place the muffin pan onto the center of the rack, and close the door.
6. Serve and enjoy.

Kale Egg Cups

Servings: 6
Cooking Time: 15 Minutes
Ingredients:
- 5 eggs
- 3 oz cheddar cheese, shredded
- 1 cup kale, chopped
- 1/4 tsp garlic powder
- Pepper
- Salt

Directions:
1. Spray 6-cups muffin pan with cooking spray and set aside.
2. In a bowl, whisk eggs with garlic powder, pepper, and salt. Stir in cheese and kale.
3. Pour egg mixture into the greased muffin pan.
4. Select bake then set the temperature to 400°F and time to 15 minutes. Press start.
5. Once the Ninja Foodi Digital Air Fryer Oven is preheated then place the muffin pan into the oven.
6. Serve and enjoy.

Puffed Egg Tarts

Servings: 4
Cooking Time: 21 Minutes.
Ingredients:
- ½ frozen puff pastry, thawed
- ¾ cup Cheddar cheese, shredded
- 4 large eggs
- 1 tablespoon fresh parsley, minced

Directions:
1. Spread the pastry sheet on a floured surface and cut it into 4 squares of equal size.
2. Place the four squares in the SearPlate of Ninja Foodi Digital Air Fryer Oven.
3. Transfer the SearPlate to Ninja Foodi Digital Air Fryer Oven and close the door.
4. Select "Air Fry" mode by rotating the dial.
5. Press the TEMP/SHADE button and change the value to 300 °F.
6. Press the TIME/SLICES button and change the value to 10 minutes, then press Start/Stop to begin cooking.

7. Press the center of each pastry square using the back of a metal spoon.

8. Divide cheese into these indentations and crack one egg into each pastry.

9. Return to the oven and close its oven door.

10. Rotate the dial to select the "Air Fry" mode.

11. Press the TIME/SLICES button and again use the dial to set the cooking time to 11 minutes.

12. Now Press the TEMP/SHADE button and rotate the dial to set the temperature at 350 °F.

13. Garnish the squares with parsley.

14. Serve warm.

Baked Berry Oatmeal

Servings: 6
Cooking Time: 20 Minutes

Ingredients:
- 1 egg
- 2 cups old fashioned oats
- 1 cup strawberries, sliced
- 1 1/2 tsp baking powder
- 1/4 cup maple syrup
- 1 1/2 cups almond milk
- 1 cup blueberries
- 1/2 tsp salt

Directions:
1. Place rack in the bottom position and close door. Select bake mode set the temperature to 375°F and set the timer to 20 minutes. Press the setting dial to preheat.

2. In a bowl, mix together oats, baking powder, and salt.

3. Add egg, maple syrup, vanilla, and milk and stir well.

4. Add berries and stir well.

5. Pour the mixture into the greased baking dish.

6. Once the unit is preheated, open the door, and place the baking dish onto the center of the rack, and close the door.

7. Serve and enjoy.

Blueberry-lemon Scones

Servings: 6
Cooking Time: 25 Minutes.

Ingredients:
- 2 cups all-purpose flour
- 1 tablespoon baking powder
- 2 teaspoons sugar
- 1 teaspoon kosher salt
- 2 ounces refined coconut oil
- 1 cup fresh blueberries
- ¼ ounce lemon zest
- 8 ounces coconut milk

Directions:
1. Blend coconut oil with salt, sugar, baking powder, and flour in a food processor.

2. Transfer this flour mixture to a mixing bowl.

3. Now add coconut milk and lemon zest to the flour mixture, then mix well.

4. Fold in blueberries and mix the prepared dough well until smooth.

5. Spread this blueberry dough into a 7-inch round and place it in a pan.

6. Refrigerate the blueberry dough for 15 minutes, then slice it into 6 wedges.

7. Layer the SearPlate with a parchment sheet.

8. Place the blueberry wedges in the lined SearPlate.

9. Transfer the scones to Ninja Foodi Digital Air Fryer Oven and close the door.

10. Select "Bake" mode by rotating the dial.

11. Press the TIME/SLICES button and change the value to 25 minutes.

12. Press the TEMP/SHADE button and change the value to 400 °F.

13. Press Start/Stop to begin cooking.

14. Serve fresh.

Breakfast Bake

Servings: 6
Cooking Time: 50 Minutes.

Ingredients:
- 24 ounces bulk pork sausage
- 1 medium bell pepper, chopped
- 1 medium onion, chopped
- 3 cups frozen hash brown potatoes
- 2 cups shredded Cheddar cheese
- 1 cup Bisquick mix
- 2 cups milk
- ¼ teaspoon pepper
- 4 eggs

Directions:
1. Whisk Bisquick with milk, eggs, and pepper in a mixer.

2. Sauté pork sausage, onion, and bell pepper in a 10-inch skillet over medium heat.

3. Stir cook until the sausage turns brown in color, then transfer to SearPlate.

4. Toss in potatoes, 1 ½ cups of cheese, and the Bisquick mixture.

5. Transfer the SearPlate to Ninja Foodi Digital Air Fryer Oven and close the door.

6. Select "Bake" mode by rotating the dial.

7. Press the TIME/SLICES button and change the value to 45 minutes.

8. Press the TEMP/SHADE button and change the value to 350 °F.

9. Press Start/Stop to begin cooking.

10. Drizzle the remaining cheese over the casserole and bake for 5 minutes.

11. Serve.

French Toast

Servings: 4
Cooking Time: 6 Minutes
Ingredients:
- 1 cup heavy cream
- 1 egg, beaten
- ¼ powdered sugar
- 1 teaspoon cinnamon
- 8 slices of bread

Directions:
1. Place your bread on the wire rack.
2. Turn on your Ninja Foodi Digital Air Fryer Oven and rotate the knob to select "Air Roast".
3. Select the timer for 4 minutes and the temperature for 390°F.
4. While the bread is toasting, combine the remaining ingredients in a mixing bowl.
5. Dip bread in batches into the mixture, making sure both sides are covered.
6. Place them on the air fry basket.
7. Now again, turn on your Ninja Foodi Digital Air Fryer Oven and rotate the knob to select "Air Fry".
8. Select the timer for 4 minutes and the temperature for 390 °F.
9. Serve.

Ham & Egg Cups

Servings: 6

Cooking Time: 18 Minutes
Ingredients:
- 6 ham slices
- 6 eggs
- 6 tablespoons cream
- 3 tablespoons mozzarella cheese, shredded
- ¼ teaspoon dried basil, crushed

Directions:
1. Lightly grease 6 cups of a silicone muffin tin.
2. Line each prepared muffin cup with 1 ham slice.
3. Crack 1 egg into each muffin cup and top with cream.
4. Sprinkle with cheese and basil.
5. Press AIR OVEN MODE button of Ninja Foodi Digital Air Fryer Oven and turn the dial to select "Air Fry" mode.
6. Press TIME/SLICES button and again turn the dial to set the cooking time to 18 minutes.
7. Now push TEMP/SHADE button and rotate the dial to set the temperature at 350 °F.
8. Press "Start/Stop" button to start.
9. When the unit beeps to show that it is preheated, open the oven door.
10. Arrange the muffin tin over the wire rack and insert in the oven.
11. When cooking time is completed, open the oven door and place the muffin tin onto a wire rack to cool for about 5 minutes.
12. Carefully invert the muffins onto the platter and serve warm.

Snacks & Appetizer Recipes

Buttermilk Biscuits

Servings: 8
Cooking Time: 8 Minutes
Ingredients:
- ½ cup cake flour
- 1¼ cups all-purpose flour
- ¼ teaspoon baking soda
- ½ teaspoon baking powder
- 1 teaspoon granulated sugar
- Salt, to taste
- ¼ cup cold unsalted butter, cut into cubes
- ¾ cup buttermilk
- 2 tablespoons butter, melted

Directions:
1. In a large bowl, sift together flours, baking soda, baking powder, sugar, and salt.
2. With a pastry cutter, cut cold butter and mix until coarse crumb forms.
3. Slowly, add buttermilk and mix until a smooth dough forms.
4. Place the dough onto a floured surface and with your hands, press it into ½-inch thickness.
5. With a 1¾-inch-round cookie cutter, cut the biscuits.
6. Arrange the biscuits into SearPlate in a single layer and coat with the butter.
7. Press AIR OVEN MODE button of Ninja Foodi Digital Air Fryer Oven and turn the dial to select "Air Fry" mode.
8. Press TIME/SLICES button and again turn the dial to set the cooking time to 8 minutes.
9. Now push TEMP/SHADE button and rotate the dial to set the temperature at 400 °F.
10. Press "Start/Stop" button to start.
11. When the unit beeps to show that it is preheated, open the oven door.
12. Insert the SearPlate in the oven.
13. When cooking time is completed, open the oven door and place the SearPlate onto a wire rack for about 5 minutes.

14. Carefully invert the biscuits onto the wire rack to cool completely before serving.

Tofu Nuggets

Servings: 4
Cooking Time: 30 Minutes
Ingredients:
- 1 lb firm tofu, cut into cubes
- 1/2 tsp paprika
- 1 tsp Italian seasoning
- 1/2 tsp garlic powder
- 1 tsp onion powder
- 1/4 cup rice flour
- 1/4 cup Nutritional yeast flakes
- 1 tbsp liquid aminos
- 1 tsp salt

Directions:
1. Add tofu and liquid aminos into the mixing bowl. Mix well and let it marinate for 20 minutes.
2. In a separate bowl, add remaining ingredients and mix well. Add tofu and coat well.
3. Spray sheet pan with cooking spray.
4. Arrange tofu cubes on a greased sheet pan.
5. Select bake mode then set the temperature to 400°F and time for 30 minutes. Press start.
6. Once the Ninja Foodi Digital Air Fryer Oven is preheated then place the sheet pan into the oven.
7. Turn tofu pieces halfway through.
8. Serve and enjoy.

Zucchini Crisps

Servings: 2
Cooking Time: 30 Minutes
Ingredients:
- 2 larges zucchinis cut in sticks or round
- salt, to taste
- 1 cup all-purpose flour
- 3 eggs, beaten
- 2 ½ cups bread crumbs
- ⅓ cup Parmesan cheese, grated
- 1 tablespoon garlic powder
- 1 teaspoon onion powder

Directions:
1. Put zucchini in a bowl and add salt; let it sit for a while to drain excess liquid.
2. In a medium-sized bowl, mix the cheese, garlic powder, bread crumbs, onion powder, and salt. Whisk the eggs in a bowl.
3. Place flour in a shallow bowl separately. Toss zucchini in egg wash, then in flour, and at the end in bread crumb mixture.
4. Please put it on a crisper plate and add it to the basket. Put the basket in the on your Ninja Foodi Digital Air Fryer Oven, Air Fry at 360 °F for 30 minutes.
5. Halfway through, toss the zucchini.
6. Once it's done, serve.

Delicious Bean Dip

Servings: 8
Cooking Time: 25 Minutes
Ingredients:
- 32 oz can refried beans
- 1 cup Monterey jack cheese, shredded
- 1 cup cheddar cheese, shredded
- 1 oz taco seasoning
- 1 cup sour cream
- 8 oz cream cheese, softened

Directions:
1. Add refried beans and remaining ingredients into the large mixing bowl and mix until well combined.
2. Pour mixture into the greased baking dish.
3. Select bake mode then set the temperature to 350°F and time for 25 minutes. Press start.
4. Once the Ninja Foodi Digital Air Fryer Oven is preheated then place the baking dish into the oven.
5. Serve and enjoy.

Chipotle Potato Fries

Servings: 6
Cooking Time: 25 Minutes
Ingredients:
- 2 sweet potatoes, cut into fries shape
- 1/4 tsp pepper
- 1/2 tsp chipotle chili powder
- 1/2 tsp paprika
- 2 tbsp olive oil
- Salt
- Cooking spray

Directions:
1. Add sweet potato fries, pepper, chili powder, paprika, oil, and salt into the large bowl and toss well.
2. Spray sheet pan with cooking spray.
3. Spread sweet potato fries on a greased sheet pan.
4. Select bake mode then set the temperature to 450°F and time for 25 minutes. Press start.
5. Once the Ninja Foodi Digital Air Fryer Oven is preheated then place the sheet pan into the oven.
6. Stir fries after 15 minutes.
7. Serve and enjoy.

Mini Hot Dogs

Servings: 8
Cooking Time: 4 Minutes.
Ingredients:
- 8 ounces refrigerated crescent rolls
- 24 cocktail hot dogs

Directions:
1. Spread the crescent rolls into 8 triangles and cut each into 3 triangles.
2. Place one mini hot dog at the center of each crescent roll.
3. Wrap the rolls around the hot dog and place them in the air fry basket.

4. Transfer the basket to Ninja Foodi Digital Air Fryer Oven and close the door.
5. Select "Air Fry" mode by rotating the dial.
6. Press the TIME/SLICES button and change the value to 4 minutes.
7. Press the TEMP/SHADE button and change the value to 325 °F.
8. Press Start/Stop to begin cooking.
9. Serve warm.

Crispy Cauliflower Bites

Servings: 4
Cooking Time: 15 Minutes
Ingredients:
- 1 egg, lightly beaten
- 1 cauliflower head, cut into florets
- 1/2 cup almond flour
- 1 tbsp heavy cream
- 1 1/2 tbsp Ranch seasoning
- Pepper
- Salt

Directions:
1. Select air fry mode set the temperature to 350°F and set the timer to 15 minutes. Press the setting dial to preheat.
2. In a small bowl, whisk egg and cream.
3. In a shallow bowl, mix almond flour, ranch seasoning, pepper, and salt.
4. Dip each cauliflower floret in egg then coat with almond flour mixture.
5. Place coated cauliflower florets in an air fryer basket.
6. Once the unit is preheated, open the door, and place the air fryer basket on the top level of the oven, and close the door.
7. Serve and enjoy.

Potato Wedges

Servings: 4
Cooking Time: 45 Minutes
Ingredients:
- 5 potatoes, cut into wedges
- 2 thyme sprigs
- ½ cup parmesan cheese, grated
- 2 tablespoon lemon juice
- ⅓ cup olive oil
- 2 garlic cloves, minced
- Salt and pepper to taste

Directions:
1. Add potato wedges into the bowl.
2. Add lemon juice, oil, garlic, thyme, cheese, pepper, and salt, and toss well.
3. Place potato wedges onto the sheet pan. Place the wire rack inside.
4. Select BAKE mode set the temperature to 325 °F, on your Ninja Foodi Digital Air Fryer Oven.
5. And set time to 45 minutes. Press start to begin preheating.

6. Once the Ninja Foodi Digital Air Fryer Oven is preheated, place a sheet pan on a wire rack and close the oven door to start cooking. Cook for 45 minutes.
7. Serve and enjoy.

Pasta Chips

Servings: 4
Cooking Time: 10 Minutes.
Ingredients:
- ½ tablespoon olive oil
- ½ tablespoon nutritional yeast
- 1 cup bow tie pasta
- ⅔ teaspoon Italian Seasoning Blend
- ¼ teaspoon salt

Directions:
1. Cook and boil the pasta in salted water in half of the time as stated on the box, then drain it.
2. Toss the boiled pasta with salt, Italian seasoning, nutritional yeast, and olive oil in a bowl.
3. Spread this pasta in the air fry basket.
4. Transfer the basket to Ninja Foodi Digital Air Fryer Oven and close the door.
5. Select "Air Fry" mode by rotating the dial.
6. Press the TIME/SLICES button and change the value to 5 minutes.
7. Press the TEMP/SHADE button and change the value to 390 °F.
8. Press Start/Stop to begin cooking.
9. Toss the pasta and continue air frying for another 5 minutes.
10. Enjoy.

Spicy Carrot Fries

Servings: 2
Cooking Time: 12 Minutes
Ingredients:
- 1 large carrot, peeled and cut into sticks
- 1 tablespoon fresh rosemary, chopped finely
- 1 tablespoon olive oil
- ¼ teaspoon cayenne pepper
- Salt and ground black pepper, as required

Directions:
1. In a bowl, add all the ingredients and mix well.
2. Press AIR OVEN MODE button of Ninja Foodi Digital Air Fryer Oven and turn the dial to select "Air Fry" mode.
3. Press TIME/SLICES button and again turn the dial to set the cooking time to 12 minutes.
4. Now push TEMP/SHADE button and rotate the dial to set the temperature at 390 °F.
5. Press "Start/Stop" button to start.
6. When the unit beeps to show that it is preheated, open the oven door.
7. Arrange the carrot fries into the air fry basket and insert in the oven.
8. When cooking time is completed, open the oven door and transfer the carrot fries onto a platter.

9. Serve warm.

Rosemary Cashews

Servings: 8
Cooking Time: 8 Minutes
Ingredients:
- 1 lb cashews
- 2 tsp brown sugar
- 1/2 tsp mustard powder
- 1/2 tsp chili powder
- 2 tbsp rosemary
- 1 tsp Worcestershire sauce
- 1 tbsp butter, melted

Directions:
1. Add cashews and remaining ingredients into the mixing bowl and toss well to coat.
2. Spread cashews in an air fryer basket.
3. Select air fry mode then set the temperature to 300°F and time for 8 minutes. Press start.
4. Once the Ninja Foodi Digital Air Fryer Oven is preheated then place the basket into the top rails of the oven.
5. Stir cashews halfway through.
6. Serve and enjoy.

Fiesta Chicken Fingers

Servings: 4
Cooking Time: 12 Minutes.
Ingredients:
- ¾ pound boneless chicken breasts, cut into strips
- ½ cup buttermilk
- ¼ teaspoon pepper
- 1 cup all-purpose flour
- 3 cups corn chips, crushed
- 1 envelope taco seasoning
- For Serving:
- Sour cream ranch dip or Fresh salsa
- Cooking spray

Directions:
1. Coat the chicken with pepper and flour.
2. Mix corn chips with taco seasoning.
3. Dip the chicken fingers in the buttermilk, then coat with the corn chips.
4. Place the chicken fingers in the air fry basket and spray with cooking oil.
5. Transfer the basket to Ninja Foodi Digital Air Fryer Oven and close the door.
6. Select "Air Fry" mode by rotating the dial.
7. Press the TIME/SLICES button and change the value to 12 minutes.
8. Press the TEMP/SHADE button and change the value to 325 °F.
9. Press Start/Stop to begin cooking.
10. Flip the Chicken fingers once cooked halfway through, then resume cooking.
11. Serve warm with sour cream ranch dip or fresh salsa.

French Toast Bites

Servings: 2
Cooking Time: 10 Minutes
Ingredients:
- ½ loaf of brioche bread
- 3 eggs
- 1 tablespoon milk
- 1 teaspoon vanilla
- ½ teaspoon cinnamon

Directions:
1. In a large mixing bowl, cut half a loaf of bread into cubes.
2. Combine the eggs, milk, vanilla, and cinnamon in a small mixing dish.
3. Pour the mixture over the slices and toss to coat.
4. In greased air fry basket, arrange bread slices in a single layer.
5. Place inside the oven.
6. Turn on Ninja Foodi Digital Air Fryer Oven and rotate the knob to select "Air Fry".
7. Select the timer for 10 minutes and the temperature for 390 °F.
8. Remove from Ninja Foodi Digital Air Fryer Oven to serve.

Garlicky Almonds

Servings: 8
Cooking Time: 6 Minutes
Ingredients:
- 2 cups almonds
- 1/4 tsp pepper
- 1 tsp paprika
- 1 tbsp garlic powder
- 1 tbsp soy sauce

Directions:
1. Add soy sauce, garlic powder, paprika, and pepper into the mixing bowl and mix well.
2. Add almonds and toss until well coated.
3. Spread almonds in an air fryer basket.
4. Select air fry mode then set the temperature to 300°F and time for 6 minutes. Press start.
5. Once the Ninja Foodi Digital Air Fryer Oven is preheated then place the basket into the top rails of the oven.
6. Stir almonds halfway through.
7. Serve and enjoy.

Eggplant Fries

Servings: 4
Cooking Time: 10 Minutes.
Ingredients:
- 2 large eggs
- ½ cup grated Parmesan cheese
- ½ cup toasted wheat germ
- 1 teaspoon Italian seasoning
- ¾ teaspoon garlic salt

- 1 eggplant, peeled
- Cooking spray
- 1 cup meatless pasta sauce, warmed

Directions:
1. Cut the eggplant into sticks.
2. Mix parmesan cheese, wheat germ, seasoning, and garlic salt in a bowl.
3. Coat the eggplant sticks with the parmesan mixture.
4. Place the eggplant fries in the air fry basket and spray them with cooking spray.
5. Transfer the basket to Ninja Foodi Digital Air Fryer Oven and close the door.
6. Select "Air Fry" mode by rotating the dial.
7. Press the TIME/SLICES button and change the value to 10 minutes.
8. Press the TEMP/SHADE button and change the value to 375 °F.
9. Press Start/Stop to begin cooking.
10. Serve warm.

Crispy Avocado Fries

Servings: 2
Cooking Time: 7 Minutes
Ingredients:
- ¼ cup all-purpose flour
- Salt and ground black pepper, as required
- 1 egg
- 1 teaspoon water
- ½ cup panko breadcrumbs
- 1 avocado, peeled, pitted, and sliced into 8 pieces
- Non-stick cooking spray

Directions:
1. In a shallow bowl, mix the flour, salt, and black pepper together.
2. In a second bowl, mix well egg and water.
3. In a third bowl, put the breadcrumbs.
4. Coat the avocado slices with flour mixture, then dip into egg mixture and finally, coat evenly with the breadcrumbs.
5. Now, spray the avocado slices evenly with cooking spray.
6. Press AIR OVEN MODE button of Ninja Foodi Digital Air Fryer Oven and turn the dial to select "Air Fry" mode.
7. Press TIME/SLICES button and again turn the dial to set the cooking time to 7 minutes.
8. Now push TEMP/SHADE button and rotate the dial to set the temperature at 400 °F.
9. Press "Start/Stop" button to start.
10. When the unit beeps to show that it is preheated, open the oven door.
11. Arrange the avocado fries into the air fry basket and insert in the oven.
12. When cooking time is completed, open the oven door and transfer the avocado fries onto a platter.
13. Serve warm.

Bacon-wrapped Filled Jalapeno

Servings: 6
Cooking Time: 15 Minutes
Ingredients:
- 12 jalapenos
- 226g cream cheese
- ½ cup cheddar cheese, shredded
- ¼ teaspoon garlic powder
- 1/8 teaspoon onion powder
- 12 slices bacon, thinly cut
- Salt and pepper, to taste

Directions:
1. Discard the seeds from the jalapenos by cutting them in half and removing the stems.
2. Combine cream cheese, shredded cheddar cheese, garlic powder, onion powder, salt, and pepper. To blend, stir everything together.
3. Fill each jalapeno just to the top with the cream mixture using a tiny spoon.
4. Turn on Ninja Foodi Digital Air Fryer Oven and rotate the knob to select "Bake".
5. Preheat by selecting the timer for 15 minute and temperature for 350 °F. Press START/STOP to begin.
6. Cut each slice of bacon in half.
7. Wrap one piece of bacon around each half of a jalapeño.
8. In the SearPlate, arrange the bacon-wrapped filled jalapenos in an even layer.
9. When the unit beeps to signify it has preheated, insert the SearPlate in the oven. Close the oven and let it cook.
10. Serve and enjoy!

Zucchini Fritters

Servings: 4
Cooking Time: 7 Minutes
Ingredients:
- 10 ½ ounces zucchini, grated and squeezed
- 7 ounces Halloumi cheese
- ¼ cup all-purpose flour
- 2 eggs
- 1 teaspoon fresh dill, minced
- Salt and ground black pepper, to taste

Directions:
1. In a large bowl and mix together all the ingredients.
2. Make small-sized fritters from the mixture.
3. Select the "AIR FRY" function on your Ninja Foodi Digital Air Fryer Oven.
4. Press "Temp Button" to set the temperature at 355 °F.
5. Now press the "Time Button" and use the dial to set the cooking time to 7 minutes.
6. Press the "START/PAUSE" button to start. When the unit beeps to show that it is preheated, open the door.
7. Arrange fritters into the greased sheet pan and insert them in the oven.
8. When cooking time is completed, open the door and serve warm.

Onion Rings

Servings: 4
Cooking Time: 15 Minutes.
Ingredients:
- ½ cup all-purpose flour
- 1 teaspoon paprika
- 1 teaspoon salt, divided
- ½ cup buttermilk
- 1 egg
- 1 cup panko breadcrumbs
- 2 tablespoons olive oil
- 1 large yellow sweet onion, sliced ½-inch-thick rings

Directions:
1. Mix flour with paprika and salt on a plate.
2. Coat the onion rings with the flour mixture.
3. Beat egg with buttermilk in a bowl. Dip all the onion rings with the egg mixture.
4. Spread the breadcrumbs in a bowl.
5. Coat the onion rings with breadcrumbs.
6. Place the onion rings in the air fry basket and spray them with cooking oil.
7. Transfer the basket to Ninja Foodi Digital Air Fryer Oven and close the door.
8. Select "Air Fry" mode by rotating the dial.
9. Press the TEMP/SHADE button and change the value to 400 °F.
10. Press the TIME/SLICES button and change the value to 15 minutes, then press Start/Stop to begin cooking.
11. Serve warm.

Cauliflower Poppers

Servings: 6
Cooking Time: 20 Minutes
Ingredients:
- 3 tablespoons olive oil
- 1 teaspoon paprika
- ½ teaspoon ground cumin
- ¼ teaspoon ground turmeric
- Salt and ground black pepper, as required
- 1 medium head cauliflower, cut into florets

Directions:
1. In a bowl, place all ingredients and toss to coat well.
2. Place the cauliflower mixture in the greased SearPlate.
3. Press AIR OVEN MODE button of Ninja Foodi Digital Air Fryer Oven and turn the dial to select the "Bake" mode.
4. Press TIME/SLICES button and again turn the dial to set the cooking time to 20 minutes.
5. Now push TEMP/SHADE button and rotate the dial to set the temperature at 450 °F.
6. Press "Start/Stop" button to start.
7. When the unit beeps to show that it is preheated, open the oven door and insert the SearPlate in oven.
8. Flip the cauliflower mixture once halfway through.
9. When cooking time is completed, open the oven door and transfer the cauliflower poppers onto a platter.

10. Serve warm.

Glazed Chicken Wings

Servings: 4
Cooking Time: 25 Minutes
Ingredients:
- 1½ pounds chicken wingettes and drumettes
- ⅓ cup tomato sauce
- 2 tablespoons balsamic vinegar
- 2 tablespoons maple syrup
- ½ teaspoon liquid smoke
- ¼ teaspoon red pepper flakes, crushed
- Salt, as required

Directions:
1. Arrange the wings onto the greased SearPlate.
2. Press AIR OVEN MODE button of Ninja Foodi Digital Air Fryer Oven and turn the dial to select "Air Fry" mode.
3. Press TIME/SLICES button and again turn the dial to set the cooking time to 25 minutes.
4. Now push TEMP/SHADE button and rotate the dial to set the temperature at 380 °F.
5. Press "Start/Stop" button to start.
6. When the unit beeps to show that it is preheated, open the oven door and insert the SearPlate in oven.
7. Meanwhile, in a small pan, add the remaining ingredients over medium heat and cook for about 10 minutes stirring occasionally.
8. When cooking time is completed, open the oven door and place the chicken wings into a bowl.
9. Add the sauce and toss to coat well.
10. Serve immediately.

Carrot Chips

Servings: 8
Cooking Time: 15 Minutes.
Ingredients:
- 2 pounds carrots, sliced
- ¼ cup olive oil
- 1 tablespoon sea salt
- 1 teaspoon ground cumin
- 1 teaspoon ground cinnamon

Directions:
1. Toss the carrot slices with oil, sea salt, cumin, and cinnamon in a large bowl.
2. Grease the SearPlate and spread the carrot slices in it.
3. Transfer the SearPlate to Ninja Foodi Digital Air Fryer Oven and close the door.
4. Select "Bake" mode by rotating the dial.
5. Press the TIME/SLICES button and change the value to 15 minutes.
6. Press the TEMP/SHADE button and change the value to 450 °F.
7. Press Start/Stop to begin cooking.
8. Flip the chips after 7-8 minutes of cooking and resume baking.
9. Serve fresh.

Butternut Squash

Servings: 4
Cooking Time: 20 Minutes
Ingredients:
- 4 cups butternut squash, cubed
- 1 teaspoon cinnamon
- Olive oil cooking spray

Directions:
1. Spray the air fry basket or line it with foil and spray it with olive oil cooking spray.
2. Place the butternut squash in the basket.
3. Coat with olive oil and sprinkle with cinnamon.
4. Place inside the oven.
5. Turn on Ninja Foodi Digital Air Fryer Oven and rotate the knob to select "Bake".
6. Select the timer for 20 minutes and the temperature for 390 °F.
7. Serve immediately after cooking.

Cod Nuggets

Servings: 5
Cooking Time: 8 Minutes
Ingredients:
- 1 cup all-purpose flour
- 2 eggs
- ¾ cup breadcrumbs
- Pinch of salt
- 2 tablespoons olive oil
- 1 pound cod, cut into 1x2½-inch strips

Directions:
1. In a shallow dish, place the flour.
2. Crack the eggs in a second dish and beat well.
3. In a third dish, mix together the breadcrumbs, salt and oil.
4. Coat the nuggets with flour, then dip into beaten eggs and finally, coat with the breadcrumbs.
5. Press AIR OVEN MODE button of Ninja Foodi Digital Air Fryer Oven and turn the dial to select "Air Fry" mode.
6. Press TIME/SLICES button and again turn the dial to set the cooking time to 8 minutes.
7. Now push TEMP/SHADE button and rotate the dial to set the temperature at 390 °F.
8. Press "Start/Stop" button to start.
9. When the unit beeps to show that it is preheated, open the oven door.
10. Arrange the nuggets in air fry basket and insert in the oven.
11. When cooking time is completed, open the oven door and transfer the nuggets onto a platter.
12. Serve warm.

Potato Chips

Servings: 2
Cooking Time: 25 Minutes.
Ingredients:
- 1 medium Russet potato, sliced

- 1 tablespoon canola oil
- ¼ teaspoon sea salt
- ¼ teaspoon black pepper
- 1 teaspoon chopped fresh rosemary

Directions:
1. Fill a suitable glass bowl with cold water and add sliced potatoes.
2. Leave the potatoes for 20 minutes, then drain them. Pat dry the chips with a paper towel.
3. Toss the potatoes with salt, black pepper, and oil to coat well.
4. Spread the potato slices in the air fry basket evenly.
5. Transfer the basket to Ninja Foodi Digital Air Fryer Oven and close the door.
6. Select "Air Fry" mode by rotating the dial.
7. Press the TIME/SLICES button and change the value to 25 minutes.
8. Press the TEMP/SHADE button and change the value to 375 °F.
9. Press Start/Stop to begin cooking.
10. Garnish with rosemary.
11. Serve warm.

Tasty Sweet Potato Wedges

Servings: 4
Cooking Time: 25 Minutes
Ingredients:
- 3 sweet potatoes, peeled & cut into wedges
- 1/4 cup parsley, chopped
- 1/8 tsp cayenne pepper
- 1/4 tsp cinnamon
- 1 tsp garlic powder
- 1 tsp onion powder
- 1 tsp oregano
- 1 tsp chili powder
- 1/2 tsp ground cumin
- 2 tsp olive oil
- Pepper
- Salt
- Cooking spray

Directions:
1. Add sweet potato wedges and remaining ingredients into the large bowl and toss well.
2. Spray sheet pan with cooking spray.
3. Spread sweet potato wedges on a greased sheet pan.
4. Select bake mode then set the temperature to 425 °F and time for 25 minutes. Press start.
5. Once the Ninja Foodi Digital Air Fryer Oven is preheated then place the sheet pan into the oven.
6. Serve and enjoy.

Broccoli Balls

Servings: 4
Cooking Time: 25 Minutes
Ingredients:
- 2 eggs
- 2 cups broccoli, cooked & chopped
- 1/2 tsp garlic, minced
- 2 shallots, minced
- 3/4 cup cheddar cheese, shredded
- 1 cup breadcrumbs
- Pepper
- Salt
- Cooking spray

Directions:
1. Add all ingredients into the mixing bowl and mix until well combined.
2. Spray sheet pan with cooking spray.
3. Make small balls from the mixture and place them on a greased sheet pan.
4. Select bake mode then set the temperature to 390 °F and time for 25 minutes. Press start.
5. Once the Ninja Foodi Digital Air Fryer Oven is preheated then place the sheet pan into the oven.
6. Serve and enjoy.

Roasted Peanuts

Servings: 6
Cooking Time: 14 Minutes
Ingredients:
- 1½ cups raw peanuts
- Nonstick cooking spray

Directions:
1. Press AIR OVEN MODE button of Ninja Foodi Digital Air Fryer Oven and turn the dial to select "Air Fry" mode.
2. Press TIME/SLICES button and again turn the dial to set the cooking time to 14 minutes.
3. Now push TEMP/SHADE button and rotate the dial to set the temperature at 320 °F.
4. Press "Start/Stop" button to start.
5. When the unit beeps to show that it is preheated, open the oven door.
6. Arrange the peanuts in air fry basket and insert in the oven.
7. While cooking, toss the peanuts twice.
8. After 9 minutes of cooking, spray the peanuts with cooking spray.
9. When cooking time is completed, open the oven door and transfer the peanuts into a heatproof bowl.
10. Serve warm.

Easy Tofu Nuggets

Servings: 4
Cooking Time: 15 Minutes
Ingredients:
- 14 oz extra-firm tofu, cut into chunks
- 1 tsp poultry seasoning
- 1/4 cup water
- 2 tbsp soy sauce
- 1/3 cup nutritional yeast
- 1 tsp sweet paprika
- 1 tsp onion powder
- 1 tbsp garlic powder

Directions:
1. Select air fry mode set the temperature to 400 °F and set the timer to 15 minutes. Press the setting dial to preheat.
2. In a mixing bowl, add tofu chunks and remaining ingredients and mix until tofu is well coated.
3. Add tofu into the air fryer basket.
4. Once the unit is preheated, open the door, and place the air fryer basket on the top level of the oven, and close the door.
5. Serve and enjoy.

Zucchini Fries

Servings: 4
Cooking Time: 12 Minutes
Ingredients:
- 1 pound zucchini, sliced into 2½-inch sticks
- Salt, as required
- 2 tablespoons olive oil
- ¾ cup panko breadcrumbs

Directions:
1. In a colander, add the zucchini and sprinkle with salt. Set aside for about 10 minutes.
2. Gently pat dry the zucchini sticks with the paper towels and coat with oil.
3. In a shallow dish, add the breadcrumbs.
4. Coat the zucchini sticks with breadcrumbs evenly.
5. Press AIR OVEN MODE button of Ninja Foodi Digital Air Fryer Oven and turn the dial to select "Air Fry" mode.
6. Press TIME/SLICES button and again turn the dial to set the cooking time to 12 minutes.
7. Now push TEMP/SHADE button and rotate the dial to set the temperature at 400 °F.
8. Press "Start/Stop" button to start.
9. When the unit beeps to show that it is preheated, open the oven door.
10. Arrange the zucchini fries in air fry basket and insert in the oven.
11. When cooking time is completed, open the oven door and transfer the zucchini fries onto a platter.
12. Serve warm.

Easy Roasted Peanuts

Servings: 6
Cooking Time: 14 Minutes
Ingredients:
- 1 ½ cups raw peanuts
- Nonstick cooking spray

Directions:
1. Turn on your Ninja Foodi Digital Air Fryer Oven and select the "AIR FRY" function.

2. Set the temperature at 320 °F and cooking time to 14 minutes.
3. Press the "START/PAUSE" button to start. When the unit beeps to show that it is preheated, open the door.
4. Arrange the peanuts in the Air Crisp Basket and insert them in the oven.
5. While cooking, toss the peanuts twice. After 9 minutes of cooking, spray the peanuts with cooking spray.
6. When cooking time is completed, open the door and transfer the peanuts into a heatproof bowl.
7. Serve warm.

Crispy Prawns

Servings: 4
Cooking Time: 8 Minutes
Ingredients:
- 1 egg
- ½ pound nacho chips, crushed
- 12 prawns, peeled and deveined

Directions:
1. In a shallow dish, beat the egg.
2. In another shallow dish, place the crushed nacho chips.
3. Coat the prawn with the beaten egg and then roll into nacho chips.
4. Press AIR OVEN MODE button of Ninja Foodi Digital Air Fryer Oven and turn the dial to select "Air Fry" mode.
5. Press TIME/SLICES button and again turn the dial to set the cooking time to 8 minutes.
6. Now push TEMP/SHADE button and rotate the dial to set the temperature at 355 °F.
7. Press "Start/Stop" button to start.
8. When the unit beeps to show that it is preheated, open the oven door.
9. Arrange the prawns into the air fry basket and insert in the oven.
10. When cooking time is completed, open the oven door and serve immediately.

Flavors Stuffed Jalapeno Poppers

Servings: 4
Cooking Time: 20 Minutes
Ingredients:
- 10 jalapeno peppers, halved & seeded
- 1/2 tsp onion powder
- 1/4 tsp pepper
- 1 cup parmesan cheese, shredded
- 8 oz cream cheese, softened
- 1 cup ground sausage, browned

Directions:
1. In a mixing bowl, mix together sausage, cream cheese, parmesan cheese, onion powder, and pepper.
2. Stuff sausage mixture into each jalapeno halves.
3. Arrange stuffed peppers on a greased sheet pan.
4. Select bake mode then set the temperature to 425 °F and time for 20 minutes. Press start.

5. Once the Ninja Foodi Digital Air Fryer Oven is preheated then place the sheet pan into the oven.
6. Serve and enjoy.

Tortilla Chips

Servings: 3
Cooking Time: 3 Minutes
Ingredients:
- 4 corn tortillas, cut into triangles
- 1 tablespoon olive oil
- Salt, to taste

Directions:
1. Coat the tortilla chips with oil and then sprinkle each side of the tortillas with salt.
2. Press AIR OVEN MODE button of Ninja Foodi Digital Air Fryer Oven and turn the dial to select "Air Fry" mode.
3. Press TIME/SLICES button and again turn the dial to set the cooking time to 3 minutes.
4. Now push TEMP/SHADE button and rotate the dial to set the temperature at 390 °F.
5. Press "Start/Stop" button to start.
6. When the unit beeps to show that it is preheated, open the oven door.
7. Arrange the tortilla chips in air fry basket and insert in the oven.
8. When cooking time is completed, open the oven door and transfer the tortilla chips onto a platter.
9. Serve warm.

Zucchini Cheese Balls

Servings: 4
Cooking Time: 10 Minutes
Ingredients:
- 2 eggs, lightly beaten
- 1 medium zucchini, grated & squeezed
- 1 1/2 cups pepper jack cheese, shredded
- 1/3 cup breadcrumbs
- 1/4 tsp onion powder
- 1/2 tsp paprika
- 1 tsp garlic powder
- Pepper
- Salt

Directions:
1. Select air fry mode set the temperature to 380 °F and set the timer to 10 minutes. Press the setting dial to preheat.
2. In a bowl, mix grated zucchini and remaining ingredients until well combined.
3. Make small balls from the zucchini mixture and place into the air fryer basket.
4. Once the unit is preheated, open the door, and place the air fryer basket on the top level of the oven, and close the door.
5. Serve and enjoy.

Carrot Fries

Servings: 2
Cooking Time: 12 Minutes
Ingredients:
- 1 large carrot, peeled and cut into sticks
- 1 tablespoon fresh rosemary, chopped finely
- 1 tablespoon olive oil
- ¼ teaspoon cayenne pepper
- Salt and ground black pepper, to taste

Directions:
1. In a bowl, add all the ingredients and mix well.
2. Turn on your Ninja Foodi Digital Air Fryer Oven and select the "AIR FRY" function.
3. Set the temperature at 390 °F. and set the time to 12 minutes.
4. Press the "START/PAUSE" button to start. When the unit beeps to show that it is preheated, open the door. Arrange the carrot fries into the Air Crisp Basket and insert them in the oven.
5. When cooking time is completed, open the door and transfer the carrot fries onto a platter.
6. Serve warm.

Creamy & Spicy Dip

Servings: 16
Cooking Time: 30 Minutes
Ingredients:
- 15 oz cream cheese, softened
- 2 tbsp butter, melted
- 1 cup breadcrumbs
- 1 1/2 jalapeno pepper, minced
- 3.5 oz green chilies, diced
- 1 cup cheddar cheese, shredded
- 1 cup mayonnaise

Directions:
1. In a mixing bowl, mix cream cheese, jalapeno pepper, green chilies, cream cheese, and mayonnaise.
2. Pour cream cheese mixture into the baking dish.
3. Mix together breadcrumbs and melted butter and sprinkle over cream cheese mixture.
4. Select bake mode then set the temperature to 350 °F and time for 30 minutes. Press start.
5. Once the Ninja Foodi Digital Air Fryer Oven is preheated then place the baking dish into the oven.
6. Serve and enjoy.

Salt & Pepper Cashews

Servings: 6
Cooking Time: 6 Minutes
Ingredients:
- 2 cups cashews
- 1 tsp nutritional yeast
- 2 tbsp rice flour
- 1/2 tsp onion powder
- 2 tbsp olive oil
- 1/2 tsp garlic powder
- 1/2 tsp pepper
- 1 tsp salt

Directions:
1. Select air fry mode set the temperature to 350 °F and set the timer to 6 minutes. Press the setting dial to preheat.
2. In a bowl, toss cashews with oil, garlic powder, onion powder, flour, nutritional yeast, pepper, and salt until well coated.
3. Add cashews into the air fryer basket.
4. Once the unit is preheated, open the door, and place the air fryer basket on the top level of the oven, and close the door.
5. Serve and enjoy.

Baked Zucchini Tots

Servings: 4
Cooking Time: 30 Minutes
Ingredients:
- 1 egg
- 2 cups zucchini, grated & squeezed
- 1/4 tsp onion powder
- 1 tsp Italian seasoning
- 1/2 cup breadcrumbs
- 1/2 cup cheddar cheese, shredded
- Pepper
- Salt

Directions:
1. Add zucchini and remaining ingredients into the large bowl and mix until well combined.
2. Spray sheet pan with cooking spray.
3. Make small tots from the mixture and place them on a greased sheet pan.
4. Select bake mode then set the temperature to 400 °F and time for 30 minutes. Press start.
5. Once the Ninja Foodi Digital Air Fryer Oven is preheated then place the sheet pan into the oven.
6. Serve and enjoy.

Persimmon Chips

Servings: 2
Cooking Time: 10 Minutes
Ingredients:
- 2 ripe persimmons, cut into slices horizontally
- Salt and ground black pepper, as required

Directions:
1. Arrange the persimmons slices onto the greased SearPlate.
2. Press AIR OVEN MODE button of Ninja Foodi Digital Air Fryer Oven and turn the dial to select "Air Fry" mode.
3. Press TIME/SLICES button and again turn the dial to set the cooking time to 10 minutes.
4. Now push TEMP/SHADE button and rotate the dial to set the temperature at 400 °F.
5. Press "Start/Stop" button to start.

6. When the unit beeps to show that it is preheated, open the oven door.
7. Insert the SearPlate in oven.
8. Flip the chips once halfway through.
9. When cooking time is completed, open the oven door and transfer the chips onto a platter.
10. Serve warm.

Spicy Spinach Chips

Servings: 4
Cooking Time: 10 Minutes
Ingredients:
- 2 cups fresh spinach leaves, torn into bite-sized pieces
- ½ tablespoon coconut oil, melted
- ⅛ teaspoon garlic powder
- Salt, as required

Directions:
1. In a large bowl and mix together all the ingredients.
2. Arrange the spinach pieces onto the greased SearPlate.
3. Press AIR OVEN MODE button of Ninja Foodi Digital Air Fryer Oven and turn the dial to select "Air Fry" mode.
4. Press TIME/SLICES button and again turn the dial to set the cooking time to 10 minutes.
5. Now push TEMP/SHADE button and rotate the dial to set the temperature at 300 °F.
6. Press "Start/Stop" button to start.
7. When the unit beeps to show that it is preheated, open the oven door.
8. Insert the SearPlate in oven.
9. Toss the spinach chips once halfway through.
10. When cooking time is completed, open the oven door and transfer the spinach chips onto a platter.
11. Serve warm.

Spicy Chickpeas

Servings: 12
Cooking Time: 40 Minutes
Ingredients:
- 30 oz can chickpeas, drained, rinsed & pat dry
- 1/4 tsp cayenne
- 2 tsp garlic powder
- 1 tbsp paprika
- 2 tbsp olive oil
- 3 tbsp hot sauce

Directions:
1. Add chickpeas and remaining ingredients into the mixing bowl and mix until well coated.
2. Spread chickpeas on a greased sheet pan.
3. Select bake mode then set the temperature to 425 °F and time for 40 minutes. Press start.
4. Once the Ninja Foodi Digital Air Fryer Oven is preheated then place the sheet pan into the oven.
5. Serve and enjoy.

Easy Sweet Potato Tots

Servings: 6

Cooking Time: 16 Minutes
Ingredients:
- 2 sweet potatoes, peel, boil, & grated
- 1/2 tsp Cajun seasoning
- Salt

Directions:
1. Select air fry mode set the temperature to 400 °F and set the timer to 16 minutes. Press the setting dial to preheat.
2. In a bowl, mix grated sweet potatoes, Cajun seasoning, and salt until well combined.
3. Make small tots from the sweet potato mixture and place into the air fryer basket.
4. Once the unit is preheated, open the door, and place the air fryer basket on the top level of the oven, and close the door.
5. Serve and enjoy.

French Fries

Servings: 2
Cooking Time: 25 Minutes
Ingredients:
- 1 pound of potatoes, cut into sticks
- Sea salt, to taste
- ½ teaspoon. black pepper
- 1 tablespoon of canola oil

Directions:
1. Cut the potatoes into 2-inch strips and soak them in cold water for 30 minutes.
2. Drain and pat dry the potatoes.
3. Preheat the Ninja Foodi Digital Air Fryer Oven at 360 °F for 3 minutes.
4. Take a bowl and add potatoes, salt, black pepper, and canola oil. Toss all the ingredients well.
5. Transfer it to a baking dish and place it inside a ninja oven. Set a timer to 25 minutes at 390 °F by selecting "BAKE."
6. After 15 minutes, turn off the oven and toss the fries.
7. Complete the cooking cycle.
8. Once 25 minutes pass, serve hot.

Pumpkin Fries

Servings: 6
Cooking Time: 12 Minutes.
Ingredients:
- ½ cup plain Greek yogurt
- 2 tablespoons maple syrup
- 3 teaspoons chipotle peppers in adobo sauce, minced
- ⅛ teaspoon salt
- 1 medium pie pumpkin
- ¼ teaspoon garlic powder
- ¼ teaspoon ground cumin
- ¼ teaspoon chili powder
- ¼ teaspoon pepper

Directions:
1. Peel and cut the pumpkin into sticks.

2. Mix garlic powder, cumin, chili powder, salt, and black pepper.

3. Coat the pumpkin sticks with the spice mixture.

4. Spread the pumpkin fries in the air fry basket and spray them with cooking spray.

5. Transfer the basket to Ninja Foodi Digital Air Fryer Oven and close the door.

6. Select "Air Fry" mode by rotating the dial.

7. Press the TIME/SLICES button and change the value to 12 minutes.

8. Press the TEMP/SHADE button and change the value to 400 °F.

9. Press Start/Stop to begin cooking.

10. Toss the fries once cooked halfway through, then resume cooking.

11. Mix yogurt with maple syrup and adobo sauce in a bowl.

12. Serve fries with the sauce.

Roasted Cashews

Servings: 6
Cooking Time: 5 Minutes
Ingredients:
- 1½ cups raw cashew nuts
- 1 teaspoon butter, melted
- Salt and freshly ground black pepper, as required

Directions:
1. In a bowl, mix all the ingredients together.

2. Press AIR OVEN MODE button of Ninja Foodi Digital Air Fryer Oven and turn the dial to select "Air Fry" mode.

3. Press TIME/SLICES button and again turn the dial to set the cooking time to 5 minutes.

4. Now push TEMP/SHADE button and rotate the dial to set the temperature at 355 °F.

5. Press "Start/Stop" button to start.

6. When the unit beeps to show that it is preheated, open the oven door.

7. Arrange the cashews into the air fry basket and insert in the oven.

8. Shake the cashews once halfway through.

9. When cooking time is completed, open the oven door and transfer the cashews into a heatproof bowl.

10. Serve warm.

Ranch Kale Chips

Servings: 6
Cooking Time: 5 Minutes.
Ingredients:
- 2 tablespoons olive oil
- 4 cups kale leaves
- 2 teaspoons Vegan Ranch Seasoning
- 1 tablespoon nutritional yeast flakes
- ¼ teaspoon salt

Directions:
1. Toss the kale leaves with oil, salt, yeast, and Ranch seasoning in a large bowl.

2. Spread the seasoned kale leaves in the air fry basket.

3. Transfer the air fry basket to Ninja Foodi Digital Air Fryer Oven and close the door.

4. Select "Air Fry" mode by rotating the dial.

5. Press the TIME/SLICES button and change the value to 5 minutes.

6. Press the TEMP/SHADE button and change the value to 370 °F.

7. Press Start/Stop to begin cooking.

8. Serve warm.

Red Meat Recipes

Crispy Sirloin Steaks

Servings: 2
Cooking Time: 14 Minutes
Ingredients:
- ½ cup flour
- Salt and ground black pepper, as required
- 2 eggs
- ¾ cup breadcrumbs
- 3 sirloin steaks, pounded

Directions:
1. In a shallow bowl, place the flour, salt and black pepper and mix well.
2. In a second shallow bowl, beat the eggs.
3. In a third shallow bowl, place the breadcrumbs.
4. Coat the steak with flour, then dip into eggs, and finally coat with the panko mixture.
5. Press AIR OVEN MODE button of Ninja Foodi Digital Air Fryer Oven and turn the dial to select "Air Fry" mode.
6. Press TIME/SLICES button and again turn the dial to set the cooking time to 14 minutes.
7. Now push TEMP/SHADE button and rotate the dial to set the temperature at 360 °F.
8. Press "Start/Stop" button to start.
9. When the unit beeps to show that it is preheated, open the oven door.
10. Arrange the steaks into the greased air fry basket and insert in the oven.
11. When the cooking time is completed, open the oven door and serve hot.

Citrus Pork Chops

Servings: 6
Cooking Time: 15 Minutes
Ingredients:
- ½ cup olive oil
- 1 teaspoon fresh orange zest, grated
- 3 tablespoons fresh orange juice
- 1 teaspoon fresh lime zest, grated
- 3 tablespoons fresh lime juice
- 8 garlic cloves, minced
- 1 cup fresh cilantro, chopped finely
- ¼ cup fresh mint leaves, chopped finely
- 1 teaspoon dried oregano, crushed
- 1 teaspoon ground cumin
- Salt and ground black pepper, as required
- 6 thick-cut pork chops

Directions:
1. In a bowl, place the oil, orange zest, orange juice, lime zest, lime juice, garlic, fresh herbs, oregano, cumin, salt and black pepper and beat until well combined.
2. In a small bowl, reserve ¼ cup of the marinade.

3. In a large zip lock bag, place the remaining marinade and pork chops.
4. Seal the bag and shake to coat well.
5. Refrigerate to marinate overnight.
6. Remove the pork chops from the bag and shake off to remove the excess marinade.
7. Press AIR OVEN MODE button of Ninja Foodi Digital Air Fryer Oven and turn the dial to select the "Broil" mode.
8. Press the TEMP/SHADE button and use the dial to select high. To set the temperature, press the TEMP/SHADE button again.
9. Press TIME/SLICES button and again turn the dial to set the cooking time to 15 minutes.
10. Press "Start/Stop" button to start.
11. When the unit beeps to show that it is preheated, open the oven door.
12. Place the pork chops over the wire rack and insert in oven.
13. After 8 minutes of cooking, flip the chops once.
14. When the cooking time is completed, open the oven door and serve hot.

Lemon Herb Pork Chops

Servings: 2
Cooking Time: 15 Minutes
Ingredients:
- 2 pork chops
- 1/2 tsp red pepper flakes
- 1 tsp fennel seeds, crushed
- 1 tsp fresh sage, chopped
- 1 tbsp canola oil
- 1 lemon zest
- 2 garlic cloves, minced
- 2 tsp fresh rosemary, chopped
- Pepper
- Salt

Directions:
1. Select air fry mode set the temperature to 380 °F and set the timer to 15 minutes. Press the setting dial to preheat.
2. In a small bowl, mix oil, lemon zest, garlic, red pepper flakes, fennel seeds, sage, rosemary, pepper, and salt.
3. Brush pork chops with oil mixture and place into the air fryer basket.
4. Once the unit is preheated, open the door, and place the air fryer basket on the top level of the oven, and close the door.
5. Serve and enjoy.

Lamb Chops With Rosemary Sauce

Servings: 8
Cooking Time: 45 Minutes.
Ingredients:
- 8 lamb loin chops
- 1 small onion, peeled and chopped
- Salt and black pepper, to taste
- For the sauce:
- 1 onion, peeled and chopped
- 1 tablespoon rosemary leaves
- 1 ounce butter
- 1 ounce plain flour
- 6 ounces milk
- 6 ounces vegetable stock
- 2 tablespoons cream, whipping
- Salt and black pepper, to taste

Directions:
1. Place the lamb loin chops and onion in a SearPlate, then drizzle salt and black pepper on top.
2. Transfer the SearPlate to Ninja Foodi Digital Air Fryer Oven and close the door.
3. Select "Air Fry" mode by rotating the dial.
4. Press the TIME/SLICES button and change the value to 45 minutes.
5. Press the TEMP/SHADE button and change the value to 350 °F.
6. Press Start/Stop to begin cooking.
7. Prepare the white sauce by melting butter in a suitable saucepan, then stir in onions.
8. Sauté for 5 minutes, then stir flour and stir cook for 2 minutes.
9. Stir in the rest of the ingredients and mix well.
10. Pour the sauce over baked chops and serve.

Lamb Burgers

Servings: 6
Cooking Time: 8 Minutes
Ingredients:
- 2 pounds ground lamb
- ½ tablespoon onion powder
- ½ tablespoon garlic powder
- ¼ teaspoon ground cumin
- Salt and ground black pepper, as required

Directions:
1. In a bowl, add all the ingredients and mix well.
2. Make 6 equal-sized patties from the mixture.
3. Arrange the patties onto the greased SearPlate in a single layer.
4. Press AIR OVEN MODE button of Ninja Foodi Digital Air Fryer Oven and turn the dial to select "Air Fry" mode.
5. Press TIME/SLICES button and again turn the dial to set the cooking time to 8 minutes.
6. Now push TEMP/SHADE button and rotate the dial to set the temperature at 360 °F.
7. Press "Start/Stop" button to start.

8. When the unit beeps to show that it is preheated, open the oven door.
9. Insert the SearPlate in oven.
10. Flip the burgers once halfway through.
11. When cooking time is completed, open the oven door and serve hot.

Garlicky Lamb Steaks

Servings: 4
Cooking Time: 15 Minutes
Ingredients:
- ½ onion, roughly chopped
- 5 garlic cloves, peeled
- 1 tablespoon fresh ginger, peeled
- 1 teaspoon ground fennel
- ½ teaspoon ground cumin
- ½ teaspoon ground cinnamon
- ½ teaspoon cayenne pepper
- Salt and ground black pepper, as required
- 1½ pounds boneless lamb sirloin steaks

Directions:
1. In a blender, add the onion, garlic, ginger, and spices and pulse until smooth.
2. Transfer the mixture into a large bowl.
3. Add the lamb steaks and coat with the mixture generously.
4. Refrigerate to marinate for about 24 hours.
5. Press AIR OVEN MODE button of Ninja Foodi Digital Air Fryer Oven and turn the dial to select "Air Fry" mode.
6. Press TIME/SLICES button and again turn the dial to set the cooking time to 15 minutes.
7. Now push TEMP/SHADE button and rotate the dial to set the temperature at 330 °F.
8. Press "Start/Stop" button to start.
9. When the unit beeps to show that it is preheated, open the oven door and grease the air fry basket.
10. Place the lamb steaks into the prepared air fry basket and insert in the oven.
11. Flip the steaks once halfway through.
12. When cooking time is completed, open the oven door and serve hot.

Steak Veggie Bites

Servings: 2
Cooking Time: 8 Minutes
Ingredients:
- 1 lb ribeye steak, cut into cubes
- 2 cups broccoli florets
- 2 tbsp butter, melted
- 8 oz mushrooms, sliced
- 1 tbsp garlic, minced
- 1 tsp Worcestershire sauce
- Pepper
- Salt

Directions:

1. Select air fry mode set the temperature to 400 °F and set the timer to 8 minutes. Press the setting dial to preheat.
2. In a bowl, toss steak cubes with mushrooms, Worcestershire sauce, butter, broccoli, garlic, pepper, and salt.
3. Add steak and vegetable mixture into the air fryer basket.
4. Once the unit is preheated, open the door, and place the air fryer basket on the top level of the oven, and close the door.
5. Serve and enjoy.

Sauce Glazed Meatloaf

Servings: 6
Cooking Time: 60 Minutes.
Ingredients:
- 1 pound ground beef
- ½ onion chopped
- 1 egg
- 1 ½ garlic clove, minced
- 1 ½ tablespoons ketchup
- 1 ½ tablespoons fresh parsley, chopped
- ¼ cup breadcrumbs
- 2 tablespoons milk
- Salt to taste
- 1 ½ teaspoons herb seasoning
- ¼ teaspoon black pepper
- ½ teaspoon ground paprika
- Glaze
- ¾ cup ketchup
- 1 ½ teaspoons white vinegar
- 2 ½ tablespoons brown sugar
- 1 teaspoon garlic powder
- ½ teaspoon onion powder
- ¼ teaspoon ground black pepper
- ¼ teaspoon salt

Directions:
1. Thoroughly mix ground beef with egg, onion, garlic, crumbs, and all the ingredients in a bowl.
2. Grease SearPlate with oil or butter and spread the minced beef in.
3. Transfer the SearPlate to Ninja Foodi Digital Air Fryer Oven and close the door.
4. Select "Air Fry" mode by rotating the dial.
5. Press the TIME/SLICES button and change the value to 40 minutes.
6. Press the TEMP/SHADE button and change the value to 375 °F.
7. Press Start/Stop to begin cooking.
8. Meanwhile, prepare the glaze by whisking its ingredients in a suitable saucepan.
9. Stir cook for 5 minutes until it thickens.
10. Brush this glaze over the meatloaf and bake it again for 15 minutes.
11. Slice and serve.

Simple Pork Chops

Servings: 2
Cooking Time: 18 Minutes
Ingredients:
- 2 (½-inch thick) pork chops
- Salt and ground black pepper, as required

Directions:
1. Season the pork chops with salt and black pepper evenly.
2. Arrange the pork chops onto a greased SearPlate.
3. Press AIR OVEN MODE button of Ninja Foodi Digital Air Fryer Oven and turn the dial to select the "Broil" mode.
4. Press the TEMP/SHADE button and use the dial to select high. To set the temperature, press the TEMP/SHADE button again.
5. Press TIME/SLICES button and again turn the dial to set the cooking time to 18 minutes.
6. Press "Start/Stop" button to start.
7. When the unit beeps to show that it is preheated, open the oven door and insert the SearPlate in oven.
8. After 12 minutes of cooking, flip the chops once.
9. When cooking time is completed, open the oven door and serve hot.

Baked Pork Chops

Servings: 2
Cooking Time: 20 Minutes
Ingredients:
- 2 boneless pork chops
- ½ tablespoon olive oil
- ¾ tablespoon brown sugar
- ½ teaspoon onion powder
- 1 teaspoon paprika
- ½ teaspoon dried thyme
- ¼ teaspoon black pepper
- ½ teaspoon salt

Directions:
1. Turn on your Ninja Foodi Digital Air Fryer Oven and rotate the knob to select "Bake".
2. Preheat by selecting the timer for 3 minutes and temperature for 425 °F.
3. Take a dish and line SearPlate with parchment paper.
4. Arrange the pork chops on the prepared SearPlate.
5. Take a small bowl and combine the brown sugar, onion powder, dried thyme, salt, pepper and paprika.
6. Rub the prepared mixture over pork chops evenly.
7. Bake the pork chops in the preheated Ninja Foodi Digital Air Fryer Oven for 20 minutes at 425 °F.
8. After done, set them aside for 5 minutes and then serve.
9. Enjoy!

Simple New York Strip Steak

Servings: 1
Cooking Time: 8 Minutes
Ingredients:
- ½ teaspoon olive oil
- ½ New York strip steak
- Kosher salt and ground black pepper, to taste

Directions:
1. Coat the steak with oil and then, generously season with salt and black pepper.
2. Grease an air fry basket.
3. Place steak into the prepared air fry basket.
4. Turn on your Ninja Foodi Digital Air Fryer Oven and rotate the knob to select "Air Fry".
5. Select the timer for about 7 to 8 minutes and temperature for 400 °F.
6. Remove from the oven and place the steak onto a cutting board for about 10 minutes before slicing.
7. Cut the steak into desired-size slices and transfer onto serving plates.
8. Serve immediately.

Garlic Balsamic Lamb Chops

Servings: 4
Cooking Time: 15 Minutes
Ingredients:
- 4 lamb chops
- 1 tsp garlic, crushed
- 2 tbsp canola oil
- 1/4 cup balsamic vinegar
- 1/2 tsp onion powder
- 1/2 tsp paprika
- Pepper
- Salt

Directions:
1. Select air fry mode set the temperature to 400 F and set the timer to 15 minutes. Press the setting dial to preheat.
2. Add lamb chops and remaining ingredients into the zip-lock bag. Seal bag and place in refrigerator for 60 minutes.
3. Place lamb chops into the air fryer basket.
4. Once the unit is preheated, open the door, and place the air fryer basket on the top level of the oven, and close the door.
5. Serve and enjoy.

Mustard Lamb Loin Chops

Servings: 2
Cooking Time: 15 Minutes
Ingredients:
- 1 tablespoon Dijon mustard
- ½ tablespoon white wine vinegar
- 1 teaspoon olive oil
- ½ teaspoon dried tarragon
- Salt and ground black pepper, as required
- 4 lamb loin chops

Directions:
1. In a large bowl, mix together the mustard, vinegar, oil, tarragon, salt, and black pepper.
2. Add the chops and coat with the mixture generously.
3. Arrange the chops onto the greased SearPlate.
4. Press AIR OVEN MODE button of Ninja Foodi Digital Air Fryer Oven and turn the dial to select "Bake" mode.
5. Press TIME/SLICES button and again turn the dial to set the cooking time to 15 minutes.
6. Now push TEMP/SHADE button and rotate the dial to set the temperature at 390 °F.
7. Press "Start/Stop" button to start.
8. When the unit beeps to show that it is preheated, open the oven door and insert the SearPlate in the oven.
9. When the cooking time is completed, open the oven door and serve hot.

Baked Beef Stew

Servings: 4
Cooking Time: 2 Hours
Ingredients:
- 1 pound beef-stew, cut into cubes
- ½ cup water
- 2 tablespoons instant tapioca
- ½ can dried tomatoes with juice
- 1 teaspoon white sugar
- ½ tablespoon beef bouillon granules
- ¾ teaspoon salt
- ⅛ teaspoon ground black pepper
- 1 strip celery, cut into ¾ inch pieces
- ½ onion, chopped
- 2 carrots, cut into 1-inch pieces
- ½ slice bread, cubed
- 2 potatoes, peeled and cubed

Directions:
1. Turn on your Ninja Foodi Digital Air Fryer Oven and rotate the knob to select "Bake".
2. Preheat by selecting the timer for 2 hours and temperature for 375 °F.
3. Grease a SearPlate.
4. Take a large pan over medium heat and brown the stew meat.
5. Meanwhile, take a bowl and mix together tomatoes, water, tapioca, beef bouillon granules, sugar, salt and pepper
6. Add prepared brown beef, celery, potatoes, carrots, onion and bread cubes.
7. Pour in the greased SearPlate.
8. Bake for about 2 hours in preheated Ninja Foodi Digital Air Fryer Oven at 375 °F.
9. Remove from oven and set aside for 2 minutes.
10. Serve warm and enjoy!

Russian Baked Beef

Servings: 3
Cooking Time: 1 Hour
Ingredients:
- ½ beef tenderloin
- 1 onion, sliced
- ¾ cup Cheddar cheese, grated
- ½ cup milk
- 1½ tablespoons mayonnaise
- Salt and black pepper, to taste

Directions:
1. Turn on your Ninja Foodi Digital Air Fryer Oven and rotate the knob to select "Bake".
2. Preheat by selecting the timer for 60 minutes and temperature for 350 °F.
3. Grease a SearPlate.
4. Cut the beef into thick slices and place in the SearPlate.
5. Season beef with salt and pepper and cover with onion slices. Also, spread cheese on top.
6. Take a bowl and stir together milk and mayonnaise and pour over cheese.
7. Bake for about an hour in preheated Ninja Foodi Digital Air Fryer Oven at 350 °F.
8. Remove from oven and set aside for 2 minutes.
9. Serve warm and enjoy!

Herbed Lamb Loin Chops

Servings: 2
Cooking Time: 12 Minutes
Ingredients:
- 4 (½-inch thick) lamb loin chops
- 1 teaspoon fresh thyme, minced
- 1 teaspoon fresh rosemary, minced
- 1 teaspoon fresh oregano, minced
- 2 garlic cloves, crushed
- Salt and ground black pepper, as required

Directions:
1. In a large bowl, place all ingredients and mix well.
2. Refrigerate to marinate overnight.
3. Arrange the chops onto the greased SearPlate.
4. Press AIR OVEN MODE button of Ninja Foodi Digital Air Fryer Oven and turn the dial to select "Bake" mode.
5. Press TIME/SLICES button and again turn the dial to set the cooking time to 12 minutes.
6. Now push TEMP/SHADE button and rotate the dial to set the temperature at 400 °F.
7. Press "Start/Stop" button to start.
8. When the unit beeps to show that it is preheated, open the oven door and insert the SearPlate in the oven.
9. Flip the chops once halfway through.
10. When the cooking time is completed, open the oven door and serve hot.

Bbq Pork Chops

Servings: 6
Cooking Time: 16 Minutes

Ingredients:
- 6 pork loin chops
- Salt and ground black pepper, as required
- ½ cup BBQ sauce

Directions:
1. With a meat tenderizer, tenderize the chops completely.
2. Sprinkle the chops with a little salt and black pepper.
3. In a large bowl, add the BBQ sauce and chops and mix well.
4. Refrigerate, covered for about 6-8 hours.
5. Press AIR OVEN MODE button of Ninja Foodi Digital Air Fryer Oven and turn the dial to select "Air Fry" mode.
6. Press TIME/SLICES button and again turn the dial to set the cooking time to 16 minutes.
7. Now push TEMP/SHADE button and rotate the dial to set the temperature at 355 °F.
8. Press "Start/Stop" button to start.
9. When the unit beeps to show that it is preheated, open the oven door.
10. Arrange the pork chops into the greased air fry basket and insert in the oven.
11. Flip the chops once halfway through.
12. When the cooking time is completed, open the oven door and serve hot.

Buttered Strip Steak

Servings: 4
Cooking Time: 15 Minutes
Ingredients:
- 2 New York strip steaks
- 2 tablespoons butter, melted
- Salt and ground black pepper, as required

Directions:
1. Brush each steak with the melted butter evenly and then season with salt and black pepper.
2. Press AIR OVEN MODE button of Ninja Foodi Digital Air Fryer Oven and turn the dial to select the "Broil" mode.
3. Press the TEMP/SHADE button and use the dial to select high. To set the temperature, press the TEMP/SHADE button again.
4. Press TIME/SLICES button and again turn the dial to set the cooking time to 15 minutes.
5. Press "Start/Stop" button to start.
6. When the unit beeps to show that it is preheated, open the oven door.
7. Place the steaks over the wire rack and insert in oven.
8. When cooking time is completed, open the oven door and place the steaks onto a cutting board for about 5 minutes before slicing.
9. Cut each steak into 2 portions and serve.

Tasty Steak Bites

Servings: 4
Cooking Time: 10 Minutes
Ingredients:
- 16 oz top sirloin filet, cut into 1-inch pieces
- 1 tsp chili powder
- 1/2 tbsp canola oil
- 1/2 tbsp brown sugar
- 1/4 tsp onion powder
- 1/4 tsp garlic powder
- Pepper
- Salt

Directions:
1. Select air fry mode set the temperature to 400 °F and set the timer to 10 minutes. Press the setting dial to preheat.
2. In a bowl, toss meat pieces with chili powder, oil, brown sugar, onion powder, garlic powder, pepper, and salt until well coated.
3. Add meat pieces into the air fryer basket.
4. Once the unit is preheated, open the door, and place the air fryer basket on the top level of the oven, and close the door.
5. Serve and enjoy.

Lime Mint Lamb Chops

Servings: 4
Cooking Time: 15 Minutes
Ingredients:
- 12 lamb loin chops
- 1/2 cup olive oil
- 3 lime juice
- 6 garlic cloves, minced
- 1/4 cup fresh mint, chopped
- 1 tbsp lime zest
- Pepper
- Salt

Directions:
1. Select air fry mode set the temperature to 370 °F and set the timer to 15 minutes. Press the setting dial to preheat.
2. Add lamb chops and remaining ingredients into the zip-lock bag. Seal bag and place in refrigerator for 4 hours.
3. Remove lamb chops from the marinade and place into the air fryer basket.
4. Once the unit is preheated, open the door, and place the air fryer basket on the top level of the oven, and close the door.
5. Serve and enjoy.

Flavors Pork Chops

Servings: 2
Cooking Time: 10 Minutes
Ingredients:
- 2 pork chops, boneless
- 1 tbsp canola oil
- 1/2 tsp lemon zest
- 1/2 tsp paprika
- 3/4 tsp rosemary, chopped
- 1/8 tsp red pepper flakes, crushed
- 1/4 tsp onion powder
- 1/4 tsp garlic powder
- Pepper
- Salt

Directions:
1. Select air fry mode set the temperature to 390 °F and set the timer to 10 minutes. Press the setting dial to preheat.
2. In a small bowl, mix rosemary, paprika, lemon zest, garlic powder, onion powder, red pepper flakes, pepper, and salt.
3. Brush pork chops with oil and rub with spice mixture.
4. Place pork chops into the air fryer basket.
5. Once the unit is preheated, open the door, and place the air fryer basket on the top level of the oven, and close the door.
6. Serve and enjoy.

Tarragon Beef Shanks

Servings: 4
Cooking Time: 15 Minutes.
Ingredients:
- 2 tablespoons olive oil
- 2 pounds beef shank
- Salt and black pepper to taste
- 1 onion, diced
- 2 stalks celery, diced
- 1 cup Marsala wine
- 2 tablespoons dried tarragon

Directions:
1. Place the beef shanks in a baking pan.
2. Whisk the rest of the ingredients in a bowl and pour over the shanks.
3. Place these shanks in the air fry basket.
4. Transfer the basket to Ninja Foodi Digital Air Fryer Oven and close the door.
5. Select "Air Fry" mode by rotating the dial.
6. Press the TIME/SLICES button and change the value to 15 minutes.
7. Press the TEMP/SHADE button and change the value to 375 °F.
8. Press Start/Stop to begin cooking.
9. Serve warm.

Meatballs

Servings: 6
Cooking Time: 8 Minutes
Ingredients:
- 1 egg
- 1 tsp Italian seasoning
- 4 oz ground pork
- 16 oz lean ground beef
- 1/3 cup Italian breadcrumbs

- 1/2 cup parmesan cheese, grated
- 1 tsp garlic, minced
- Pepper
- Salt

Directions:
1. Select air fry mode set the temperature to 350 °F and set the timer to 8 minutes. Press the setting dial to preheat.
2. Add meat and remaining ingredients into the bowl and mix until well combined.
3. Make small balls from the meat mixture and place them into the air fryer basket.
4. Once the unit is preheated, open the door, and place the air fryer basket on the top level of the oven, and close the door.
5. Serve and enjoy.

Mint Lamb With Toasted Hazelnuts

Servings: 2
Cooking Time: 25 Minutes.

Ingredients:
- ¼ cup hazelnuts, toasted
- ⅔ pound shoulder lamb, cut into strips
- 1 tablespoon hazelnut oil
- 2 tablespoons mint leaves, chopped
- ½ cup frozen peas
- ¼ cup water
- ½ cup white wine
- Salt and black pepper to taste

Directions:
1. Toss lamb with hazelnuts, spices, and all the ingredients in a SearPlate.
2. Transfer the SearPlate to Ninja Foodi Digital Air Fryer Oven and close the door.
3. Select "Bake" mode by rotating the dial.
4. Press the TIME/SLICES button and change the value to 25 minutes.
5. Press the TEMP/SHADE button and change the value to 370 °F.
6. Press Start/Stop to begin cooking.
7. Serve warm.

Pork Chops With Cashew Sauce

Servings: 8
Cooking Time: 52 Minutes.

Ingredients:
- 8 pork loin chops
- 1 small onion, peeled and chopped
- Salt and black pepper, to taste
- For the Sauce:
- ¼ cup cashews, finely chopped
- 1 cup cashew butter
- 1 ounce wheat flour
- 6 fl. oz. milk
- 6 fl. oz. beef stock
- 2 tablespoons coconut cream, whipping

- Salt and black pepper, to taste

Directions:
1. Place the pork loin chops and onion in the SearPlate, then drizzle salt and black pepper on top.
2. Transfer the SearPlate to Ninja Foodi Digital Air Fryer Oven and close the door.
3. Select "Bake" mode by rotating the dial.
4. Press the TIME/SLICES button and change the value to 45 minutes.
5. Press the TEMP/SHADE button and change the value to 375 °F.
6. Press Start/Stop to begin cooking.
7. Prepare the white sauce by first melting butter in a suitable saucepan, then stir in cashews.
8. Sauté for 5 minutes, then stir flour and stir cook for 2 minutes.
9. Stir in the rest of the sauce ingredients and mix well.
10. Pour the sauce over baked chops and serve.

Herbs Crumbed Rack Of Lamb

Servings: 5
Cooking Time: 30 Minutes

Ingredients:
- 1 tablespoon butter, melted
- 1 garlic clove, finely chopped
- 1¾ pounds rack of lamb
- Salt and ground black pepper, as required
- 1 egg
- ½ cup panko breadcrumbs
- 1 tablespoon fresh thyme, minced
- 1 tablespoon fresh rosemary, minced

Directions:
1. In a bowl, mix together the butter, garlic, salt, and black pepper.
2. Coat the rack of lamb evenly with garlic mixture.
3. In a shallow dish, beat the egg.
4. In another dish, mix together the breadcrumbs and herbs.
5. Dip the rack of lamb in beaten egg and then coat with breadcrumbs mixture.
6. Press AIR OVEN MODE button of Ninja Foodi Digital Air Fryer Oven and turn the dial to select "Air Fry" mode.
7. Press TIME/SLICES button and again turn the dial to set the cooking time to 25 minutes.
8. Now push TEMP/SHADE button and rotate the dial to set the temperature at 250 °F.
9. Press "Start/Stop" button to start.
10. When the unit beeps to show that it is preheated, open the oven door and grease the air fry basket.
11. Place the rack of lamb into the prepared air fry basket and insert in the oven.
12. After 25 minutes of cooking,
13. When cooking time is completed, open the oven door and set the temperature at 390 °F for 5 minutes.
14. When cooking time is completed, open the oven door and place the rack of lamb onto a cutting board for about 5-10 minutes.

15. With a sharp knife, cut the rack of lamb into individual chops and serve.

Herby Pork Bake

Servings: 2
Cooking Time: 40 Minutes
Ingredients:
- 1 pork loin steak, cut into bite-sized pieces
- ½ red onion, cut into wedges
- 1 potato, halved
- ½ carrot, halved
- ½ tablespoon olive oil
- 1 tablespoon mixed dried herbs
- 4 tablespoons Cider Pour Over Sauce

Directions:
1. Turn on your Ninja Foodi Digital Air Fryer Oven and rotate the knob to select "Bake".
2. Preheat by selecting the timer for 3 minutes and temperature for 420 °F.
3. Take the SearPlate and toss pork, onion, potatoes and carrots with herbs and olive oil.
4. Bake for about 25 minutes in preheated Ninja Foodi Digital Air Fryer Oven at 420 °F.
5. Remove from the oven and add sauce on top.
6. Bake for 5 more minutes so that you have a bubbling sauce.
7. Serve and enjoy!

Sage Garlic Pork Chops

Servings: 4
Cooking Time: 12 Minutes
Ingredients:
- 4 pork chops
- 1 tbsp dried sage
- 2 tbsp canola oil
- 2 tsp garlic, minced
- 1 tbsp apple cider vinegar
- Pepper
- Salt

Directions:
1. Select air fry mode set the temperature to 400 °F and set the timer to 12 minutes. Press the setting dial to preheat.
2. In a bowl, mix pork chops with oil, sage, vinegar, garlic, pepper, and salt and set aside for 15 minutes.
3. Place pork chops into the air fryer basket.
4. Once the unit is preheated, open the door, and place the air fryer basket on the top level of the oven, and close the door.
5. Serve and enjoy.

Spiced Pork Shoulder

Servings: 4
Cooking Time: 55 Minutes
Ingredients:
- 1 teaspoon ground cumin
- 1 teaspoon cayenne pepper
- ½ teaspoon garlic powder
- ½ teaspoon onion powder
- Salt and ground black pepper, as required
- 2 pounds skin-on pork shoulder

Directions:
1. In a small bowl, place the spices, salt and black pepper and mix well.
2. Arrange the pork shoulder onto a cutting board, skin-side down.
3. Season the inner side of pork shoulder with salt and black pepper.
4. With kitchen twines, tie the pork shoulder into a long round cylinder shape.
5. Season the outer side of pork shoulder with spice mixture.
6. Press AIR OVEN MODE button of Ninja Foodi Digital Air Fryer Oven and turn the dial to select the "Air Roast" mode.
7. Press TIME/SLICES button and again turn the dial to set the cooking time to 55 minutes.
8. Now push TEMP/SHADE button and rotate the dial to set the temperature at 350 °F.
9. Press "Start/Stop" button to start.
10. When the unit beeps to show that it is preheated, open the oven door and grease the air fry basket.
11. Arrange the pork shoulder into air fry basket and insert in the oven.
12. When cooking time is completed, open the oven door and place the pork shoulder onto a platter for about 10 minutes before slicing.
13. With a sharp knife, cut the pork shoulder into desired sized slices and serve.

Czech Roast Pork

Servings: 4
Cooking Time: 3 Hours And 30 Minutes
Ingredients:
- 1 tablespoon caraway seeds
- ½ tablespoon garlic powder
- 1 tablespoon vegetable oil
- ½ tablespoon prepared mustard
- ½ tablespoon salt
- 1½ medium onions, chopped
- 2 pounds pork shoulder blade roast
- 1 teaspoon ground black pepper
- ¼ cup beer

Directions:
1. Take a bowl and add garlic powder, mustard, vegetable oil, caraway seeds, salt and pepper to form a paste.
2. Rub the paste over pork roast and let it sit for about 30 minutes.
3. Turn on your Ninja Foodi Digital Air Fryer Oven and rotate the knob to select "Air Roast".
4. Preheat by selecting the timer for 3 minutes and temperature for 350 °F.

5. Take a SearPlate and add onions, pour in the beer and place pork.
6. Cover it with a foil.
7. Roast for about an hour in preheated Ninja Foodi Digital Air Fryer Oven at 350 °F.
8. Remove foil, turn roast and let it roast for 2 hours and 30 minutes more.
9. Remove from oven and set aside for 10 minutes before slicing.
10. Serve warm and enjoy!

Steak With Bell Peppers

Servings: 4
Cooking Time: 11 Minutes
Ingredients:
- 1 teaspoon dried oregano, crushed
- 1 teaspoon onion powder
- 1 teaspoon garlic powder
- 1 teaspoon red chili powder
- 1 teaspoon paprika
- Salt, as required
- 1¼ pounds flank steak, cut into thin strips
- 3 green bell peppers, seeded and cubed
- 1 red onion, sliced
- 2 tablespoons olive oil
- 3-4 tablespoons feta cheese, crumbled

Directions:
1. In a large bowl, mix together the oregano and spices.
2. Add the steak strips, bell peppers, onion, and oil and mix until well combined.
3. Press AIR OVEN MODE button of Ninja Foodi Digital Air Fryer Oven and turn the dial to select "Air Fry" mode.
4. Press TIME/SLICES button and again turn the dial to set the cooking time to 11 minutes.
5. Now push TEMP/SHADE button and rotate the dial to set the temperature at 390 °F.
6. Press "Start/Stop" button to start.
7. When the unit beeps to show that it is preheated, open the oven door and grease the air fry basket.
8. Place the steak mixture into the prepared air fry basket and insert in the oven.
9. When cooking time is completed, open the oven door and transfer the steak mixture onto serving plates.
10. Serve immediately with the topping of feta.

Lamb Rack With Lemon Crust

Servings: 3
Cooking Time: 25 Minutes.
Ingredients:
- 1 ⅔ pounds Frenched rack of lamb
- Salt and black pepper, to taste
- ¼ pound dry breadcrumbs
- 1 teaspoon garlic, grated
- ½ teaspoon salt
- 1 teaspoon cumin seeds
- 1 teaspoon ground cumin

- 1 teaspoon oil
- ½ teaspoon grated lemon rind
- 1 egg, beaten

Directions:
1. Place the lamb rack in a SearPlate and pour the whisked egg on top.
2. Whisk the rest of the crusting ingredients in a bowl and spread over the lamb.
3. Transfer the SearPlate to Ninja Foodi Digital Air Fryer Oven and close the door.
4. Select "Air Fry" mode by rotating the dial.
5. Press the TIME/SLICES button and change the value to 25 minutes.
6. Press the TEMP/SHADE button and change the value to 350 °F.
7. Press Start/Stop to begin cooking.
8. Serve warm.

Rosemary Lamb Chops

Servings: 2
Cooking Time: 6 Minutes
Ingredients:
- 1 tablespoon olive oil, divided
- 2 garlic cloves, minced
- 1 tablespoon fresh rosemary, chopped
- Salt and ground black pepper, as required
- 4 lamb chops

Directions:
1. In a large bowl, mix together the oil, garlic, rosemary, salt and black pepper.
2. Coat the chops with half of the garlic mixture.
3. Press AIR OVEN MODE button of Ninja Foodi Digital Air Fryer Oven and turn the dial to select "Air Fry" mode.
4. Press TIME/SLICES button and again turn the dial to set the cooking time to 6 minutes.
5. Now push TEMP/SHADE button and rotate the dial to set the temperature at 390 °F.
6. Press "Start/Stop" button to start.
7. When the unit beeps to show that it is preheated, open the oven door and grease the air fry basket.
8. Place the lamb chops into the prepared air fry basket and insert in the oven.
9. Flip the chops once halfway through.
10. When cooking time is completed, open the oven door and serve hot with the topping of the remaining garlic mixture.

Garlicky Lamb Chops

Servings: 8
Cooking Time: 45 Minutes.
Ingredients:
- 8 medium lamb chops
- ¼ cup olive oil
- 3 thin lemon slices
- 2 garlic cloves, crushed
- 1 teaspoon dried oregano

- 1 teaspoon salt
- ½ teaspoon black pepper

Directions:

1. Place the medium lamb chops in a SearPlate and rub them with olive oil.
2. Add lemon slices, garlic, oregano, salt, and black pepper on top of the lamb chops.
3. Transfer the SearPlate to Ninja Foodi Digital Air Fryer Oven and close the door.
4. Select "Air Roast" mode by rotating the dial.
5. Press the TIME/SLICES button and change the value to 45 minutes.
6. Press the TEMP/SHADE button and change the value to 400 °F.
7. Press Start/Stop to begin cooking.
8. Serve warm.

Bacon-wrapped Pork Tenderloin

Servings: 4
Cooking Time: 30 Minutes

Ingredients:

- 1 pork tenderloin
- 2 tablespoons Dijon mustard
- 1 tablespoon honey
- 4 bacon strips

Directions:

1. Coat the tenderloin with mustard and honey.
2. Wrap the pork tenderloin with bacon strips.
3. Press AIR OVEN MODE button of Ninja Foodi Digital Air Fryer Oven and turn the dial to select "Air Fry" mode.
4. Press TIME/SLICES button and again turn the dial to set the cooking time to 30 minutes.
5. Now push TEMP/SHADE button and rotate the dial to set the temperature at 360 °F.
6. Press "Start/Stop" button to start.
7. When the unit beeps to show that it is preheated, open the oven door and grease the air fry basket.
8. Place the pork tenderloin into the prepared air fry basket and insert in the oven.
9. Flip the pork tenderloin once halfway through.
10. When cooking time is completed, open the oven door and place the pork loin onto a cutting board for about 10 minutes before slicing.
11. With a sharp knife, cut the tenderloin into desired sized slices and serve.

Herbed Chuck Roast

Servings: 6
Cooking Time: 45 Minutes

Ingredients:

- 1 beef chuck roast
- 1 tablespoon olive oil
- 1 teaspoon dried rosemary, crushed
- 1 teaspoon dried thyme, crushed
- Salt, as required

Directions:

1. In a bowl, add the oil, herbs and salt and mix well.
2. Coat the beef roast with herb mixture generously.
3. Arrange the beef roast onto the greased SearPlate.
4. Press AIR OVEN MODE button of Ninja Foodi Digital Air Fryer Oven and turn the dial to select "Air Fry" mode.
5. Press TIME/SLICES button and again turn the dial to set the cooking time to 45 minutes.
6. Now push TEMP/SHADE button and rotate the dial to set the temperature at 360 °F.
7. Press "Start/Stop" button to start.
8. When the unit beeps to show that it is preheated, open the oven door and insert the SearPlate in the oven.
9. When cooking time is completed, open the oven door and place the roast onto a cutting board.
10. With a piece of foil, cover the beef roast for about 20 minutes before slicing.
11. With a sharp knife, cut the beef roast into desired size slices and serve.

Greek Lamb Farfalle

Servings: 6
Cooking Time: 20 Minutes.

Ingredients:

- 1 tablespoon olive oil
- 1 onion, chopped
- 2 garlic cloves, chopped
- 2 teaspoons dried oregano
- 1 pound pack lamb mince
- ¾ pound tin tomatoes, chopped
- ¼ cup black olives pitted
- ½ cup frozen spinach, defrosted
- 2 tablespoons dill, removed and chopped
- 9 ounces farfalle paste, boiled
- 1 ball half-fat mozzarella, torn

Directions:

1. Sauté onion and garlic with oil in a pan over moderate heat for 5 minutes.
2. Stir in tomatoes, spinach, dill, oregano, lamb, and olives then stir cook for 5 minutes.
3. Spread the lamb in the SearPlate and toss in the boiled Farfalle pasta.
4. Top the pasta lamb mix with mozzarella cheese.
5. Transfer the SearPlate into Ninja Foodi Digital Air Fryer Oven and close the door.
6. Select "Air Fry" mode by rotating the dial.
7. Press the TIME/SLICES button and change the value to 10 minutes.
8. Press the TEMP/SHADE button and change the value to 350 °F.
9. Press Start/Stop to begin cooking.
10. Serve warm.

Juicy Lamb Chops

Servings: 4
Cooking Time: 15 Minutes
Ingredients:

- 8 loin lamb chops
- 1/2 tsp canola oil
- 2 tbsp mustard
- 1 tbsp fresh lemon juice
- 1 tsp tarragon
- Pepper
- Salt

Directions:

1. Select air fry mode set the temperature to 390 °F and set the timer to 15 minutes. Press the setting dial to preheat.
2. Add lamb chops and remaining ingredients into the zip-lock bag. Seal bag and place in refrigerator for 60 minutes.
3. Place marinated lamb chops into the air fryer basket.
4. Once the unit is preheated, open the door, and place the air fryer basket on the top level of the oven, and close the door.
5. Serve and enjoy.

Glazed Beef Short Ribs

Servings: 4
Cooking Time: 8 Minutes
Ingredients:

- 2 pounds bone-in beef short ribs
- 3 tablespoons scallions, chopped
- ½ tablespoon fresh ginger, finely grated
- ½ cup low-sodium soy sauce
- ¼ cup balsamic vinegar
- ½ tablespoon Sriracha
- 1 tablespoon sugar
- ½ teaspoon ground black pepper

Directions:

1. In a resealable bag, place all the ingredients.
2. Seal the bag and shake to coat well.
3. Refrigerate overnight.
4. Press AIR OVEN MODE button of Ninja Foodi Digital Air Fryer Oven and turn the dial to select "Air Fry" mode.
5. Press TIME/SLICES button and again turn the dial to set the cooking time to 8 minutes.
6. Now push TEMP/SHADE button and rotate the dial to set the temperature at 380 °F.
7. Press "Start/Stop" button to start.
8. When the unit beeps to show that it is preheated, open the oven door.
9. Place the ribs into the greased air fry basket and insert in the oven.
10. Flip the ribs once halfway through.
11. When the cooking time is completed, open the oven door and serve hot.

Roasted Pork Belly

Servings: 8

Cooking Time: 1 Hour And 30 Minutes
Ingredients:

- ¾ teaspoon dried oregano
- ¾ teaspoon ground cumin
- ¾ teaspoon ground black pepper
- ¾ teaspoon salt
- ¾ teaspoon paprika
- ¾ teaspoon onion powder
- ¾ teaspoon ground turmeric
- ¾ teaspoon garlic powder
- 2 pounds whole pork belly
- Cayenne pepper, to taste
- 1 tablespoon lemon juice

Directions:

1. Take a bowl and add garlic powder, onion powder, turmeric, cayenne pepper, paprika, oregano, cumin, salt and pepper.
2. Rub the mixture onto pork belly.
3. Cover with a plastic wrap and refrigerate for at least 2 hours.
4. Turn on your Ninja Foodi Digital Air Fryer Oven and rotate the knob to select "Air Roast".
5. Preheat by selecting the timer for 3 minutes and temperature for 450 °F.
6. Line a SearPlate with parchment paper.
7. Place pork belly onto the prepared dish, with shallow cuts.
8. Rub lemon juice on top.
9. Roast for about 40 minutes in preheated Ninja Foodi Digital Air Fryer Oven at 350 °F until fat is crispy.
10. Remove from oven and set aside for 10 minutes before slicing.
11. Serve warm and enjoy!

Minced Lamb Casserole

Servings: 6
Cooking Time: 31 Minutes.
Ingredients:

- 2 tablespoons olive oil
- 1 medium onion, chopped
- ½ pound ground lamb
- 4 fresh mushrooms, sliced
- 1 cup small pasta shells, cooked
- 2 cups bottled marinara sauce
- 1 teaspoon butter
- 4 teaspoons flour
- 1 cup milk
- 1 egg, beaten
- 1 cup cheddar cheese, grated

Directions:

1. Put a wok on moderate heat and add oil to heat.
2. Toss in onion and sauté until soft.
3. Stir in mushrooms and lamb, then cook until meat is brown.
4. Add marinara sauce and cook it to a simmer.

5. Stir in pasta, then spread this mixture in the SearPlate.
6. Prepare the sauce by melting butter in a suitable saucepan over moderate heat.
7. Stir in flour and whisk well, pour in the milk.
8. Mix well and whisk ¼ cup of sauce with egg, then return it to the saucepan.
9. Stir, cook for 1 minute, then pour this sauce over the lamb.
10. Drizzle cheese over the lamb casserole.
11. Transfer the SearPlate to Ninja Foodi Digital Air Fryer Oven and close the door.
12. Select "Bake" mode by rotating the dial.
13. Press the TIME/SLICES button and change the value to 30 minutes.
14. Press the TEMP/SHADE button and change the value to 350 °F.
15. Press Start/Stop to begin cooking.
16. Serve warm.

Marinated Steak Bites

Servings: 6
Cooking Time: 10 Minutes
Ingredients:
- 1 lb ribeye steak, cut into pieces
- 1/4 tsp red pepper flakes
- 1/2 tsp garlic powder
- 1 tbsp lemon juice
- 1 tbsp lemon zest
- 1 stick butter, melted
- 1 tbsp parsley, chopped
- 1/2 tsp Worcestershire sauce
- 1/2 tbsp Dijon mustard
- Pepper
- Salt

Directions:
1. Select air fry mode set the temperature to 400 °F and set the timer to 10 minutes. Press the setting dial to preheat.
2. Add steak pieces and remaining ingredients into the bowl and mix well.
3. Cover and set aside for 30 minutes.
4. Remove steak pieces from the marinade and place into the air fryer basket.
5. Once the unit is preheated, open the door, and place the air fryer basket on the top level of the oven, and close the door.
6. Serve and enjoy.

Za'atar Chops

Servings: 8
Cooking Time: 20 Minutes.
Ingredients:
- 8 pork loin chops, bone-in
- 1 tablespoon Za'atar
- 3 garlic cloves, crushed
- 1 teaspoon avocado oil
- 2 tablespoons lemon juice
- 1 ¼ teaspoons salt
- Black pepper, to taste

Directions:
1. Rub the pork chops with oil, za'atar, salt, lemon juice, garlic, and black pepper.
2. Place these chops in the air fry basket.
3. Transfer the basket to Ninja Foodi Digital Air Fryer Oven and close the door.
4. Select "Air Fry" mode by rotating the dial.
5. Press the TIME/SLICES button and change the value to 20 minutes.
6. Press the TEMP/SHADE button and change the value to 400 °F.
7. Press Start/Stop to begin cooking.
8. Flip the chops when cooked halfway through, then resume cooking.
9. Serve warm.

Zucchini Beef Meatloaf

Servings: 4
Cooking Time: 40 Minutes.
Ingredients:
- 2 pounds ground beef
- 1 cup zucchini, shredded
- 2 eggs
- ½ cup onion, chopped
- 3 garlic cloves minced
- 3 tablespoons Worcestershire sauce
- 3 tablespoons fresh parsley, chopped
- ¾ cup Panko breadcrumbs
- ⅓ cup beef broth
- Salt to taste
- ¼ teaspoon ground black pepper
- ½ teaspoon ground paprika

Directions:
1. Thoroughly mix ground beef with egg, zucchini, onion, garlic, crumbs, parsley, Worcestershire sauce, broth and all the seasoning ingredients in a bowl.
2. Grease the SearPlate with oil and spread the minced beef in the pan.
3. Transfer the SearPlate to Ninja Foodi Digital Air Fryer Oven and close the door.
4. Select "Air Fry" mode by rotating the dial.
5. Press the TIME/SLICES button and change the value to 40 minutes.
6. Press the TEMP/SHADE button and change the value to 375 °F.
7. Press Start/Stop to begin cooking.
8. Slice and serve.

Roast Beef And Yorkshire Pudding

Servings: 2
Cooking Time: 1 Hour 50 Minutes
Ingredients:
- 1 egg, beaten
- ½ cup milk
- ½ cup flour
- 1/8 teaspoon salt
- Salt, to taste
- Freshly ground pepper, to taste
- 1 pound rump roast
- Garlic powder, to taste

Directions:
1. Turn on your Ninja Foodi Digital Air Fryer Oven and rotate the knob to select "Air Roast".
2. Set the timer for 90 minutes and temperature for 375 °F.
3. When the unit beeps to signify it has preheated, place beef in a SearPlate and season with salt, garlic powder and pepper.
4. Roast in oven for about 90 minutes until the thickest part of the beef is at 135 °F.
5. Remove from oven, reserving drippings.
6. Take a small bowl, beat egg until foamy.
7. Take another bowl, stir salt and flour. Pour in the beaten egg and add milk.
8. Now, preheat by selecting the timer for 3 minutes and temperature for 400 °F.
9. Pour the reserved drippings to a tin. Place in the preheated oven for about 3 minutes.
10. Remove from oven, add the flour mixture into the hot drippings.
11. Return to oven and set the timer for 20 minutes or until brown.
12. Serve warm and enjoy!

Ground Beef Casserole

Servings: 3
Cooking Time: 25 Minutes
Ingredients:
- ¼ medium onion, chopped
- ½ pound extra lean ground beef
- ½ pound penne
- ½ tablespoon olive oil
- ½ clove garlic, minced
- ½ cup marinara sauce
- 1 cup cheddar cheese, shredded
- Salt and pepper to taste

Directions:
1. Take a large pot with lightly salted water and bring it to a boil. Add penne and let it cook for about 10 minutes.
2. Take a pan and add oil, beef and onion.
3. Fry for about 10 minutes over medium-high heat and add garlic.
4. Stir in the marinara sauce and add salt and pepper according to taste.

5. Drain the pasta and pour into the SearPlate.
6. Add the beef-marinara mixture on top of the penne pasta. Lastly, add cheese with cheese.
7. Turn on your Ninja Foodi Digital Air Fryer Oven and rotate the knob to select "Bake".
8. Select the timer for 10 minutes and temperature for 400 °F. Press Star/Stop button to begin preheating.
9. Bake for about 10 minutes in preheated Ninja Foodi Digital Air Fryer Oven until the cheese is nicely melted.
10. Serve immediately.

American Roast Beef

Servings: 3
Cooking Time: 1 Hour
Ingredients:
- 1½ pounds beef eye of round roast
- ¼ teaspoon kosher salt
- ⅛ teaspoon black pepper, freshly ground
- ¼ teaspoon garlic powder

Directions:
1. Turn on your Ninja Foodi Digital Air Fryer Oven and rotate the knob to select "Air Roast".
2. Preheat by selecting the timer for 3 minutes and temperature for 375 °F.
3. Place beef in a SearPlate and season with salt, garlic powder and pepper.
4. Roast in oven for about an hour.
5. Remove from oven and set aside for 10 minutes before slicing.
6. Serve warm and enjoy!

Easy Steak Bites

Servings: 2
Cooking Time: 6 Minutes
Ingredients:
- 2 top sirloin steaks, cut into pieces
- 1 tbsp canola oil
- 1 tsp smoked paprika
- 1/4 tsp garlic powder
- 1/2 tsp ground coriander
- Pepper
- Salt

Directions:
1. Select air fry mode set the temperature to 400 °F and set the timer to 6 minutes. Press the setting dial to preheat.
2. In a bowl, toss steak pieces with remaining ingredients until well coated.
3. Add steak pieces into the air fryer basket.
4. Once the unit is preheated, open the door, and place the air fryer basket on the top level of the oven, and close the door.
5. Serve and enjoy.

Garlic Braised Ribs

Servings: 8
Cooking Time: 20 Minutes.
Ingredients:
- 2 tablespoons vegetable oil
- 5 pounds bone-in short ribs
- Salt and black pepper, to taste
- 2 heads garlic, halved
- 1 medium onion, chopped
- 4 ribs celery, chopped
- 2 medium carrots, chopped
- 3 tablespoons tomato paste
- ¼ cup dry red wine
- ¼ cup beef stock
- 4 sprigs thyme
- 1 cup parsley, chopped
- ½ cup chives, chopped
- 1 tablespoon lemon zest, grated

Directions:
1. Toss everything in a large bowl, then add short ribs.
2. Mix well to soak the ribs and marinate for 30 minutes.
3. Transfer the soaked ribs to the SearPlate and add the marinade around them.
4. Transfer the SearPlate to Ninja Foodi Digital Air Fryer Oven and close the door.
5. Select "Air Fry" mode by rotating the dial.
6. Press the TIME/SLICES button and change the value to 20 minutes.
7. Press the TEMP/SHADE button and change the value to 400 °F.
8. Press Start/Stop to begin cooking.
9. Serve warm.

Savory Pork Roast

Servings: 3
Cooking Time: 1 Hour
Ingredients:
- ¼ teaspoon dried thyme
- 1 tablespoon fresh rosemary, divided
- 1 teaspoon garlic salt
- ⅛ teaspoon black pepper, freshly ground
- 1½ pounds pork loin roast, boneless

Directions:
1. Turn on your Ninja Foodi Digital Air Fryer Oven and rotate the knob to select "Air Roast".
2. Preheat by selecting the timer for 3 minutes and temperature for 350 °F.
3. Take a bowl mix well rosemary, garlic salt, thyme, and pepper together.
4. Now add pork to coat well.
5. Take a dish and place coated pork on it.
6. Roast pork for about an hour in preheated Ninja Foodi Digital Air Fryer Oven at 350 °F.
7. Serve and enjoy!

Beef Zucchini Shashliks

Servings: 4
Cooking Time: 25 Minutes.
Ingredients:
- 1 pound beef, boned and diced
- 1 lime, juiced, and chopped
- 3 tablespoons olive oil
- 20 garlic cloves, chopped
- 1 handful rosemary, chopped
- 3 green peppers, cubed
- 2 zucchinis, cubed
- 2 red onions, cut into wedges

Directions:
1. Toss the beef with the rest of the skewer's ingredients in a bowl.
2. Thread the beef, peppers, zucchini, and onion on the skewers.
3. Place these beef skewers in the air fry basket.
4. Transfer the basket to Ninja Foodi Digital Air Fryer Oven and close the door.
5. Select "Air Fry" mode by rotating the dial.
6. Press the TIME/SLICES button and change the value to 25 minutes.
7. Press the TEMP/SHADE button and change the value to 370 °F.
8. Press Start/Stop to begin cooking.
9. Flip the skewers when cooked halfway through, then resume cooking.
10. Serve warm.

Pork Belly Bites

Servings: 4
Cooking Time: 15 Minutes
Ingredients:
- 1 lb pork belly, cut into 3/4-inch cubes
- 2 tbsp canola oil
- 8 oz mushrooms, clean and halved
- 1/2 tsp garlic powder
- 1 tsp soy sauce
- Pepper
- Salt

Directions:
1. Select air fry mode set the temperature to 400 °F and set the timer to 15 minutes. Press the setting dial to preheat.
2. In a bowl, toss pork belly cubes with remaining ingredients until well coated.
3. Add meat mixture into the air fryer basket.
4. Once the unit is preheated, open the door, and place the air fryer basket on the top level of the oven, and close the door.
5. Serve and enjoy.

Tasty Tri-tip Steaks

Servings: 2
Cooking Time: 12 Minutes
Ingredients:

- 12 oz tri-tip steaks
- 2 tbsp butter, melted
- 1 tsp garlic, minced
- Pepper
- Salt

Directions:
1. Select air fry mode set the temperature to 400 °F and set the timer to 12 minutes. Press the setting dial to preheat.
2. In a small bowl, mix butter, garlic, pepper, and salt.
3. Brush steaks with butter mixture and place into the air fryer basket.
4. Once the unit is preheated, open the door, and place the air fryer basket on the top level of the oven, and close the door.
5. Serve and enjoy.

Pork Chops With Brussels Sprouts

Servings: 2
Cooking Time: 10 Minutes
Ingredients:

- 2 pork chops
- 1 tsp Dijon mustard
- 1 tsp maple syrup
- 1 tsp canola oil
- 6 oz Brussels sprouts, quartered
- Pepper
- Salt

Directions:
1. Select air fry mode set the temperature to 400 °F and set the timer to 10 minutes. Press the setting dial to preheat.
2. In a small bowl, mix oil, Dijon mustard, maple syrup, pepper, and salt.
3. Brush pork chops with oil mixture and place into the air fryer basket and top with Brussels sprouts.
4. Once the unit is preheated, open the door, and place the air fryer basket on the top level of the oven, and close the door.
5. Serve and enjoy.

Lamb And Potato Bake

Servings: 2
Cooking Time: 55 Minutes
Ingredients:

- 2 potatoes
- ¾ lean lamb mince
- ½ teaspoon cinnamon
- ½ tablespoon olive oil
- 4 cups tomato pasta sauce
- 1 cup cheese sauce

Directions:
1. Boil the potatoes for 12 minutes or until half cooked.

2. Meanwhile, take a pan and heat oil over medium heat.
3. Add lamb mince in to brown. Use a spoon to break up lumps.
4. Add cinnamon and fry for about a minute.
5. Pour in the tomato sauce and leave for about 5 minutes.
6. Once the potatoes are done, thinly slice them.
7. Turn on your Ninja Foodi Digital Air Fryer Oven and rotate the knob to select "Bake".
8. Select the timer for 35 minutes and temperature for 390 °F.
9. Place everything on a SearPlate and spread cheeses on top.
10. Bake until well cooked.
11. Serve and enjoy!

Beef Zucchini Patties

Servings: 6
Cooking Time: 35 Minutes
Ingredients:

- 1 lb ground beef
- 1/2 onion, chopped
- 2 medium zucchini, grated and squeezed
- 2 eggs, lightly beaten
- 1/2 tsp chili powder
- 1 tsp curry powder
- 1 cup breadcrumbs
- Pepper
- Salt

Directions:
1. Place rack in the bottom position and close door. Select bake mode set the temperature to 400 °F and set the timer to 35 minutes. Press the setting dial to preheat.
2. Add all ingredients into the large bowl and mix until well combined.
3. Make six equal shapes patties from the meat mixture and place onto a baking sheet.
4. Once the unit is preheated, open the door, and place the baking sheet onto the rack, and close the door.
5. Serve and enjoy.

Seasoned Sirloin Steak

Servings: 2
Cooking Time: 12 Minutes
Ingredients:

- 2 top sirloin steaks
- 1 tablespoon steak seasoning
- Salt and ground black pepper, as required

Directions:
1. Season each steak with steak seasoning, salt and black pepper.
2. Arrange the steaks onto the greased SearPlate.
3. Press AIR OVEN MODE button of Ninja Foodi Digital Air Fryer Oven and turn the dial to select "Air Fry" mode.
4. Press TIME/SLICES button and again turn the dial to set the cooking time to 12 minutes.

5. Now push TEMP/SHADE button and rotate the dial to set the temperature at 400 °F.

6. Press "Start/Stop" button to start.

7. When the unit beeps to show that it is preheated, open the oven door and insert the SearPlate in the oven.

8. Flip the steaks once halfway through.

9. When cooking time is completed, open the oven door and serve hot.

Pork Stuffed Bell Peppers

Servings: 4
Cooking Time: 1 Hour 10 Minutes
Ingredients:
- 4 medium green bell peppers
- ⅔ pound ground pork
- 2 cups cooked white rice
- 1½ cups marinara sauce, divided
- 1 teaspoon Worcestershire sauce
- 1 teaspoon Italian seasoning
- Salt and ground black pepper, as required
- ½ cup mozzarella cheese, shredded

Directions:
1. Cut the tops from bell peppers and then carefully remove the seeds.

2. Heat a large skillet over medium heat and cook the pork for about 6-8 minutes. Mince the pork.

3. Add the rice, ¾ cup of marinara sauce, Worcestershire sauce, Italian seasoning, salt and black pepper and stir to combine.

4. Remove from the heat.

5. Arrange the bell peppers into the greased SearPlate.

6. Carefully, stuff each bell pepper with the pork mixture and top each with the remaining sauce.

7. Press AIR OVEN MODE button of Ninja Foodi Digital Air Fryer Oven and turn the dial to select the "Bake" mode.

8. Press TIME/SLICES button and again turn the dial to set the cooking time to 60 minutes.

9. Now push TEMP/SHADE button and rotate the dial to set the temperature at 350 °F.

10. Press "Start/Stop" button to start.

11. When the unit beeps to show that it is preheated, open the oven door.

12. Insert the SearPlate in oven.

13. After 50 minutes of cooking, top each bell pepper with cheese.

14. When cooking time is completed, open the oven door and transfer the bell peppers onto a platter.

15. Serve warm.

Lamb Kebabs

Servings: 4
Cooking Time: 20 Minutes.
Ingredients:
- 18 ounces lamb mince
- 1 teaspoon chili powder
- 1 teaspoon cumin powder
- 1 egg
- 2 ounces onion, chopped
- 2 teaspoons sesame oil
- Salt

Directions:
1. Whisk onion with egg, chili powder, oil, cumin powder, and salt in a bowl.

2. Add lamb to coat well, then thread it on the skewers.

3. Place these lamb skewers in the air fry basket.

4. Transfer the basket to Ninja Foodi Digital Air Fryer Oven and close the door.

5. Select "Air Fry" mode by rotating the dial.

6. Press the TIME/SLICES button and change the value to 20 minutes.

7. Press the TEMP/SHADE button and change the value to 395 °F.

8. Press Start/Stop to begin cooking.

9. Serve warm.

Garlic Herb Lamb Chops

Servings: 8
Cooking Time: 6 Minutes
Ingredients:
- 8 lamb chops
- 1/4 cup olive oil
- 1 tbsp thyme, chopped
- 2 garlic cloves, minced
- 1 lemon zest
- 1 tbsp rosemary, chopped
- 1/2 tsp dried oregano
- 2 tbsp lemon juice
- Pepper
- Salt

Directions:
1. Select air fry mode set the temperature to 400 °F and set the timer to 6 minutes. Press the setting dial to preheat.

2. Add lamb chops and remaining ingredients into the ziplock bag. Seal bag and place in refrigerator for 60 minutes.

3. Place lamb chops into the air fryer basket.

4. Once the unit is preheated, open the door, and place the air fryer basket on the top level of the oven, and close the door.

5. Serve and enjoy.

Balsamic Beef Top Roast

Servings: 10
Cooking Time: 45 Minutes
Ingredients:
- 1 tablespoon butter, melted
- 1 tablespoon balsamic vinegar
- ½ teaspoon ground cumin
- ½ teaspoon smoked paprika
- ½ teaspoon red pepper flakes, crushed
- Salt and ground black pepper, as required
- 3 pounds beef top roast

Directions:
1. In a bowl, add butter, vinegar, spices, salt and black pepper and mix well.

2. Coat the roast with spice mixture generously.

3. With kitchen twines, tie the roast to keep it compact.
4. Arrange the roast onto the greased SearPlate.
5. Press AIR OVEN MODE button of Ninja Foodi Digital Air Fryer Oven and turn the dial to select "Air Fry" mode.
6. Press TIME/SLICES button and again turn the dial to set the cooking time to 45 minutes.
7. Now push TEMP/SHADE button and rotate the dial to set the temperature at 360 °F.
8. Press "Start/Stop" button to start.
9. When the unit beeps to show that it is preheated, open the oven door and insert the SearPlate in the oven.
10. When the cooking time is completed, open the oven door and place the roast onto a cutting board for about 10 minutes before slicing.
11. With a sharp knife, cut the roast into desired sized slices and serve.

Herbed Leg Of Lamb

Servings: 6
Cooking Time: 1¼ Hours
Ingredients:
- 2¼ pounds boneless leg of lamb
- 2 tablespoons olive oil
- Salt and ground black pepper, as required
- 2 fresh rosemary sprigs
- 2 fresh thyme sprigs

Directions:
1. Coat the leg of lamb with oil and sprinkle with salt and black pepper.
2. Wrap the leg of lamb with herb sprigs.
3. Press AIR OVEN MODE button of Ninja Foodi Digital Air Fryer Oven and turn the dial to select "Air Fry" mode.
4. Press TIME/SLICES button and again turn the dial to set the cooking time to 75 minutes.
5. Now push TEMP/SHADE button and rotate the dial to set the temperature at 300 °F.
6. Press "Start/Stop" button to start.
7. When the unit beeps to show that it is preheated, open the oven door.
8. Arrange the leg of lamb into the greased air fry basket and insert in the oven.
9. Immediately set the temperature at 355 °F.
10. When the cooking time is completed, open the oven door and place the leg of lamb onto a cutting board for about 10 minutes.
11. Cut the leg of lamb into desired-sized pieces and serve.

Simple Beef Tenderloin

Servings: 10
Cooking Time: 50 Minutes
Ingredients:
- 1 beef tenderloin, trimmed
- 2 tablespoons olive oil
- Salt and ground black pepper, as required

Directions:
1. With kitchen twine, tie the tenderloin.

2. Rub the tenderloin with oil and season with salt and black pepper.
3. Place the tenderloin into the greased SearPlate.
4. Press AIR OVEN MODE button of Ninja Foodi Digital Air Fryer Oven and turn the dial to select the "Air Roast" mode.
5. Press TIME/SLICES button and again turn the dial to set the cooking time to 50 minutes.
6. Now push TEMP/SHADE button and rotate the dial to set the temperature at 400 °F.
7. Press "Start/Stop" button to start.
8. When the unit beeps to show that it is preheated, open the oven door and insert the SearPlate in the oven.
9. When cooking time is completed, open the oven door and place the tenderloin onto a platter for about 10 minutes before slicing.
10. With a sharp knife, cut the tenderloin into desired sized slices and serve.

Lamb Chops With Carrots

Servings: 4
Cooking Time: 10 Minutes
Ingredients:
- 2 tablespoons fresh rosemary, minced
- 2 tablespoons fresh mint leaves, minced
- 1 garlic clove, minced
- 3 tablespoons olive oil
- Salt and ground black pepper, as required
- 4 lamb chops
- 2 large carrots, peeled and cubed

Directions:
1. In a large bowl, mix together the herbs, garlic, oil, salt, and black pepper.
2. Add the chops and generously coat with mixture.
3. Refrigerate to marinate for about 3 hours.
4. In a large pan of water, soak the carrots for about 15 minutes.
5. Drain the carrots completely.
6. Press AIR OVEN MODE button of Ninja Foodi Digital Air Fryer Oven and turn the dial to select "Air Fry" mode.
7. Press TIME/SLICES button and again turn the dial to set the cooking time to 10 minutes.
8. Now push TEMP/SHADE button and rotate the dial to set the temperature at 390 °F.
9. Press "Start/Stop" button to start.
10. When the unit beeps to show that it is preheated, open the oven door.
11. Arrange chops into the greased air fry basket in a single layer and insert in the oven.
12. After 2 minutes of cooking, arrange carrots into the air fry basket and top with the chops in a single layer.
13. Insert the basket in oven.
14. When the cooking time is completed, open the oven door and transfer the chops and carrots onto serving plates.
15. Serve hot.

Beef, Pork & Lamb Recipes

Baked Pork Ribs

Servings: 8
Cooking Time: 30 Minutes
Ingredients:
- 2 lbs pork ribs, boneless
- 1 ½ tablespoon garlic powder
- 1 tablespoon onion powder
- Salt and pepper to taste

Directions:
1. Place pork ribs on a sheet pan and season with onion powder, garlic powder, pepper, and salt.
2. Place the wire rack inside.
3. Select "BAKE" mode, set the temperature to 350 °F, and set the time to 30 minutes.
4. Press "START/PAUSE" to begin preheating.
5. Once the Ninja Foodi Digital Air Fryer Oven is preheated, place the sheet pan on a wire rack and close the oven door to start cooking.
6. Cook for 30 minutes.
7. Serve and enjoy.

Glazed Lamb Chops

Servings: 4
Cooking Time: 15 Minutes
Ingredients:
- 1 tablespoon Dijon mustard
- ½ tablespoon fresh lime juice
- 1 teaspoon honey
- ½ teaspoon olive oil
- Salt and black pepper, to taste
- 4 lamb loin chops

Directions:
1. Mix the mustard, black pepper, lemon juice, oil, honey, salt, and black pepper in a bowl.
2. Add the chops and coat with the mixture generously.
3. Place the chops onto the greased sheet pan.
4. Insert the sheet pan in oven. Flip the chops once halfway through.
5. Select "BAKE" mode.
6. Press the "Time" button and turn the dial to set the cooking time to 15 minutes.
7. Now push the "Temp" button and rotate the dial to set the temperature at 390 °F.
8. Press the "START/PAUSE" button to start.
9. When the unit beeps to show that cooking time is completed, press the "Power" button to stop cooking and open the door.
10. Serve hot.

Herb Pork Chops

Servings: 4
Cooking Time: 15 Minutes
Ingredients:
- 4 pork chops
- 1/2 tsp mixed herbs
- 1/2 tsp paprika
- Pepper
- Salt
- Cooking spray

Directions:
1. Spray pork chops with cooking spray.
2. Mix together mix herbs, paprika, pepper, and salt, and rub over pork chops.
3. Place pork chops in an air fryer basket.
4. Select air fry then set the temperature to 350 °F and time for 15 minutes. Press start.
5. Once the Ninja Foodi Digital Air Fryer Oven is preheated then place the basket into the top rails of the oven.
6. Turn pork chops halfway through.
7. Serve and enjoy.

Simple Pork Tenderloin

Servings: 6
Cooking Time: 30 Minutes
Ingredients:
- 2 lbs pork tenderloin
- 1 tbsp smoked paprika
- 1/2 tsp chili powder
- 1/2 tbsp salt

Directions:
1. In a small bowl, mix together paprika, chili powder, and salt and rub over pork tenderloin.
2. Place pork tenderloin on a sheet pan.
3. Select bake mode then set the temperature to 425 °F and time for 30 minutes. Press start.
4. Once the Ninja Foodi Digital Air Fryer Oven is preheated then place the sheet pan into the oven.
5. Serve and enjoy.

Greek Pork Chops

Servings: 6
Cooking Time: 25 Minutes
Ingredients:
- 6 pork chops
- 1/2 cup basil pesto
- 2 tbsp olive oil
- Pepper
- Salt

Directions:
1. Brush pork chops with oil and season with pepper and salt.
2. Place pork chops into the baking dish.
3. Pour pesto over pork chops.
4. Select bake mode then set the temperature to 425 °F and time for 25 minutes. Press start.

5. Once the Ninja Foodi Digital Air Fryer Oven is preheated then place the baking dish into the oven.
6. Serve and enjoy.

Breaded Pork Chops

Servings: 3
Cooking Time: 19 Minutes
Ingredients:
- 3 pork chops, rinsed
- Salt and black pepper, to taste
- Garlic powder, to taste
- Smoked paprika, to taste
- ½ cup breadcrumbs
- 2 large eggs

Directions:
1. Rub the pork chops with garlic powder, black pepper, salt, and smoked paprika.
2. Spread the breadcrumbs in a shallow bowl and beat the eggs in another bowl.
3. Dip each chop in egg first, and then coat it well with breadcrumbs. Place these chops in the Air Fryer basket.
4. Transfer these chops to the Ninja Foodi Digital Air Fryer Oven and Close its door.
5. Select the "AIR FRY" mode using the dial.
6. Set its cooking time to 13 minutes and temperature to 350 °F, then press "START/PAUSE" to initiate preheating.
7. Flip the chops after 6 minutes and resume cooking.
8. Serve warm.

Lamb Loin Chops

Servings: 2
Cooking Time: 15 Minutes
Ingredients:
- 1 tablespoon Dijon mustard
- ½ tablespoon white wine vinegar
- 1 teaspoon olive oil
- ½ teaspoon dried tarragon
- Salt and ground black pepper, to taste
- 4 lamb loin chops

Directions:
1. In a large bowl, mix the mustard, vinegar, oil, tarragon, salt, and black pepper.
2. Add the chops and coat with the mixture generously.
3. Arrange the chops onto the greased sheet pan.
4. Insert the sheet pan in the oven.
5. Select the "BAKE" function on your Ninja Foodi Digital Air Fryer Oven.
6. Press "Temp Button" and use the dial to set the temperature at 390 °F.
7. Now press the "Time Button" and use the dial to set the cooking time to 15 minutes.
8. Press the "START/PAUSE" button to start.
9. When the cooking time is completed, open the door and serve hot.

Beef Short Ribs

Servings: 4
Cooking Time: 8 Minutes
Ingredients:
- 2 pounds bone-in beef short ribs
- 3 tablespoons scallions, chopped
- ½ tablespoon fresh ginger, finely grated
- ½ cup low-sodium soy sauce
- ¼ cup balsamic vinegar
- ½ tablespoon Sriracha
- 1 tablespoon sugar
- ½ teaspoon ground black pepper

Directions:
1. In a resalable bag, place all the ingredients. Seal the bag and shake to coat well. Refrigerate overnight.
2. Select the "AIR FRY" function on your Ninja Foodi Digital Air Fryer Oven.
3. Press "Temp Button" and use the dial to set the temperature at 380 °F.
4. Now press the "Time Button" and use the dial to set the cooking time to 8 minutes.
5. Press the "START/PAUSE" button to start.
6. Place the ribs into the greased Air Crisp Basket and insert them in the oven.
7. Flip the ribs once halfway through.
8. When the cooking time is completed, open the door and serve hot.

Easy Pork Ribs

Servings: 8
Cooking Time: 30 Minutes
Ingredients:
- 2 lbs pork ribs, boneless
- 1 tsp Italian seasoning
- Pepper
- Salt

Directions:
1. Place pork ribs in a baking dish and season with Italian seasoning, pepper, and salt.
2. Select bake mode then set the temperature to 350 °F and time for 30 minutes. Press start.
3. Once the Ninja Foodi Digital Air Fryer Oven is preheated then place the baking dish into the oven.
4. Serve and enjoy.

Lamb Patties

Servings: 4
Cooking Time: 15 Minutes
Ingredients:
- 1 lb ground lamb
- 1/4 cup onion, minced
- 1 tbsp garlic, minced
- 1/4 tsp cayenne pepper
- 1 tsp ground coriander
- 1 tsp ground cumin

- 1 tsp ground cinnamon
- 1/4 tsp pepper
- 1 tsp kosher salt

Directions:
1. Add all ingredients into the mixing bowl and mix until well combined.
2. Make small patties from the meat mixture and place them onto the sheet pan.
3. Select bake mode then set the temperature to 450 °F and time for 15 minutes. Press start.
4. Once the Ninja Foodi Digital Air Fryer Oven is preheated then place the sheet pan into the oven.
5. Serve and enjoy.

Flavorful Pork Patties

Servings: 2
Cooking Time: 10 Minutes
Ingredients:
- 1/2 lb ground pork
- 1 egg, lightly beaten
- 1/2 cup breadcrumbs
- 1/4 tsp paprika
- 1/8 tsp cayenne
- 1/2 tsp Italian seasoning
- Pepper
- Salt

Directions:
1. Add all ingredients into the large bowl and mix until well combined.
2. Make patties from the meat mixture and place them in an air fryer basket.
3. Select air fry then set the temperature to 360 °F and time for 10 minutes. Press start.
4. Once the Ninja Foodi Digital Air Fryer Oven is preheated then place the basket into the top rails of the oven.
5. Turn patties halfway through.
6. Serve and enjoy.

Meatloaf

Servings: 8
Cooking Time: 60 Minutes
Ingredients:
- 3 eggs
- 4 oz sharp cheddar cheese, shredded
- 1/4 cup green pepper, diced
- 1/2 cup onion, chopped
- 1/4 tsp black pepper
- 45 crackers, crushed
- 1 1/2 lbs lean ground beef
- 1/2 cup milk
- 1 tsp salt

Directions:
1. In a mixing bowl, beat the eggs then add cheese, green pepper, onion, cracker crumbs, milk pepper, and salt. Stir well to combine.

2. Add ground meat and mix well.
3. Make a loaf of meat mixture and place on a sheet pan.
4. Select bake mode then set the temperature to 350 °F and time for 60 minutes. Press start.
5. Once the Ninja Foodi Digital Air Fryer Oven is preheated then place the sheet pan into the oven.
6. Serve and enjoy.

Rosemary Beef Roast

Servings: 6
Cooking Time: 45 Minutes
Ingredients:
- 2 lbs beef roast
- 1 tsp rosemary
- 1 tbsp olive oil
- 1 tsp salt
- 1 tsp pepper

Directions:
1. Mix together oil, rosemary, pepper, and salt and rub all over the meat.
2. Place beef roast in an air fryer basket.
3. Select air fry then set the temperature to 360 °F and time for 45 minutes. Press start.
4. Once the Ninja Foodi Digital Air Fryer Oven is preheated then place the basket into the top rails of the oven.
5. Serve and enjoy.

Meatloaf

Servings: 6
Cooking Time: 50 Minutes
Ingredients:
- 2 lbs ground beef
- 1 tsp oregano
- 1 red bell pepper, diced and sautéed
- 1 tsp paprika
- 1/2 cup sunflower seed flour
- 1/2 cup of salsa
- 2 eggs, lightly beaten
- 1 tsp cumin
- 1/2 tsp salt

Directions:
1. Add all ingredients into the mixing bowl and mix until well combined.
2. Transfer meat mixture into the greased loaf pan.
3. Select bake mode then set the temperature to 375 °F and time for 50 minutes. Press start.
4. Once the Ninja Foodi Digital Air Fryer Oven is preheated then place the loaf pan into the oven.
5. Serve and enjoy.

Lamb Steaks

Servings: 4
Cooking Time: 15 Minutes
Ingredients:

- ½ onion, roughly chopped
- 5 garlic cloves, peeled
- 1 tablespoon fresh ginger, peeled
- 1 teaspoon ground fennel
- ½ teaspoon ground cumin
- ½ teaspoon ground cinnamon
- ½ teaspoon cayenne pepper
- Salt and ground black pepper, to taste
- 1 ½ pound boneless lamb sirloin steaks

Directions:

1. In a blender, add the onion, garlic, ginger, and spices and pulse until smooth.
2. Transfer the mixture into a large bowl. Add the lamb steaks and coat with the mixture generously. Refrigerate to marinate for about 24 hours.
3. Select the "AIR FRY" function on your Ninja Foody Digital Air Fry Oven.
4. And set the temperature at 330 °F.
5. Now press the "Time Button" and use the dial to set the cooking time to 15 minutes.
6. Press the "START/PAUSE" button to start. Grease the Air Crisp Basket.
7. Place the lamb steaks into the prepared Air Crisp Basket and insert them in the oven.
8. Flip the steaks once halfway through. When cooking time is completed, open the door and serve hot.

Garlic Ranch Pork Chops

Servings: 5
Cooking Time: 30 Minutes
Ingredients:

- 5 pork chops
- 1/4 cup olive oil
- 1 tsp garlic, minced
- 1 1/2 tbsp ranch seasoning
- Pepper
- Salt

Directions:

1. Season pork chops with pepper and salt and place on a sheet pan.
2. Mix together olive oil, garlic, and ranch seasoning.
3. Pour oil mixtures over pork chops.
4. Select bake mode then set the temperature to 425 °F and time for 30 minutes. Press start.
5. Once the Ninja Foodi Digital Air Fryer Oven is preheated then place the sheet pan into the oven.
6. Serve and enjoy.

Rump Steak

Servings: 2
Cooking Time: 15 Minutes

Ingredients:

- 2 pounds of rump steak
- 2 onions, sliced
- 1 green bell pepper, sliced
- Salt and black pepper, to taste
- ½ cup parmesan cheese
- 4 Hoagies roll, as needed

Directions:

1. Take a Ninja Foodi Digital Air Fryer Oven and grease it with a mesh tray.
2. Place the steak, bell pepper, and onion in a bowl and season it with salt and black pepper. Then place it on a baking tray.
3. Preheat the Ninja Foodi Digital Air Fryer Oven for 390 °F for 5 minutes.
4. Put the tray in the Oven and bake for 10 minutes at 350 °F.
5. Once done, place it on a hoagie roll and layer the shredded parmesan on top.
6. Serve and enjoy.

Roasted Lamb Leg

Servings: 4
Cooking Time: 75 Minutes
Ingredients:

- 2 ½ lbs. lamb leg roast, slits carved
- 1 Tablespoon of olive oil
- 2 garlic cloves, sliced into smaller slithers
- 1 Tablespoon of dried rosemary
- Cracked Himalayan rock salt to taste
- Ground peppercorns to taste

Directions:

1. Make the cuts in the lamb roast and insert them with garlic. Season with oil.
2. Sprinkle the lamb roast with kosher salt, rosemary, and ground black pepper.
3. Place the lamb roast on the Air Crisp Basket.
4. Preheat the Ninja Foodi Digital Air Fryer Oven by selecting the "AIR ROAST" mode.
5. Adjust the temperature to 380 °F, set time to 75 minutes.
6. Open the door and transfer to the Ninja Foodi Digital Air Fryer Oven.
7. Remove and allow to rest.
8. Serve and enjoy.

Pork Chops

Servings: 4
Cooking Time: 20 Minutes
Ingredients:

- 4 pork chops, cut to 1-inch thickness
- 1 bag frozen green beans
- 1 Tablespoon of coarsely crushed black peppercorns
- 2 Tablespoon of extra-virgin olive oil
- Salt and black pepper, to taste

Directions:

1. Season the pork chops with peppercorn.

2. Transfer to the Ninja Foodi digital Air Fry Oven baking sheet.
3. Add the remaining ingredients.
4. Preheat the Ninja Foodi digital Air Fry Oven by selecting "AIR FRY" mode
5. Adjust temperature to 350 °F and time to 20 minutes.
6. Open the door and transfer to the Ninja Foodi Digital Air Fryer Oven.
7. Remove and serve.

Lamb Kebab

Servings: 4
Cooking Time: 18 Minutes
Ingredients:
- A handful of thyme leaves, chopped
- 1 tablespoon honey
- 1 lime, zest, and juice
- 2 tablespoon jerk paste
- 2 pounds lamb steak

Directions:
1. Mix lamb with jerk paste, lime juice, zest, honey, and thyme.
2. Toss well to coat, then marinate for 30 minutes. Alternatively, thread the lamb on the skewers. Place these lamb skewers in the Air Crisp Basket.
3. Preheat Air Fry Oven and select the "AIR FRY" mode. Press the Time button and set the cooking time to 18 minutes.
4. Now push the Temp button set the temperature at 360 °F.
5. Once preheated, place the Air fryer basket in the oven and close its lid.
6. Flip the skewers when cooked halfway through, and then resume cooking.
7. Once ready, serve, and enjoy!

Lamb Chops

Servings: 2
Cooking Time: 5 Minutes
Ingredients:
- 4 lamb chops
- 1 garlic clove, minced
- 1 1/2 tbsp olive oil
- Pepper
- Salt

Directions:
1. Mix together garlic, olive oil, pepper, and salt and rub over lamb chops.
2. Place lamb chops in an air fryer basket.
3. Select air fry then set the temperature to 400 °F and time for 5 minutes. Press start.
4. Once the Ninja Foodi Digital Air Fryer Oven is preheated then place the basket into the top rails of the oven.
5. Serve and enjoy.

Beef Patties

Servings: 6
Cooking Time: 25 Minutes
Ingredients:
- 2 eggs, lightly beaten
- 1 lb ground beef
- 1/2 tsp chili powder
- 1 cup breadcrumbs
- 1/2 onion, chopped
- 2 zucchinis, grated and squeezed
- Pepper
- Salt

Directions:
1. Add all ingredients into the large bowl and mix until well combined.
2. Make small patties from the meat mixture and place them on a sheet pan.
3. Select bake mode then set the temperature to 400 °F and time for 25 minutes. Press start.
4. Once the Ninja Foodi Digital Air Fryer Oven is preheated then place the sheet pan into the oven.
5. Serve and enjoy.

Dill Beef Roast

Servings: 8
Cooking Time: 45 Minutes
Ingredients:
- 2 1/2 lbs beef roast
- 1/2 tsp garlic powder
- 1/2 tsp onion powder
- 2 tbsp olive oil
- 1 tsp dill

Directions:
1. Mix together garlic powder, onion powder, dill, and olive oil. Rub all over the beef roast.
2. Place beef roast in the air fryer basket.
3. Select air fry then set the temperature to 360 °F and time for 45 minutes. Press start.
4. Once the Ninja Foodi Digital Air Fryer Oven is preheated then place the basket into the top rails of the oven.
5. Serve and enjoy.

Glazed Pork Tenderloin

Servings: 3
Cooking Time: 20 Minutes
Ingredients:
- 2 tablespoons Sriracha
- 2 tablespoons maple syrup
- ¼ teaspoon red pepper flakes, crushed salt, as required
- 1pound pork tenderloin

Directions:
1. In a small bowl, add the Sriracha, maple syrup, red pepper flakes, and salt and mix well. Brush the pork tenderloin with the mixture evenly.

2. Select "AIR FRY" mode. Press the "Time" button and turn the dial to set the cooking time to 20 minutes.
3. Now push the "Temp" button and rotate the dial to set the temperature at 350 °F.
4. Press the "START/PAUSE" button to start.
5. Grease the Air Crisp Basket, arrange the pork tenderloin into the Air Crisp Basket and insert it in the oven.
6. When the unit beeps to show that cooking time is completed, press the "Power" button to stop cooking and open the door.
7. Remove from oven and place the pork tenderloin onto a platter to rest for 15 minutes before slicing.
8. Chop the roast into desired sizes s and serve.

Poultry Recipes

Crispy Chicken Cutlets

Servings: 4
Cooking Time: 30 Minutes
Ingredients:
- ¾ cup flour
- 2 large eggs
- 1½ cups breadcrumbs
- ¼ cup Parmesan cheese, grated
- 1 tablespoon mustard powder
- Salt and ground black pepper, as required
- 4 (¼-inch thick) skinless, boneless chicken cutlets

Directions:
1. In a shallow bowl, add the flour.
2. In a second bowl, crack the eggs and beat well.
3. In a third bowl, mix together the breadcrumbs, cheese, mustard powder, salt, and black pepper.
4. Season the chicken with salt, and black pepper.
5. Coat the chicken with flour, then dip into beaten eggs and finally coat with the breadcrumbs mixture.
6. Press AIR OVEN MODE button of Ninja Foodi Digital Air Fryer Oven and turn the dial to select "Air Fry" mode.
7. Press TIME/SLICES button and again turn the dial to set the cooking time to 30 minutes.
8. Now push TEMP/SHADE button and rotate the dial to set the temperature at 355 °F.
9. Press "Start/Stop" button to start.
10. When the unit beeps to show that it is preheated, open the oven door and grease the air fry basket.
11. Place the chicken cutlets into the prepared air fry basket and insert in the oven.
12. When cooking time is completed, open the oven door and serve hot.

Crispy Chicken Legs

Servings: 3
Cooking Time: 20 Minutes
Ingredients:
- 3 chicken legs
- 1 cup buttermilk
- 2 cups white flour
- 1 teaspoon garlic powder
- 1 teaspoon onion powder
- 1 teaspoon ground cumin
- 1 teaspoon paprika
- Salt and ground black pepper, as required
- 1 tablespoon olive oil

Directions:
1. In a bowl, place the chicken legs and buttermilk and refrigerate for about 2 hours.
2. In a shallow dish, mix together the flour and spices.
3. Remove the chicken from buttermilk.
4. Coat the chicken legs with flour mixture, then dip into buttermilk and finally, coat with the flour mixture again.
5. Press AIR OVEN MODE button of Ninja Foodi Digital Air Fryer Oven and turn the dial to select "Air Fry" mode.
6. Press TIME/SLICES button and again turn the dial to set the cooking time to 20 minutes.
7. Now push TEMP/SHADE button and rotate the dial to set the temperature at 355 °F.
8. Press "Start/Stop" button to start.
9. When the unit beeps to show that it is preheated, open the oven door and grease the air fry basket.
10. Arrange chicken legs into the prepared air fry basket and drizzle with the oil.
11. Insert the basket in the oven.
12. When cooking time is completed, open the oven door and serve hot.

Thanksgiving Turkey

Servings: 4
Cooking Time: 35 Minutes
Ingredients:
- 1 turkey breast
- Kosher salt and black pepper, to taste
- 1 teaspoon thyme, chopped
- 1 teaspoon rosemary, chopped
- 1 teaspoon sage, chopped
- ¼ cup maple syrup
- 2 tablespoons Dijon mustard
- 1 tablespoon. butter, melted

Directions:
1. Rub the turkey breast with maple syrup, Dijon mustard, butter, black pepper, and herbs.
2. Place the turkey in a baking tray and set it in the Ninja Foodi Digital Air Fryer Oven.
3. Select the "AIR FRY" mode using the function keys.
4. Set its cooking time to 35 minutes and temperature to 390 °F
5. Press "START/PAUSE" to initiate preheating.
6. Serve warm.

Tasty Chicken Drumsticks

Servings: 4
Cooking Time: 20 Minutes
Ingredients:
- 4 chicken drumsticks
- 3/4 cup teriyaki sauce
- 4 tbsp green onion, chopped
- 1 tbsp sesame seeds, toasted

Directions:
1. Select air fry mode set the temperature to 360 °F and set the timer to 20 minutes. Press the setting dial to preheat.
2. Add chicken drumsticks and teriyaki sauce into the zip-lock bag. Seal bag and place in refrigerator for 1 hour.
3. Arrange marinated chicken drumsticks in the air fryer basket.
4. Once the unit is preheated, open the door, and place the air fryer basket on the top level of the oven, and close the door.
5. Garnish with green onion and sprinkle with sesame seeds.
6. Serve and enjoy.

Maple Chicken Thighs

Servings: 4
Cooking Time: 25 Minutes
Ingredients:
- ½ cup maple syrup
- 1 cup buttermilk
- 1 egg
- 1 teaspoon garlic powder
- 4 chicken thighs, skin-on, bone-in
Dry Rub:

- ½ cup all-purpose flour
- ½ teaspoons honey powder
- 1 tablespoon of salt
- 1 teaspoon sweet Paprika
- ¼ teaspoons smoked Paprika
- 1 teaspoon onion powder
- ¼ teaspoons ground black pepper
- ¼ cup tapioca flour
- ½ teaspoons cayenne pepper
- ½ teaspoons garlic powder

Directions:
1. Whisk buttermilk, egg, maple syrup, and a teaspoon of garlic in a Ziplock bag.
2. Add the chicken thighs to the buttermilk and seal this bag. Shake it to coat the chicken well, then refrigerator for 1 hour.
3. Meanwhile, whisk the flour with salt, tapioca, pepper, smoked Paprika, Sweet Paprika, honey powder, granulated garlic, cayenne pepper, and granulated onion in a bowl.
4. Remove the marinated chicken from its bag and coat it with the flour mixture.
5. Shake off the excess and place the chicken in the Oven.
6. Place this sheet inside the Ninja Foodi Digital Air Fryer Oven and Close its door.
7. Select the "AIR FRY" mode using the Function Keys.
8. Set its cooking time to 12 minutes and temperature to 380 °F, then press "START/PAUSE" to initiate preheating.
9. Flip the chicken thighs and continue baking for another 13 minutes at the same temperature.
10. Serve warm.

Parmesan Chicken Bake

Servings: 3
Cooking Time: 50 Minutes
Ingredients:
- 3 skinless, boneless chicken breast halves
- 1 cup prepared marinara sauce
- ¼ cup grated Parmesan cheese, divided
- ½ package garlic croutons
- ½ package shredded mozzarella cheese, divided
- 2 tablespoons chopped fresh basil
- 1 tablespoon olive oil
- 1 clove garlic, crushed and finely chopped
- Red pepper flakes, to taste

Directions:
1. Turn on your Ninja Foodi Digital Air Fryer Oven and rotate the knob to select "Bake".
2. Preheat by selecting the timer for 3 minutes and temperature for 350 °F.
3. Grease the SearPlate and sprinkle garlic and red pepper flakes.
4. Arrange the chicken breasts on SearPlate and pour marinara sauce over chicken.
5. Also, top with half of the mozzarella cheese and Parmesan cheese and then sprinkle the croutons.

6. Lastly, add remaining mozzarella cheese on top, followed by half the Parmesan cheese.

7. Select the timer for about 50 minutes and temperature for 160 °F.

8. Bake until cheese and croutons are golden brown and the chicken is no longer pink inside.

9. Serve and enjoy!

Baked Chicken Wings

Servings: 4

Cooking Time: 30 Minutes

Ingredients:

- 2 lbs fresh chicken wings
- 1 tbsp Worcestershire sauce
- 4 tbsp butter
- 4 tbsp cayenne pepper sauce
- 2 tbsp spring onion, chopped
- 1 tbsp brown sugar
- 1 tsp sea salt

Directions:

1. Place rack in the bottom position and close door. Select bake mode set the temperature to 350 °F and set the timer to 30 minutes. Press the setting dial to preheat.

2. Arrange chicken wings on a sheet pan.

3. Once the unit is preheated, open the door, and place the sheet pan onto the center of the rack, and close the door.

4. In a large bowl, mix together brown sugar, cayenne pepper sauce, Worcestershire sauce, butter, and salt.

5. Remove wings from the oven and place in a bowl and toss until wings are well coated.

6. Garnish with spring onion and serve.

Herbed Turkey Legs

Servings: 2

Cooking Time: 30 Minutes

Ingredients:

- 1 tablespoon butter, melted
- 2 garlic cloves, minced
- ¼ teaspoon dried rosemary
- ¼ teaspoon dried thyme
- ¼ teaspoon dried oregano
- Salt and ground black pepper, as required
- 2 turkey legs

Directions:

1. In a large bowl, mix together the butter, garlic, herbs, salt, and black pepper.

2. Add the turkey legs and coat with mixture generously.

3. Press AIR OVEN MODE button of Ninja Foodi Digital Air Fryer Oven and turn the dial to select "Air Fry" mode.

4. Press TIME/SLICES button and again turn the dial to set the cooking time to 27 minutes.

5. Now push TEMP/SHADE button and rotate the dial to set the temperature at 350 °F.

6. Press "Start/Stop" button to start.

7. When the unit beeps to show that it is preheated, open the oven door.

8. Arrange the turkey wings into the greased air fry basket and insert in the oven.

9. When the cooking time is completed, open the oven door and serve hot.

Chicken Kabobs

Servings: 2

Cooking Time: 9 Minutes

Ingredients:

- 1 chicken breast, cut into medium-sized pieces
- 1 tablespoon fresh lemon juice
- 3 garlic cloves, grated
- 1 tablespoon fresh oregano, minced
- ½ teaspoon lemon zest, grated
- Salt and ground black pepper, as required
- 1 teaspoon plain Greek yogurt
- 1 teaspoon olive oil

Directions:

1. In a large bowl, add the chicken, lemon juice, garlic, oregano, lemon zest, salt and black pepper and toss to coat well.

2. Cover the bowl and refrigerate overnight.

3. Remove the bowl from the refrigerator and stir in the yogurt and oil.

4. Thread the chicken pieces onto the metal skewers.

5. Press AIR OVEN MODE button of Ninja Foodi Digital Air Fryer Oven and turn the dial to select "Air Fry" mode.

6. Press TIME/SLICES button and again turn the dial to set the cooking time to 9 minutes.

7. Now push TEMP/SHADE button and rotate the dial to set the temperature at 350 °F.

8. Press "Start/Stop" button to start.

9. When the unit beeps to show that it is preheated, open the oven door and grease the air fry basket.

10. Place the skewers into the prepared air fry basket and insert in the oven.

11. Flip the skewers once halfway through.

12. When cooking time is completed, open the oven door and serve hot.

Meatballs

Servings: 2

Cooking Time: 8 Minutes

Ingredients:

- 1/2 lb ground chicken
- 1 zucchini, shredded & squeezed
- 2 tsp smoked paprika
- 1/2 cup breadcrumbs
- Pepper
- Salt

Directions:

1. Select air fry mode set the temperature to 360 °F and set the timer to 8 minutes. Press the setting dial to preheat.

2. In a bowl, mix chicken, paprika, breadcrumbs, zucchini, pepper, and salt until well combined.

3. Make small balls from the chicken mixture and place in the air fryer basket.

4. Once the unit is preheated, open the door, and place the air fryer basket on the top level of the oven, and close the door.

5. Serve and enjoy.

Turkey Breast

Servings: 8
Cooking Time: 60 Minutes
Ingredients:
- 2 lbs turkey breast
- 1/4 tsp pepper
- 1/2 tsp sage leaves, chopped
- 1 tbsp butter
- 1 tsp salt

Directions:
1. Rub butter all over the turkey breast and season with pepper, sage, and salt.
2. Place turkey breast in an air fryer basket.
3. Select air fry then set the temperature to 325 °F and time for 60 minutes. Press start.
4. Once the Ninja Foodi Digital Air Fryer Oven is preheated then place the basket into the top rails of the oven.
5. Turn turkey breast halfway through.
6. Serve and enjoy.

Marinated Spicy Chicken Legs

Servings: 4
Cooking Time: 20 Minutes
Ingredients:
- 4 chicken legs
- 3 tablespoons fresh lemon juice
- 3 teaspoons ginger paste
- 3 teaspoons garlic paste
- Salt, as required
- 4 tablespoons plain yogurt
- 2 teaspoons red chili powder
- 1 teaspoon ground cumin
- 1 teaspoon ground coriander
- 1 teaspoon ground turmeric
- Ground black pepper, as required

Directions:
1. In a bowl, mix together the chicken legs, lemon juice, ginger, garlic and salt. Set aside for about 15 minutes.
2. Meanwhile, in another bowl, mix together the yogurt and spices.
3. Add the chicken legs and coat with the spice mixture generously.
4. Cover the bowl and refrigerate for at least 10-12 hours.
5. Press AIR OVEN MODE button of Ninja Foodi Digital Air Fryer Oven and turn the dial to select "Air Fry" mode.
6. Press TIME/SLICES button and again turn the dial to set the cooking time to 20 minutes.
7. Now push TEMP/SHADE button and rotate the dial to set the temperature at 440 °F.

8. Press "Start/Stop" button to start.
9. When the unit beeps to show that it is preheated, open the oven door and grease the air fry basket.
10. Place the chicken legs into the prepared air fry basket and insert in the oven.
11. When cooking time is completed, open the oven door and serve hot.

Crispy Roasted Chicken

Servings: 8
Cooking Time: 40 Minutes
Ingredients:
- 1 whole chicken, cut into 8 pieces
- Salt and ground black pepper, as required
- 2 cups buttermilk
- 2 cups all-purpose flour
- 1 tablespoon ground mustard
- 1 tablespoon garlic powder
- 1 tablespoon onion powder
- 1 tablespoon paprika

Directions:
1. Rub the chicken pieces with salt and black pepper.
2. In a large bowl, add the chicken pieces and buttermilk and refrigerate to marinate for at least 1 hour.
3. Meanwhile, in a large bowl, place the flour, mustard, spices, salt and black pepper and mix well.
4. Remove the chicken pieces from bowl and drip off the excess buttermilk.
5. Coat the chicken pieces with the flour mixture, shaking any excess off.
6. Press AIR OVEN MODE button of Ninja Foodi Digital Air Fryer Oven and turn the dial to select "Air Fry" mode.
7. Press TIME/SLICES button and again turn the dial to set the cooking time to 20 minutes.
8. Now push TEMP/SHADE button and rotate the dial to set the temperature at 390 °F.
9. Press "Start/Stop" button to start.
10. When the unit beeps to show that it is preheated, open the oven door and grease air fry basket.
11. Arrange half of the chicken pieces into air fry basket and insert in the oven.
12. Repeat with the remaining chicken pieces.
13. When the cooking time is completed, open the oven door and serve immediately.

Gingered Chicken Drumsticks

Servings: 3
Cooking Time: 25 Minutes
Ingredients:
- ¼ cup full-fat coconut milk
- 2 teaspoons fresh ginger, minced
- 2 teaspoons galangal, minced
- 2 teaspoons ground turmeric
- Salt, as required
- 3 chicken drumsticks

Directions:

1. Place the coconut milk, galangal, ginger, and spices in a large bowl and mix well.
2. Add the chicken drumsticks and coat with the marinade generously.
3. Refrigerate to marinate for at least 6-8 hours.
4. Press AIR OVEN MODE button of Ninja Foodi Digital Air Fryer Oven and turn the dial to select "Air Fry" mode.
5. Press TIME/SLICES button and again turn the dial to set the cooking time to 25 minutes.
6. Now push TEMP/SHADE button and rotate the dial to set the temperature at 375 °F.
7. Press "Start/Stop" button to start.
8. When the unit beeps to show that it is preheated, open the oven door and grease the air fry basket.
9. Place the chicken drumsticks into the prepared air fry basket and insert in the oven.
10. When cooking time is completed, open the oven door and serve hot.

Chicken Nuggets

Servings: 6
Cooking Time: 10 Minutes
Ingredients:
- 2 large chicken breasts, cut into cubes
- 1 cup breadcrumbs
- ⅓ tablespoon Parmesan cheese, shredded
- 1 teaspoon onion powder
- ¼ teaspoon smoked paprika
- Salt and ground black pepper, as required

Directions:
1. In a large resalable bag, add all the ingredients.
2. Seal the bag and shake well to coat thoroughly.
3. Select the "AIR FRY" function on your Ninja Foodi Digital Air Fryer Oven.
4. Press, "Temp Button" and use the dial to set the temperature at 400 °F and the cooking time to 10 minutes.
5. Press the "START/PAUSE" button to start.
6. Arrange the nuggets into the Air Crisp Basket and insert them in the oven.
7. When cooking time is completed, open the door and transfer the nuggets onto a platter.
8. Serve warm.

Turkey Patties

Servings: 9
Cooking Time: 25 Minutes
Ingredients:
- 1 egg, lightly beaten
- 2 tbsp cilantro, chopped
- 1 lb ground turkey
- 1/2 tsp garlic, minced
- 1/3 cup breadcrumbs
- 1 tsp Italian seasoning
- 2 tbsp lemon juice
- Pepper
- Salt

Directions:
1. Add all ingredients into the mixing bowl and mix until well combined.
2. Make patties from meat mixture and place sheet pan.
3. Select bake mode then set the temperature to 400 °F and time for 25 minutes. Press start.
4. Once the Ninja Foodi Digital Air Fryer Oven is preheated then place the sheet pan into the oven.
5. Serve and enjoy.

Chicken Stew

Servings: 6
Cooking Time: 1 Hour And 10 Minutes
Ingredients:
- 1 rotisserie chicken, roughly shredded
- 1 package precooked chicken sausages, sliced
- 3 medium carrots, diced
- 1 bag frozen pearl onions
- 1 can cannellini beans, drained and rinsed
- 3 garlic cloves, minced
- 2 cups chicken stock
- Kosher salt and freshly ground black pepper, to taste

Directions:
1. In a large bowl, combine the chicken, sausages, carrots, pearl onions, beans, garlic, stock, salt, and pepper. Pour the mixture into a casserole dish.
2. Select "AIR ROAST," on your Ninja Foodi Digital Air Fryer Oven.
3. Set the temperature to 325 °F, and set the time to 60 minutes.
4. Press "START/PAUSE" to begin preheating.
5. When the unit has preheated, place the casserole dish on the wire rack inside.
6. Close the oven door to begin cooking.
7. When cooking is completed, let the stew cool for 10 minutes before serving.

Crispy Cheese Chicken

Servings: 4
Cooking Time: 35 Minutes
Ingredients:
- 4 chicken breasts
- ¼ cup olive oil
- 1 cup breadcrumbs
- 1 cup parmesan cheese, shredded
- ¼ teaspoon garlic powder
- ¼ teaspoon Italian seasoning
- Salt and pepper to taste

Directions:
1. Season chicken with pepper and salt and brush with olive oil.
2. In a shallow dish, mix parmesan cheese, garlic powder, Italian seasoning, and breadcrumbs.
3. Coat chicken with parmesan and breadcrumb mixture and place in the baking dish.

4. Place the wire rack inside your Ninja Foodi Digital Air Fryer Oven.
5. Select "BAKE" mode, set the temperature to 350 °F, and set time to 35 minutes. Press start to begin preheating.
6. Once the Ninja Foodi Digital Air Fryer Oven is preheated, place the baking dish on a wire rack and close the oven door to start cooking. Cook for 35 minutes.
7. Serve and enjoy.

Gingered Chicken Drumsticks

Servings: 6
Cooking Time: 25 Minutes
Ingredients:
- 4 teaspoons fresh ginger, minced
- 4 teaspoons galangal, minced
- ½ cup full-fat coconut milk
- 4 teaspoons ground turmeric
- Salt, to taste
- 6 chicken drumsticks

Directions:
1. Take a bowl and mix together galangal, ginger, coconut milk and spices.
2. Add chicken drumsticks to the bowl for well coating.
3. Refrigerate for at least 6 to 8 hours.
4. Turn on your Ninja Foodi Digital Air Fryer Oven and rotate the knob to select "Air Fry".
5. Select the timer for about 20 to 25 minutes and temperature for 375 °F.
6. Grease the air fry basket and place the drumsticks into the prepared basket.
7. Remove from the oven and serve on a platter.
8. Serve hot and enjoy!

Creamy Chicken Casserole

Servings: 4
Cooking Time: 47 Minutes.
Ingredients:
- Chicken Mushroom Casserole
- 2 ½ pounds chicken breasts, cut into strips
- 1 ½ teaspoons salt
- ¼ teaspoon black pepper
- 1 cup all-purpose flour
- 6 tablespoons olive oil
- 1 pound white mushrooms, sliced
- 1 medium onion, diced
- 3 garlic cloves, minced
- Sauce
- 3 tablespoons unsalted butter
- 3 tablespoons all-purpose flour
- ½ cup milk, optional
- 1 cups chicken broth, optional
- 1 tablespoon lemon juice
- 1 cup half and half cream

Directions:

1. Butter a casserole dish and toss in chicken with mushrooms and all the casserole ingredients.
2. Prepare the sauce in a suitable pan. Add butter and melt over moderate heat.
3. Stir in all-purpose flour and whisk well for 2 minutes, then pour in milk, chicken broth, lemon juice, and cream.
4. Mix well and pour this creamy white sauce over the chicken mix in the SearPlate.
5. Transfer the SearPlate to Ninja Foodi Digital Air Fryer Oven and close the door.
6. Select "Bake" mode by rotating the dial.
7. Press the TIME/SLICES button and change the value to 45 minutes.
8. Press the TEMP/SHADE button and change the value to 350 °F.
9. Press Start/Stop to begin cooking.
10. Serve warm.

Blackened Chicken Bake

Servings: 4
Cooking Time: 18 Minutes.
Ingredients:
- 4 chicken breasts
- 2 teaspoons olive oil
- Chopped parsley, for garnish
Seasoning:
- 1 ½ tablespoons brown sugar
- 1 teaspoon paprika
- 1 teaspoon dried oregano
- ¼ teaspoon garlic powder
- ½ teaspoon salt and pepper

Directions:
1. Mix olive oil with brown sugar, paprika, oregano, garlic powder, salt, and black pepper in a bowl.
2. Place the chicken breasts in the SearPlate of Ninja Foodi Digital Air Fryer Oven.
3. Transfer the SearPlate to Ninja Foodi Digital Air Fryer Oven and close the door.
4. Select "Bake" mode by rotating the dial.
5. Press the TIME/SLICES button and change the value to 18 minutes.
6. Press the TEMP/SHADE button and change the value to 425 °F.
7. Press Start/Stop to begin cooking.
8. Serve warm.

Buttered Turkey Breast

Servings: 10
Cooking Time: 1¼ Hours
Ingredients:
- ¼ cup butter
- 5 carrots, peeled and cut into chunks
- 1 boneless turkey breast
- Salt and ground black pepper, as required
- 1 cup chicken broth
Directions:

1. In a pan, heat the oil over medium heat and the carrots for about 4-5 minutes.
2. Add the turkey breast and cook for about 10 minutes or until golden brown from both sides.
3. Remove from the heat and stir in salt, black pepper and broth.
4. Transfer the mixture into SearPlate.
5. Press AIR OVEN MODE button of Ninja Foodi Digital Air Fryer Oven and turn the dial to select "Bake" mode.
6. Press TIME/SLICES button and again turn the dial to set the cooking time to 60 minutes.
7. Now push TEMP/SHADE button and rotate the dial to set the temperature at 375 °F.
8. Press "Start/Stop" button to start.
9. When the unit beeps to show that it is preheated, open the oven door.
10. Insert the SearPlate in the oven.
11. When the cooking time is completed, open the oven door and with tongs, place the turkey onto a cutting board for about 5 minutes before slicing.
12. Cut into desired-sized slices and serve alongside carrots.

Herbed Duck Breast

Servings: 2
Cooking Time: 20 Minutes
Ingredients:
- 1 duck breast
- Olive oil cooking spray
- ½ tablespoon fresh thyme, chopped
- ½ tablespoon fresh rosemary, chopped
- 1 cup chicken broth
- 1 tablespoon fresh lemon juice
- Salt and ground black pepper, as required

Directions:
1. Spray the duck breast with cooking spray evenly.
2. In a bowl, mix well the remaining ingredients.
3. Add the duck breast and coat with the marinade generously.
4. Refrigerate, covered for about 4 hours.
5. With a piece of foil, cover the duck breast
6. Press AIR OVEN MODE button of Ninja Foodi Digital Air Fryer Oven and turn the dial to select "Air Fry" mode.
7. Press TIME/SLICES button and again turn the dial to set the cooking time to 15 minutes.
8. Now push TEMP/SHADE button and rotate the dial to set the temperature at 390 °F.
9. Press "Start/Stop" button to start.
10. When the unit beeps to show that it is preheated, open the oven door and grease the air fry basket.
11. Place the duck breast into the prepared air fry basket and insert in the oven.
12. After 15 minutes of cooking, set the temperature to 355 °F for 5 minutes.
13. When cooking time is completed, open the oven door and serve hot.

Mustard Chicken

Servings: 4
Cooking Time: 22 Minutes
Ingredients:
- 4 chicken breast, boneless & halves
- 1 cup breadcrumbs
- 1/3 cup maple syrup
- 3/4 cup Dijon mustard
- Pepper
- Salt

Directions:
1. Select air fry mode set the temperature to 325 °F and set the timer to 22 minutes. Press the setting dial to preheat.
2. In a shallow dish, mix together breadcrumbs, pepper, and salt.
3. In a separate shallow dish, mix maple syrup and Dijon mustard.
4. Dip each chicken breast in maple syrup mixture and coat with breadcrumbs.
5. Arrange coated chicken breasts in the air fryer basket.
6. Once the unit is preheated, open the door, and place the air fryer basket on the top level of the oven, and close the door.
7. Serve and enjoy.

Meatballs

Servings: 6
Cooking Time: 18 Minutes
Ingredients:
- 2 eggs, lightly beaten
- 1 lb ground turkey
- 1 tsp dried oregano
- 1 tbsp garlic, minced
- 1 tbsp nutritional yeast
- 1 tsp cumin
- 1 tbsp dried onion flakes
- 1 tbsp basil, chopped
- 1/3 cup breadcrumbs
- 2 cups zucchini, grated
- Pepper
- Salt

Directions:
1. Add all ingredients into the mixing bowl and mix until well combined.
2. Make small balls from the meat mixture and place them on a sheet pan.
3. Select bake mode then set the temperature to 400 °F and time for 18 minutes. Press start.
4. Once the Ninja Foodi Digital Air Fryer Oven is preheated then place the sheet pan into the oven.
5. Serve and enjoy.

Herb Chicken

Servings: 4
Cooking Time: 60 Minutes

Ingredients:
- 3 lbs whole chicken, remove giblets
- 1 tbsp olive oil
- 1/8 tsp ground black pepper
- 1 garlic clove, minced
- 1 tsp dried parsley
- 1 tsp dried rosemary, crushed
- 1/4 tsp salt

Directions:
1. Select air fry mode set the temperature to 350 °F and set the timer to 60 minutes. Press the setting dial to preheat.
2. In a small bowl, mix together olive oil, rosemary, pepper, garlic, parsley, and salt.
3. Rub oil mixture all over the chicken.
4. Arrange chicken in the air fryer basket.
5. Once the unit is preheated, open the door, and place the air fryer basket on the top level of the oven, and close the door.
6. Serve and enjoy.

Turkey Patties

Servings: 4
Cooking Time: 30 Minutes
Ingredients:
- 1 lb ground turkey
- 2 tbsp vinegar
- 1/2 onion, diced
- 1 tsp garlic, minced
- 1 cup spinach, sautéed
- 1/4 cup breadcrumbs
- 4 oz mozzarella cheese, cubed
- 2 tbsp Worcestershire sauce
- 1 tsp lemon zest
- 1 tbsp olive oil
- Pepper
- Salt

Directions:
1. Add all ingredients into the large bowl and mix until well combined.
2. Make patties from the mixture and place them on a sheet pan.
3. Select bake mode then set the temperature to 350 °F and time for 30 minutes. Press start.
4. Once the Ninja Foodi Digital Air Fryer Oven is preheated then place the sheet pan into the oven.
5. Turn patties halfway through.
6. Serve and enjoy.

Oat Crusted Chicken Breasts

Servings: 2
Cooking Time: 12 Minutes
Ingredients:
- 2 chicken breasts
- Salt and ground black pepper, as required
- ¾ cup oats

- 2 tablespoons mustard powder
- 1 tablespoon fresh parsley
- 2 medium eggs

Directions:
1. Place the chicken breasts onto a cutting board and with a meat mallet, flatten each into even thickness.
2. Then, cut each breast in half.
3. Sprinkle the chicken pieces with salt and black pepper and set aside.
4. In a blender, add the oats, mustard powder, parsley, salt and black pepper and pulse until a coarse breadcrumb-like mixture is formed.
5. Transfer the oat mixture into a shallow bowl.
6. In another bowl, crack the eggs and beat well.
7. Coat the chicken with oats mixture and then, dip into beaten eggs and again, coat with the oats mixture.
8. Press AIR OVEN MODE button of Ninja Foodi Digital Air Fryer Oven and turn the dial to select "Air Fry" mode.
9. Press TIME/SLICES button and again turn the dial to set the cooking time to 12 minutes.
10. Now push TEMP/SHADE button and rotate the dial to set the temperature at 350 °F.
11. Press "Start/Stop" button to start.
12. When the unit beeps to show that it is preheated, open the oven door and grease the air fry basket.
13. Place the chicken breasts into the prepared air fry basket and insert in the oven.
14. Flip the chicken breasts once halfway through.
15. When cooking time is completed, open the oven door and serve hot.

Delicious Chicken Thighs

Servings: 6
Cooking Time: 60 Minutes
Ingredients:
- 6 chicken thighs, clean and pat dry
- 2 1/2 tbsp fresh mint, minced
- 2 1/2 tsp ground cinnamon
- 2 tbsp chicken broth
- 1/2 cup coconut milk
- 1 tsp dried basil
- 1 tsp sea salt

Directions:
1. In a small bowl, mix together basil, mint, salt, and cinnamon and rub over chicken.
2. Place chicken into the baking dish.
3. Add broth and coconut milk around the chicken in a baking dish.
4. Select bake mode then set the temperature to 425 °F and time for 60 minutes. Press start.
5. Once the Ninja Foodi Digital Air Fryer Oven is preheated then place the baking dish into the oven.
6. Serve and enjoy.

Parmesan Chicken Tenders

Servings: 4
Cooking Time: 15 Minutes
Ingredients:
- ½ cup flour
- Salt and ground black pepper, as required
- 2 eggs, beaten
- ¾ cup panko breadcrumbs
- ¾ cup Parmesan cheese, grated finely
- 1 teaspoon Italian seasoning
- 8 chicken tenders

Directions:
1. In a shallow dish, mix together the flour, salt and black pepper.
2. In a second shallow dish, place the beaten eggs.
3. In a third shallow dish, mix together the breadcrumbs, parmesan cheese and Italian seasoning.
4. Coat the chicken tenders with flour mixture, then dip into the beaten eggs and finally coat with breadcrumb mixture.
5. Arrange the tenders onto a greased SearPlate in a single layer.
6. Press AIR OVEN MODE button of Ninja Foodi Digital Air Fryer Oven and turn the dial to select "Air Fry" mode.
7. Press TIME/SLICES button and again turn the dial to set the cooking time to 15 minutes.
8. Now push TEMP/SHADE button and rotate the dial to set the temperature at 360 °F.
9. Press "Start/Stop" button to start.
10. When the unit beeps to show that it is preheated, open the oven door and insert the SearPlate in oven.
11. When the cooking time is completed, open the oven door and serve hot.

Pineapple Chicken

Servings: 4
Cooking Time: 18 Minutes
Ingredients:
- 2 lb chicken thighs, boneless
- 1/4 cup pineapple juice
- 1/4 cup soy sauce
- 1/4 cup ketchup
- 3/4 tsp garlic, minced
- 1/4 tsp ground ginger
- 1/2 cup brown sugar

Directions:
1. Select air fry mode set the temperature to 360 °F and set the timer to 18 minutes. Press the setting dial to preheat.
2. Add chicken, garlic, ginger, pineapple juice, soy sauce, ketchup, and brown sugar in a zip-lock bag. Seal bag and place in refrigerator for 2 hours.
3. Remove chicken from marinade and place in the air fryer basket.
4. Once the unit is preheated, open the door, and place the air fryer basket on the top level of the oven, and close the door.

5. Serve and enjoy.

Herb Butter Chicken

Servings: 2
Cooking Time: 15 Minutes
Ingredients:
- 1½ cloves garlic, minced
- ½ teaspoon dried parsley
- ⅛ teaspoon dried rosemary
- ⅛ teaspoon dried thyme
- 2 skinless, boneless chicken breast halves
- ¼ cup butter, softened

Directions:
1. Turn on your Ninja Foodi Digital Air Fryer Oven and rotate the knob to select "Broil".
2. Cover the SearPlate with aluminum foil and place chicken on it.
3. Take a small bowl and mix together parsley, rosemary, thyme, butter and garlic.
4. Spread the mixture on top of chicken.
5. Broil in the oven with the coating of butter and herbs for at least 30 minutes at low.
6. Serve warm and enjoy!

Meatloaf

Servings: 8
Cooking Time: 40 Minutes
Ingredients:
- 2 eggs
- 1 lb mozzarella cheese, cut into cubes
- 2 lbs ground turkey
- 2 tsp Italian seasoning
- 1/4 cup basil pesto
- 1/2 cup parmesan cheese, grated
- 1/2 cup marinara sauce, without sugar
- 1 cup cottage cheese
- 1 tsp salt

Directions:
1. Place rack in the bottom position and close door. Select bake mode set the temperature to 390 °F and set the timer to 40 minutes. Press the setting dial to preheat.
2. A grease casserole dish with butter and set aside.
3. Add all ingredients into the large bowl and mix until well combined.
4. Transfer mixture into the casserole dish.
5. Once the unit is preheated, open the door, and place the casserole dish onto the rack, and close the door.
6. Serve and enjoy.

Orange Chicken

Servings: 4
Cooking Time: 35 Minutes
Ingredients:
- 4 chicken breasts, skinless
- 1 tsp rosemary, chopped
- 1/4 cup orange juice
- 1/2 tsp olive oil
- Pepper
- Salt

Directions:
1. Rub chicken with garlic and oil. Season with rosemary and pepper.
2. Place chicken in the baking dish. Pour orange juice around the chicken.
3. Select bake mode then set the temperature to 450 °F and time for 35 minutes. Press start.
4. Once the Ninja Foodi Digital Air Fryer Oven is preheated then place the baking dish into the oven.
5. Serve and enjoy.

Cajun Roast Chicken Breast

Servings: 2
Cooking Time: 20 Minutes
Ingredients:
- 1pound chicken breast, uncooked and skinless
- 2 tablespoons oil, divided
- 2 tablespoons Cajun seasoning
- 3 sweet potatoes, peeled, cut into cubes
- 1 cup broccoli cut in florets
- Salt and black pepper to taste

Directions:
1. Take a bowl and add oil and Cajun seasoning. Rub the chicken breast with the rub.
2. Put the chicken in the Ninja Foodie pan along with broccoli and sweet potatoes. Sprinkle salt and black pepper on top.
3. Turn on the Ninja Foodi Digital Air Fryer Oven and select "AIR ROAST" on your Ninja Foodi Digital Air Fryer Oven.
4. Set the timer to 20 minutes and temperature at 400 °F.
5. Once preheating done, add the chicken pan to the oven.
6. When the internal temperature of the chicken reaches 165 °F, serve it, and enjoy it.

Roasted Goose

Servings: 12
Cooking Time: 40 Minutes.
Ingredients:
- 8 pounds goose
- Juice of a lemon
- Salt and pepper
- ½ yellow onion, peeled and chopped
- 1 head garlic, peeled and chopped
- ½ cup wine

- 1 teaspoon dried thyme

Directions:
1. Place the goose in a SearPlate and whisk the rest of the ingredients in a bowl.
2. Pour this thick sauce over the goose and brush it liberally.
3. Transfer the goose to Ninja Foodi Digital Air Fryer Oven and close the door.
4. Select "Air Roast" mode by rotating the dial.
5. Press the TEMP/SHADE button and change the value to 355 °F.
6. Press the TIME/SLICES button and change the value to 40 minutes, then press Start/Stop to begin cooking.
7. Serve warm.

Roasted Duck

Servings: 6
Cooking Time: 3 Hours
Ingredients:
- 6 pounds whole Pekin duck
- Salt, to taste
- 5 garlic cloves, chopped
- 1 lemon, chopped
- Glaze
- ½ cup balsamic vinegar
- 1 lemon, juiced
- ¼ cup honey

Directions:
1. Place the Pekin duck in a baking tray and add garlic, lemon, and salt on top.
2. Whisk honey, the juiced lemon, and vinegar in a bowl.
3. Brush this glaze over the duck liberally. Marinate overnight in the refrigerator.
4. Remove the duck from the marinade and move the duck to SearPlate.
5. Transfer the SearPlate to Ninja Foodi Digital Air Fryer Oven and close the door.
6. Select "Air Roast" mode by rotating the dial.
7. Press the TIME/SLICES button and change the value to 2 hours.
8. Press the TEMP/SHADE button and change the value to 350 °F.
9. Press Start/Stop to begin cooking.
10. When cooking completed, set the oven the temperature to 350 °F and time to 1 hour at Air Roast mode. Press Start/Stop to begin.
11. When it is cooked, serve warm.

Spiced Turkey Breast

Servings: 8
Cooking Time: 45 Minutes
Ingredients:
- 2 tablespoons fresh rosemary, chopped
- 1 teaspoon ground cumin
- 1 teaspoon ground cinnamon
- 1 teaspoon smoked paprika

- 1 teaspoon cayenne pepper
- Salt and ground black pepper, as required
- 1 turkey breast

Directions:

1. In a bowl, mix together the rosemary, spices, salt and black pepper.
2. Rub the turkey breast with rosemary mixture evenly.
3. With kitchen twines, tie the turkey breast to keep it compact.
4. Press AIR OVEN MODE button of Ninja Foodi Digital Air Fryer Oven and turn the dial to select "Air Fry" mode.
5. Press TIME/SLICES button and again turn the dial to set the cooking time to 45 minutes.
6. Now push TEMP/SHADE button and rotate the dial to set the temperature at 360 °F.
7. Press "Start/Stop" button to start.
8. When the unit beeps to show that it is preheated, open the oven door.
9. Arrange the turkey breast into the greased air fry basket and insert in oven.
10. When the cooking time is completed, open the oven door and place the turkey breast onto a platter for about 5-10 minutes before slicing.
11. With a sharp knife, cut the turkey breast into desired sized slices and serve.

Tasty Chicken Wings

Servings: 6
Cooking Time: 12 Minutes

Ingredients:

- 6 chicken wings
- 1/2 tsp red chili flakes
- 1 tbsp honey
- 2 tbsp Worcestershire sauce
- Pepper
- Salt

Directions:

1. Add all ingredients except chicken wings to a bowl and mix well.
2. Arrange chicken wings in an air fryer basket.
3. Select air fry then set the temperature to 350 °F and time for 12 minutes. Press start.
4. Once the Ninja Foodi Digital Air Fryer Oven is preheated then place the basket into the top rails of the oven.
5. Serve and enjoy.

Flavorful Chicken Thighs

Servings: 8
Cooking Time: 10 Minutes

Ingredients:

- 3 lbs chicken thigh, skinless and boneless
- 1 tbsp coriander powder
- 3 tbsp olive oil
- 1 tbsp cayenne
- 1 tbsp cinnamon
- 1/2 tsp ground nutmeg

- Pepper
- Salt

Directions:

1. In a small bowl, mix together all ingredients except chicken.
2. Rub bowl mixture all over the chicken.
3. Arrange chicken in an air fryer basket.
4. Select air fry then set the temperature to 300 °F and time for 10 minutes. Press start.
5. Once the Ninja Foodi Digital Air Fryer Oven is preheated then place the basket into the top rails of the oven.
6. Serve and enjoy.

Chinese Chicken Drumsticks

Servings: 4
Cooking Time: 20 Minutes

Ingredients:

- 1 tablespoon oyster sauce
- 1 teaspoon light soy sauce
- ½ teaspoon sesame oil
- 1 teaspoon Chinese five-spice powder
- Salt and ground white pepper, as required
- 4 chicken drumsticks
- 1 cup corn flour

Directions:

1. In a bowl, mix together the sauces, oil, five-spice powder, salt, and black pepper.
2. Add the chicken drumsticks and generously coat with the marinade.
3. Refrigerate for at least 30-40 minutes.
4. In a shallow dish, place the corn flour.
5. Remove the chicken from marinade and lightly coat with corn flour.
6. Press AIR OVEN MODE button of Ninja Foodi Digital Air Fryer Oven and turn the dial to select "Air Fry" mode.
7. Press TIME/SLICES button and again turn the dial to set the cooking time to 20 minutes.
8. Now push TEMP/SHADE button and rotate the dial to set the temperature at 390 °F.
9. Press "Start/Stop" button to start.
10. When the unit beeps to show that it is preheated, open the oven door and grease the air fry basket.
11. Place the chicken drumsticks into the prepared air fry basket and insert in the oven.
12. When cooking time is completed, open the oven door and serve hot.

Parmesan Chicken Meatballs

Servings: 4
Cooking Time: 12 Minutes.

Ingredients:

- 1 pound ground chicken
- 1 large egg, beaten
- ½ cup Parmesan cheese, grated
- ½ cup pork rinds, ground
- 1 teaspoon garlic powder

- 1 teaspoon paprika
- 1 teaspoon kosher salt
- ½ teaspoon pepper
- ½ cup ground pork rinds, for crust

Directions:
1. Toss all the meatball ingredients in a bowl and mix well.
2. Make small meatballs out of this mixture and roll them in the pork rinds.
3. Place the coated meatballs in the air fry basket.
4. Transfer the basket to Ninja Foodi Digital Air Fryer Oven and close the door.
5. Select "Bake" mode by rotating the dial.
6. Press the TIME/SLICES button and change the value to 12 minutes.
7. Press the TEMP/SHADE button and change the value to 400 °F.
8. Press Start/Stop to begin cooking.
9. Once preheated, place the air fry basket inside and close its oven door.
10. Serve warm.

Simple Chicken Thighs

Servings: 4
Cooking Time: 20 Minutes
Ingredients:
- 4 skinless, boneless chicken thighs
- Salt and ground black pepper, as required
- 2 tablespoons butter, melted

Directions:
1. Line a SearPlate with a lightly greased piece of foil.
2. Rub the chicken thighs with salt and black pepper evenly and then, brush with melted butter.
3. Place the chicken thighs into the prepared SearPlate.
4. Press AIR OVEN MODE button of Ninja Foodi Digital Air Fryer Oven and turn the dial to select "Bake" mode.
5. Press TIME/SLICES button and again turn the dial to set the cooking time to 20 minutes.
6. Now push TEMP/SHADE button and rotate the dial to set the temperature at 450 °F.
7. Press "Start/Stop" button to start.
8. When the unit beeps to show that it is preheated, open the oven door and insert the SearPlate in oven.
9. When the cooking time is completed, open the oven door and serve hot.

Tasty Chicken Bites

Servings: 4
Cooking Time: 20 Minutes
Ingredients:
- 2 lbs chicken thighs, cut into chunks
- 2 tbsp olive oil
- 1/2 tsp onion powder
- 1/2 tsp garlic powder
- 1/4 cup fresh lemon juice
- 1/4 tsp white pepper
- Pepper

- Salt

Directions:
1. Select air fry mode set the temperature to 380 °F and set the timer to 20 minutes. Press the setting dial to preheat.
2. Add chicken chunks and remaining ingredients into the large bowl and mix well.
3. Cover and place in refrigerator for overnight.
4. Arrange chicken in the air fryer basket.
5. Once the unit is preheated, open the door, and place the air fryer basket on the top level of the oven, and close the door.
6. Serve and enjoy.

Greek Meatballs

Servings: 6
Cooking Time: 10 Minutes
Ingredients:
- 2 eggs
- 2 lbs ground chicken breast
- 1/4 cup fresh parsley, chopped
- 1/2 cup breadcrumbs
- 1/2 cup ricotta cheese
- 1 tsp pepper
- 2 tsp salt

Directions:
1. Add all ingredients into the large mixing bowl and mix until well combined.
2. Make small balls from the meat mixture and place them in an air fryer basket.
3. Select air fry then set the temperature to 380 °F and time for 10 minutes. Press start.
4. Once the Ninja Foodi Digital Air Fryer Oven is preheated then place the basket into the top rails of the oven.
5. Serve and enjoy.

Feta Turkey Burgers

Servings: 2
Cooking Time: 15 Minutes
Ingredients:
- 8 ounces ground turkey breast
- 1½ tablespoons extra-virgin olive oil
- 2 garlic cloves, grated
- 2 teaspoons fresh oregano, chopped
- ½ teaspoon red pepper flakes, crushed
- Salt, as required
- ¼ cup feta cheese, crumbled

Directions:
1. In a large bowl, add all the ingredients except for feta cheese and mix until well combined.
2. Make 2 (½-inch-thick) patties from the mixture.
3. Press AIR OVEN MODE button of Ninja Foodi Digital Air Fryer Oven and turn the dial to select "Air Fry" mode.
4. Press TIME/SLICES button and again turn the dial to set the cooking time to 15 minutes.
5. Now push TEMP/SHADE button and rotate the dial to set the temperature at 360 °F.

6. Press "Start/Stop" button to start.

7. When the unit beeps to show that it is preheated, open the oven door.

8. Arrange the patties into the greased air fry basket and insert in the oven.

9. Flip the turkey burgers once halfway through.

10. When the cooking time is completed, open the oven door and serve hot with the topping of feta cheese.

Bacon-wrapped Chicken Breasts

Servings: 2

Cooking Time: 35 Minutes

Ingredients:

- 2 boneless, skinless chicken breasts
- ½ teaspoon smoked paprika
- ½ teaspoon garlic powder
- Salt and ground black pepper, as required
- 4 thin bacon slices

Directions:

1. With a meat mallet, pound each chicken breast into ¾-inch thickness.

2. In a bowl, mix together the paprika, garlic powder, salt and black pepper.

3. Rub the chicken breasts with spice mixture evenly.

4. Wrap each chicken breast with bacon strips.

5. Press AIR OVEN MODE button of Ninja Foodi Digital Air Fryer Oven and turn the dial to select "Air Fry" mode.

6. Press TIME/SLICES button and again turn the dial to set the cooking time to 35 minutes.

7. Now push TEMP/SHADE button and rotate the dial to set the temperature at 400 °F.

8. Press "Start/Stop" button to start.

9. When the unit beeps to show that it is preheated, open the oven door.

10. Arrange the chicken pieces into the greased air fry basket and insert in the oven.

11. When the cooking time is completed, open the oven door and serve hot.

Air-fried Chicken Fillet

Servings: 6

Cooking Time:9 Minutes

Ingredients:

- ½ cup fresh basil
- ¼ cup fresh cilantro
- 1 tablespoon olive oil
- 1 teaspoon garlic, minced
- 1pound chicken fillet

Directions:

1. Blend in fresh cilantro and basil in a blender.

2. Add olive oil and minced garlic, stir well. Cut fillet into medium tenders and add basil mixture and stir.

3. Arrange drip pan in the bottom of the Air Fry Oven cooking chamber.

4. Preheat your Ninja Foodi Digital Air Fryer Oven to 360 °F on "AIR FRY" mode.

5. Add tenders to Oven and cook for 9 minutes. Stir well.

6. Once cooking is done, let them chill for and serve.

7. Enjoy!

Turkey Breast With Veggies

Servings: 3

Cooking Time: 45 Minutes

Ingredients:

- 1 lb turkey breast, cut into 1-inch cubes
- 2 tbsp olive oil
- 1 cup mushrooms, cleaned
- 1/2 lb Brussels sprouts, cut in half
- Pepper
- Salt

Directions:

1. In a small bowl, mix oil, pepper, and salt.

2. In a baking dish, mix together turkey, mushrooms, and Brussels sprouts. Pour oil mixture on top.

3. Select bake mode then set the temperature to 350 °F and time for 45 minutes. Press start.

4. Once the Ninja Foodi Digital Air Fryer Oven is preheated then place the baking dish into the oven.

5. Serve and enjoy.

Tasty Japanese Chicken

Servings: 4

Cooking Time: 10 Minutes

Ingredients:

- 1 1/2 lbs chicken thighs, boneless & cut into 2-inch pieces
- 1 tsp garlic, minced
- 1 tsp brown sugar
- 1 tbsp rice wine vinegar
- 3 tbsp soy sauce
- 2 tsp ginger, grated
- 1/2 cup cornstarch

Directions:

1. Select air fry mode set the temperature to 400 °F and set the timer to 10 minutes. Press the setting dial to preheat.

2. In a mixing bowl, add chicken, ginger, garlic, brown sugar, vinegar, and soy sauce and mix well.

3. Cover and place in refrigerator for overnight.

4. Remove chicken from marinade and toss with cornstarch.

5. Arrange chicken in the air fryer basket.

6. Once the unit is preheated, open the door, and place the air fryer basket on the top level of the oven, and close the door.

7. Serve and enjoy.

Chicken Patties

Servings: 4
Cooking Time: 25 Minutes
Ingredients:
- 1 egg
- 1 lb ground chicken
- 2 cups broccoli, cooked and chopped
- 1/2 cup breadcrumbs
- 1 1/2 cups mozzarella cheese, shredded
- Pepper
- Salt

Directions:
1. Add all ingredients into the large bowl and mix until well combined.
2. Make small patties from the mixture and place them on a sheet pan.
3. Select bake mode then set the temperature to 390 °F and time for 25 minutes. Press start.
4. Once the Ninja Foodi Digital Air Fryer Oven is preheated then place the sheet pan into the oven.
5. Turn patties after 15 minutes.
6. Serve and enjoy.

Creamy Chicken Breasts

Servings: 2
Cooking Time: 30 Minutes
Ingredients:
- 2 chicken breasts, skinless and boneless
- 1/4 cup sour cream
- 3/4 cup parmesan cheese, grated
- 1/2 cup Caesar salad dressing

Directions:
1. Coat chicken with parmesan cheese and place it into the greased baking dish.
2. Mix together Caesar dressing and sour cream and pour over chicken.
3. Select bake mode then set the temperature to 375 °F and time for 30 minutes. Press start.
4. Once the Ninja Foodi Digital Air Fryer Oven is preheated then place the baking dish into the oven.
5. Serve and enjoy.

Cajun Chicken

Servings: 4
Cooking Time: 20 Minutes
Ingredients:
- 1 lb chicken breasts, boneless & halves
- 2 tsp olive oil
- 1 tsp ground thyme
- 2 tsp paprika
- 1/2 tsp onion powder
- 1/2 tsp cayenne
- 1 tsp cumin
- 1/4 tsp salt

Directions:

1. Select air fry mode set the temperature to 375 °F and set the timer to 20 minutes. Press the setting dial to preheat.
2. In a small bowl, mix paprika, thyme, cumin, cayenne, onion powder, and salt.
3. Brush chicken with oil and rub with spice mixture.
4. Arrange chicken in the air fryer basket.
5. Once the unit is preheated, open the door, and place the air fryer basket on the top level of the oven, and close the door.
6. Serve and enjoy.

Chicken Kebabs

Servings: 6
Cooking Time: 20 Minutes.
Ingredients:
- 16 ounces skinless chicken breasts, cubed
- 2 tablespoons soy sauce
- ½ zucchini sliced
- 1 tablespoon chicken seasoning
- 1 teaspoon BBQ seasoning
- salt and pepper to taste
- ½ green pepper sliced
- ½ red pepper sliced
- ½ yellow pepper sliced
- ¼ red onion sliced
- 4 cherry tomatoes
- cooking spray

Directions:
1. Toss chicken and veggies with all the spices and seasoning in a bowl.
2. Alternatively, thread them on skewers and place these skewers in the air fry basket.
3. Transfer the basket to Ninja Foodi Digital Air Fryer Oven and close the door.
4. Select "Air Fry" mode by rotating the dial.
5. Press the TIME/SLICES button and change the value to 20 minutes.
6. Press the TEMP/SHADE button and change the value to 350 °F.
7. Press Start/Stop to begin cooking.
8. Flip the skewers when cooked halfway through, then resume cooking.
9. Serve warm.

Marinated Ranch Broiled Chicken

Servings: 1
Cooking Time: 15 Minutes
Ingredients:
- 1 tablespoon olive oil
- ½ tablespoon red wine vinegar
- 2 tablespoons dry Ranch-style dressing mix
- 1 chicken breast half, skinless and boneless

Directions:
1. Take a bowl and mix together dressing mix, oil and vinegar.
2. Add chicken in it and toss to coat well.

78

3. Refrigerate for about an hour.

4. Turn on your Ninja Foodi Digital Air Fryer Oven and rotate the knob to select "Broil".

5. Set timer for 15 minutes and temperature level to high. Press Start/Stop button to begin preheating.

6. When the unit beeps to signify that it is preheated, place chicken onto the SearPlate and broil for about 15 minutes until chicken is cooked through.

7. Serve warm and enjoy!

Lemon Pepper Baked Chicken

Servings: 4
Cooking Time: 30 Minutes
Ingredients:

- 4 chicken breasts, skinless and boneless
- 1 tsp lemon pepper seasoning
- 4 tsp lemon juice
- 4 tsp butter, sliced
- 1/2 tsp paprika
- 1 tsp garlic powder
- Pepper
- Salt

Directions:

1. Place rack in the bottom position and close door. Select bake mode set the temperature to 350 °F and set the timer to 30 minutes. Press the setting dial to preheat.

2. Season chicken with pepper and salt and place in the baking dish.

3. Pour lemon juice over chicken.

4. Mix together paprika, lemon pepper seasoning, and garlic powder and sprinkle over chicken.

5. Add butter slices on top of the chicken.

6. Once the unit is preheated, open the door, and place the baking dish onto the center of the rack, and close the door.

7. Serve and enjoy.

Chicken Potato Bake

Servings: 4
Cooking Time: 25 Minutes.
Ingredients:

- 4 potatoes, diced
- 1 tablespoon garlic, minced
- 1.5 tablespoons olive oil
- 1/8 teaspoon salt
- 1/8 teaspoon pepper
- 1.5 pounds boneless skinless chicken
- 3/4 cup mozzarella cheese, shredded
- Parsley, chopped

Directions:

1. Toss chicken and potatoes with all the spices and oil in a SearPlate.

2. Drizzle the cheese on top of the chicken and potato.

3. Transfer the SearPlate to Ninja Foodi Digital Air Fryer Oven and close the door.

4. Select "Bake" mode by rotating the dial.

5. Press the TIME/SLICES button and change the value to 25 minutes.

6. Press the TEMP/SHADE button and change the value to 375 °F.

7. Press Start/Stop to begin cooking.

8. Serve warm.

Turkey Burger Patties

Servings: 4
Cooking Time: 14 Minutes
Ingredients:

- 1 egg white
- 1/2 tsp dried oregano
- 2 tbsp Worcestershire sauce
- 1 lb ground turkey
- 1/2 tsp dried basil
- Pepper
- Salt

Directions:

1. Select air fry mode set the temperature to 360 °F and set the timer to 14 minutes. Press the setting dial to preheat.

2. In a bowl, mix ground turkey, oregano, Worcestershire sauce, egg white, basil, pepper, and salt until well combined.

3. Make patties from the turkey mixture and place into the air fryer basket.

4. Once the unit is preheated, open the door, and place the air fryer basket on the top level of the oven, and close the door.

5. Serve and enjoy.

Deviled Chicken

Servings: 8
Cooking Time: 40 Minutes.
Ingredients:

- 2 tablespoons butter
- 2 cloves garlic, chopped
- 1 cup Dijon mustard
- ½ teaspoon cayenne pepper
- 1 ½ cups panko breadcrumbs
- ¾ cup Parmesan, freshly grated
- ¼ cup chives, chopped
- 2 teaspoons paprika
- 8 small bone-in chicken thighs, skin removed

Directions:

1. Toss the chicken thighs with crumbs, cheese, chives, butter, and spices in a bowl and mix well to coat.

2. Transfer the chicken along with its spice mix to a SearPlate.

3. Transfer the SearPlate to Ninja Foodi Digital Air Fryer Oven and close the door.

4. Select "Air Fry" mode by rotating the dial.

5. Press the TIME/SLICES button and change the value to 40 minutes.

6. Press the TEMP/SHADE button and change the value to 375 °F.

7. Press Start/Stop to begin cooking.

8. Serve warm.

Lemony Chicken Thighs

Servings: 6
Cooking Time: 20 Minutes
Ingredients:
- 6 chicken thighs
- 2 tablespoons olive oil
- 2 tablespoons fresh lemon juice
- 1 tablespoon Italian seasoning
- Salt and ground black pepper, as required
- 1 lemon, sliced thinly

Directions:
1. In a large bowl, add all the ingredients except for lemon slices and toss to coat well.
2. Refrigerate to marinate for 30 minutes to overnight.
3. Remove the chicken thighs from bowl and let any excess marinade drip off.
4. Press AIR OVEN MODE button of Ninja Foodi Digital Air Fryer Oven and turn the dial to select "Air Fry" mode.
5. Press TIME/SLICES button and again turn the dial to set the cooking time to 20 minutes.
6. Now push TEMP/SHADE button and rotate the dial to set the temperature at 350 °F.
7. Press "Start/Stop" button to start.
8. When the unit beeps to show that it is preheated, open the oven door.
9. Arrange the chicken thighs into the greased air fry basket and insert the basket in oven.
10. Flip the chicken thighs once halfway through.
11. When the cooking time is completed, open the oven door and serve hot alongside the lemon slices.

Fish & Seafood Recipes

Lemony Salmon

Servings: 3
Cooking Time: 8 Minutes
Ingredients:
- 1½ pounds salmon
- ½ teaspoon red chili powder
- Salt and ground black pepper, as required
- 1 lemon, cut into slices
- 1 tablespoon fresh dill, chopped

Directions:
1. Season the salmon with chili powder, salt, and black pepper.
2. Press AIR OVEN MODE button of Ninja Foodi Digital Air Fryer Oven and turn the dial to select "Air Fry" mode.
3. Press TIME/SLICES button and again turn the dial to set the cooking time to 8 minutes.
4. Now push TEMP/SHADE button and rotate the dial to set the temperature at 375 °F.
5. Press "Start/Stop" button to start.
6. When the unit beeps to show that it is preheated, open the oven door.
7. Arrange the salmon fillets into the greased air fry basket and insert in the oven.
8. When cooking time is completed, open the oven door and serve hot with the garnishing of fresh dill.

Fish Newburg With Haddock

Servings: 4
Cooking Time: 29 Minutes.
Ingredients:
- 1 ½ pounds haddock fillets
- Salt and freshly ground black pepper
- 4 tablespoons butter
- 1 tablespoon & 2 teaspoons flour
- ¼ teaspoon sweet paprika
- ¼ teaspoon ground nutmeg
- Dash cayenne pepper
- ¾ cup heavy cream
- ½ cup milk
- 3 tablespoons dry sherry
- 2 large egg yolks
- 4 pastry shells

Directions:
1. Rub haddock with black pepper and salt, then place in SearPlate.
2. Place the spiced haddock in the pastry shell and close like a calzone.
3. Drizzle 1 tablespoon of melted butter on top. Transfer the SearPlate to Ninja Foodi Digital Air Fryer Oven and close the door.
4. Select "Bake" mode by rotating the dial.
5. Press the TIME/SLICES button and change the value 25 minutes.
6. Press the TEMP/SHADE button and change the value 350 °F.
7. Press Start/Stop to begin cooking.
8. Meanwhile, melt 3 tablespoons of butter in a suitable saucepan over low heat.
9. Stir in nutmeg, cayenne, paprika, and salt, then mix well.
10. Add flour to the spice butter and whisk well to avoid lumps.

11. Cook for 2 minutes, then add milk and cream. Mix well and cook until thickens.

12. Beat egg yolks with sherry in a bowl and stir in a ladle of cream mixture.

13. Mix well and return the mixture to the saucepan.

14. Cook the mixture on low heat for 2 minutes.

15. Add the baked wrapped haddock to the sauce and cook until warm.

16. Serve warm.

Cod Parcel

Servings: 4
Cooking Time: 23 Minutes
Ingredients:
- 2 cod fillets
- 6 asparagus stalks
- ¼ cup white sauce
- 1 teaspoon oil
- ¼ cup champagne
- Salt and ground black pepper, as required

Directions:
1. In a bowl, mix together all the ingredients.
2. Divide the cod mixture over 2 pieces of foil evenly.
3. Seal the foil around the cod mixture to form the packet.
4. Press AIR OVEN MODE button of Ninja Foodi Digital Air Fryer Oven and turn the dial to select "Air Fry" mode.
5. Press TIME/SLICES button and again turn the dial to set the cooking time to 13 minutes.
6. Now push TEMP/SHADE button and rotate the dial to set the temperature at 355 °F.
7. Press "Start/Stop" button to start.
8. When the unit beeps to show that it is preheated, open the oven door.
9. Arrange the cod parcels in air fry basket and insert in the oven.
10. When cooking time is completed, open the oven door and transfer the parcels onto serving plates.
11. Carefully unwrap the parcels and serve hot.

Crispy Catfish

Servings: 5
Cooking Time: 15 Minutes
Ingredients:
- 5 catfish fillets
- 1 cup milk
- 2 teaspoons fresh lemon juice
- ½ cup yellow mustard
- ½ cup cornmeal
- ¼ cup all-purpose flour
- 2 tablespoons dried parsley flakes
- ¼ teaspoon red chili powder
- ¼ teaspoon cayenne pepper
- ¼ teaspoon onion powder
- ¼ teaspoon garlic powder
- Salt and ground black pepper, to taste

- Olive oil cooking spray

Directions:
1. In a large bowl, place the catfish, milk, and lemon juice and refrigerate for about 15 minutes.
2. In a shallow bowl, add the mustard. In another bowl, mix the cornmeal, flour, parsley flakes, and spices.
3. Remove the catfish fillets from the milk mixture, and with paper towels, pat them dry. Coat each fish fillet with mustard and then roll into cornmeal mixture.
4. Then, spray each fillet with the cooking spray.
5. Select "AIR FRY" function on your Ninja Foodi Digital Air Fryer Oven.
6. Set the temperature at 400 °F and time to 15 minutes.
7. Press the "START/PAUSE" button to start. When the unit beeps to show that it is preheated, open the door.
8. Arrange the catfish fillets into the greased Air Crisp Basket and insert them in the oven. After 10 minutes of cooking, flip the fillets and spray with the cooking spray.
9. When cooking time is completed, open the door and serve hot.

Scallops With Chanterelles

Servings: 3
Cooking Time: 15 Minutes
Ingredients:
- 1 tablespoon balsamic vinegar
- ½ pound scallops
- 3 tablespoons butter
- ½ tomato, peeled, seeded, and chopped
- 1 tablespoon butter
- ¼ pound chanterelle mushrooms

Directions:
1. Take a pan and add half tablespoon butter over medium heat.
2. Stir in chanterelles and cook for 5 to 8 minutes.
3. Transfer to a bowl.
4. Add remaining butter in the same pan over low heat and cook for 5 minutes.
5. Stir in tomato and balsamic vinegar and cook for 2 minutes.
6. Stir the tomato mixture into mushrooms.
7. Transfer the tomato-mushroom mixture into SearPlate.
8. Turn on your Ninja Foodi Digital Air Fryer Oven and rotate the knob to select "Broil".
9. Select the timer for about 2 minutes per side and temperature for high.
10. When the unit beeps to signify it has preheated, insert the SearPlate in the oven.
11. Close the oven and let it cook.
12. Serve warm and enjoy!

Tuna Patties

Servings: 4
Cooking Time: 6 Minutes
Ingredients:
- 1 egg, lightly beaten
- 8 oz can tuna, drained
- 1/4 tsp garlic powder
- 1/4 cup breadcrumbs
- 1 tbsp mustard
- Pepper
- Salt

Directions:
1. Add all ingredients into the large bowl and mix until well combined.
2. Make patties from the mixture and place them in an air fryer basket.
3. Select air fry then set the temperature to 400 °F and time for 6 minutes. Press start.
4. Once the Ninja Foodi Digital Air Fryer Oven is preheated then place the basket into the top rails of the oven.
5. Turn patties halfway through.
6. Serve and enjoy.

Herbed Shrimp

Servings: 3
Cooking Time: 7 Minutes
Ingredients:
- 4 tablespoons salted butter, melted
- 1 tablespoon fresh lemon juice
- 1 tablespoon garlic, minced
- 2 teaspoons red pepper flakes, crushed
- 1 pound shrimp, peeled and deveined
- 2 tablespoons fresh basil, chopped
- 1 tablespoon fresh chives, chopped
- 2 tablespoons chicken broth

Directions:
1. In a 7-inch round baking pan, place butter, lemon juice, garlic, and red pepper flakes and mix well.
2. Press AIR OVEN MODE button of Ninja Foodi Digital Air Fryer Oven and turn the dial to select the "Air Fry" mode.
3. Press TIME/SLICES button and again turn the dial to set the cooking time to 7 minutes.
4. Now push TEMP/SHADE button and rotate the dial to set the temperature at 325 °F.
5. Press "Start/Stop" button to start.
6. When the unit beeps to show that it is preheated, open the oven door and insert the SearPlate in the oven.
7. After 2 minutes of cooking in the SearPlate, stir in the shrimp, basil, chives, and broth.
8. When cooking time is completed, open the oven door and stir the mixture.
9. Serve hot.

Shrimp Scampi

Servings: 4
Cooking Time: 10 Minutes
Ingredients:
- 2 lbs shrimp, peeled
- 1/2 cup fresh lime juice
- 1/4 cup butter, sliced
- 3/4 cup olive oil
- 2 tsp dried oregano
- 1 tbsp garlic, minced
- Pepper
- Salt

Directions:
1. Add shrimp to a baking dish.
2. In a bowl, whisk together lemon juice, oregano, garlic, oil, pepper, and salt and pour over shrimp.
3. Spread butter on top of shrimp.
4. Select bake mode then set the temperature to 350 °F and time for 10 minutes. Press start.
5. Once the Ninja Foodi Digital Air Fryer Oven is preheated then place the baking dish into the oven.
6. Serve and enjoy.

Pesto Salmon

Servings: 4
Cooking Time: 15 Minutes
Ingredients:
- 1¼ pounds salmon fillet, cut into 4 fillets
- 2 tablespoons white wine
- 1 tablespoon fresh lemon juice
- 2 tablespoons pesto

Directions:
1. Arrange the salmon fillets onto q foil-lined SearPlate skin-side down.
2. Drizzle the salmon fillets with wine and lemon juice.
3. Set aside for about 15 minutes.
4. Spread pesto over each salmon fillet evenly.
5. Press AIR OVEN MODE button of Ninja Foodi Digital Air Fryer Oven and turn the dial to select the "Broil" mode.
6. Press TIME/SLICES button and again turn the dial to set the cooking time to 15 minutes.
7. Press TEMP/SHADE button and turn the dial to set high. To set the temperature, press the TEMP/SHADE button again.
8. Press "Start/Stop" button to start.
9. When the unit beeps to show that it is preheated, open the oven door.
10. Insert the SearPlate in oven.
11. When cooking time is completed, open the oven door and serve hot.

Greek Shrimp

Servings: 4
Cooking Time: 25 Minutes

Ingredients:

- 1 lb shrimp, peeled
- 1 tbsp garlic, sliced
- 2 cups cherry tomatoes
- 1 tbsp olive oil
- Pepper
- Salt

Directions:

1. Add shrimp, oil, garlic, tomatoes, pepper, and salt into the bowl and toss well.
2. Transfer shrimp mixture into the baking dish.
3. Select bake mode then set the temperature to 400 °F and time for 25 minutes. Press start.
4. Once the Ninja Foodi Digital Air Fryer Oven is preheated then place the baking dish into the oven.
5. Serve and enjoy.

Baked Tilapia With Buttery Crumb Topping

Servings: 4
Cooking Time: 16 Minutes.

Ingredients:

- 4 tilapia fillets
- Salt and black pepper to taste
- 1 cup bread crumbs
- 3 tablespoons butter, melted
- ½ teaspoon dried basil

Directions:

1. Rub the tilapia fillets with black pepper and salt, then place them in the SearPlate.
2. Mix butter, breadcrumbs, and seasonings in a bowl.
3. Sprinkle the breadcrumbs mixture on top of the tilapia.
4. Transfer the SearPlate to Ninja Foodi Digital Air Fryer Oven and close the door.
5. Select "Bake" mode by rotating the dial.
6. Press the TIME/SLICES button and change the value to 15 minutes.
7. Press the TEMP/SHADE button and change the value to 375 °F.
8. Press Start/Stop to begin cooking.
9. Switch to "Broil" at "high" and cook for 1 minute.
10. Serve warm.

Salmon With Prawns

Servings: 4
Cooking Time: 18 Minutes

Ingredients:

- 4 salmon fillets
- 2 tablespoons olive oil
- ½ pound cherry tomatoes, chopped
- 8 large prawns, peeled and deveined
- 2 tablespoons fresh lemon juice
- 2 tablespoons fresh thyme, chopped

Directions:

1. In the bottom of the SearPlate, place salmon fillets and tomatoes in a single layer and drizzle with the oil.
2. Arrange the prawns on top in a single layer.
3. Drizzle with lemon juice and sprinkle with thyme.
4. Press AIR OVEN MODE button of Ninja Foodi Digital Air Fryer Oven and turn the dial to select "Air Fry" mode.
5. Press TIME/SLICES button and again turn the dial to set the cooking time to 18 minutes.
6. Now push TEMP/SHADE button and rotate the dial to set the temperature at 390 °F.
7. Press "Start/Stop" button to start.
8. When the unit beeps to show that it is preheated, open the oven door.
9. Insert the SearPlate in the oven.
10. When cooking time is completed, open the oven door and serve immediately.

Coconut Prawns

Servings: 4
Cooking Time: 12 Minutes

Ingredients:

- ½ cup flour
- ¼ teaspoon paprika
- Salt and white pepper, to taste
- 2 egg whites
- ¾ cup panko breadcrumbs
- ½ cup unsweetened coconut, shredded
- 2 teaspoons lemon zest, grated finely
- 1 pound prawns, peeled and deveined

Directions:

1. On a shallow plate, place the flour, paprika, salt, and white pepper and mix well.
2. In a second shallow plate, add the egg whites and beat lightly.
3. In a third shallow plate, place the breadcrumbs, coconut, and lemon zest and mix well.
4. Coat the prawns with flour mixture, then dip into egg whites and finally coat with the coconut mixture.
5. Select "BAKE" mode and set the cooking time to 12 minutes on your Ninja Foodi Digital Air Fryer Oven.
6. Set the temperature at 400 °F.
7. Press the "START/PAUSE" button to start.
8. When the unit beeps to show that it is preheated, open the door.
9. Insert the sheet pan into the oven. Flip the prawns once halfway through.
10. When the unit beeps to show that cooking time is completed, press the "Power" button to stop cooking and open the door.
11. Serve hot.

Garlic Butter Salmon Bites

Servings: 2
Cooking Time: 10 Minutes
Ingredients:

- 1 tablespoon lemon juice
- 2 tablespoons butter
- ½ tablespoon garlic, minced
- ½ teaspoon pepper
- 4 ounces salmon
- ½ teaspoon salt
- ½ tablespoon apple cider or rice vinegar

Directions:
1. Take a large bowl and add everything except salmon and whisk together until well combined.
2. Slice the salmon into small cubes and marinade them into the mixture.
3. Cover the bowl with plastic wrap and refrigerate it for about an hour.
4. Now, spread out the marinated salmon cubes into the air fry basket.
5. Turn on your Ninja Foodi Digital Air Fryer Oven and rotate the knob to select "Air Fry".
6. Select the timer for 10 minutes and temperature for 350 °F.
7. Wait till the salmon is finely cooked.
8. Serve and enjoy!

Scallops With Spinach

Servings: 2
Cooking Time: 10 Minutes
Ingredients:

- ¾ cup heavy whipping cream
- 1 tablespoon tomato paste
- 1 teaspoon garlic, minced
- 1 tablespoon fresh basil, chopped
- Salt and ground black pepper, as required
- 8 jumbo sea scallops
- Olive oil cooking spray
- 1 package frozen spinach, thawed and drained

Directions:
1. In a bowl, place the cream, tomato paste, garlic, basil, salt, and black pepper and mix well.
2. Spray each scallop evenly with cooking spray and then, sprinkle with a little salt and black pepper.
3. In the bottom of a baking pan, place the spinach.
4. Arrange scallops on top of the spinach on SearPlate in a single layer and top with the cream mixture evenly.
5. Press AIR OVEN MODE button of Ninja Foodi Digital Air Fryer Oven and turn the dial to select "Air Fry" mode.
6. Press TIME/SLICES button and again turn the dial to set the cooking time to 10 minutes.
7. Now push TEMP/SHADE button and rotate the dial to set the temperature at 350 °F.
8. Press "Start/Stop" button to start.

9. When the unit beeps to show that it is preheated, open the oven door.
10. Place the SearPlate in the oven.
11. When cooking time is completed, open the oven door and serve hot.

Baked Honey Garlic Shrimp

Servings: 4
Cooking Time: 8 Minutes
Ingredients:

- 1 lb shrimp, peeled and deveined
- 1 1/2 tbsp soy sauce
- 1/2 tsp garlic, minced
- 2 tbsp honey

Directions:
1. Add shrimp into the baking dish.
2. In a bowl, mix together garlic, soy sauce, and honey and pour over shrimp and mix well.
3. Select bake mode then set the temperature to 375 °F and time for 8 minutes. Press start.
4. Once the Ninja Foodi Digital Air Fryer Oven is preheated then place the baking dish into the oven.
5. Serve and enjoy.

Greek Scallops

Servings: 4
Cooking Time: 15 Minutes
Ingredients:

- 1 1/2 lbs sea scallops
- 2 tbsp olives, chopped
- 8 tbsp butter, melted
- 1/2 tsp garlic, minced
- 1 tbsp dried basil
- 4 sun-dried tomatoes, minced
- Pepper
- Salt

Directions:
1. Add all ingredients into the bowl and toss well.
2. Pour scallops mixture into the baking dish.
3. Select bake mode then set the temperature to 400 °F and time for 15 minutes. Press start.
4. Once the Ninja Foodi Digital Air Fryer Oven preheated then place the baking dish into the oven.
5. Serve and enjoy.

Crispy Flounder

Servings: 3
Cooking Time: 12 Minutes
Ingredients:

- 1 egg
- 1 cup dry Italian breadcrumb
- ¼ cup olive oil
- 3 flounder fillets

Directions:
1. In a shallow bowl, beat the egg.

2. In another bowl, add the breadcrumbs and oil and mix until a crumbly mixture is formed.
3. Dip the flounder fillets into the beaten egg and then coat with the breadcrumb mixture.
4. Press AIR OVEN MODE button of Ninja Foodi Digital Air Fryer Oven and turn the dial to select "Air Fry" mode.
5. Press TIME/SLICES button and again turn the dial to set the cooking time to 12 minutes.
6. Now push TEMP/SHADE button and rotate the dial to set the temperature at 355 °F.
7. Press "Start/Stop" button to start.
8. When the unit beeps to show that it is preheated, open the oven door and grease the air fry basket.
9. Place the flounder fillets into the prepared air fry basket and insert in the oven.
10. When cooking time is completed, open the oven door and serve hot.

Salmon Patties

Servings: 4
Cooking Time: 20 Minutes
Ingredients:
- 2 eggs, lightly beaten
- 1/4 cup breadcrumbs
- 1/2 cup fresh parsley, chopped
- 1 tsp Dijon mustard
- 14 oz can salmon, drained and flaked
- 1 tbsp garlic, minced
- 1/4 tsp pepper
- 1/2 tsp kosher salt

Directions:
1. Add all ingredients into the bowl and mix until well combined.
2. Spray sheet pan with cooking spray.
3. Make patties from the mixture and place them on a greased sheet pan.
4. Select bake mode then set the temperature to 400 °F and time for 20 minutes. Press start.
5. Once the Ninja Foodi Digital Air Fryer Oven is preheated then place the sheet pan into the oven.
6. Turn patties halfway through.
7. Serve and enjoy.

Air Fried Fish Sticks

Servings: 1
Cooking Time: 15 Minutes
Ingredients:
- ½ pound fish fillets
- ¼ teaspoon ground black pepper, divided
- 1 egg
- ¼ cup flour
- ½ teaspoon salt, divided
- ½ cup breadcrumbs, dried

Directions:
1. Take a bowl and add flour, salt and pepper.

2. In a second bowl, whisk the egg. In another bowl, add breadcrumbs.
3. Dredge the fish in flour, then dip in egg and lastly coat with breadcrumbs.
4. Once they are done, put them in an air fry basket.
5. Turn on your Ninja Foodi Digital Air Fryer Oven and rotate the knob to select "Air Fry".
6. Select the timer for about 10 to 15 minutes and temperature for 400 °F.
7. Serve and enjoy!

Roasted Mussels

Servings: 4
Cooking Time: 6 Minutes
Ingredients:
- 1 pound mussels
- 1 tablespoon butter
- 1 cup of water
- 2 teaspoons garlic, minced
- 1 teaspoon chives
- 1 teaspoon basil
- 1 teaspoon parsley

Directions:
1. Toss the mussels with oil and all other ingredients in a bowl.
2. Spread the seasoned shrimp in the oven baking tray.
3. Preheat your Ninja Foodi Digital Air Fryer Oven and select the "AIR ROAST" mode.
4. Press the Time button and again turn the dial to set the cooking time to 6 minutes.
5. Now push the Temp button and rotate the dial to set the temperature at 390 °F.
6. Once preheated, place the mussel's tray in the oven and close its lid.
7. Serve warm.

Lemon Turmeric Fish

Servings: 2
Cooking Time: 20 Minutes
Ingredients:
- 1/2 lb white fish fillets
- 1/2 tsp garlic, chopped
- 1/4 tsp ground cumin
- 1/8 tsp turmeric
- 1 tsp fresh lemon juice
- 1/2 tsp olive oil
- Pepper
- Salt

Directions:
1. Mix together turmeric, cumin, pepper, garlic, oil, and lemon juice and rub all over fish fillets and place in a baking dish.
2. Select bake mode then set the temperature to 400 °F and time for 20 minutes. Press start.
3. Once the Ninja Foodi Digital Air Fryer Oven is preheated then place the baking dish into the oven.

4. Serve and enjoy.

Cajun Salmon

Servings: 2
Cooking Time: 7 Minutes
Ingredients:
- 2 (¾-inch thick) salmon fillets
- 1 tablespoon Cajun seasoning
- ½ teaspoon sugar
- 1 tablespoon fresh lemon juice

Directions:
1. Sprinkle the salmon fillets with Cajun seasoning and sugar evenly.
2. Press AIR OVEN MODE button of Ninja Foodi Digital Air Fryer Oven and turn the dial to select "Air Fry" mode.
3. Press TIME/SLICES button and again turn the dial to set the cooking time to 7 minutes.
4. Now push TEMP/SHADE button and rotate the dial to set the temperature at 355 °F.
5. Press "Start/Stop" button to start.
6. When the unit beeps to show that it is preheated, open the oven door.
7. Arrange the salmon fillets, skin-side up in the greased air fry basket and insert in the oven.
8. When cooking time is completed, open the oven door and transfer the salmon fillets onto a platter.
9. Drizzle with the lemon juice and serve hot.

Spicy Bay Scallops

Servings: 4
Cooking Time: 8 Minutes.
Ingredients:
- 1 pound bay scallops rinsed and patted dry
- 2 teaspoons smoked paprika
- 2 teaspoons chili powder
- 2 teaspoons olive oil
- 1 teaspoon garlic powder
- ¼ teaspoon ground black pepper
- ⅛ teaspoon cayenne red pepper

Directions:
1. Scallops with paprika, chili powder, olive oil, garlic powder, black pepper, and red pepper in a bowl.
2. Place the scallops in the air fry basket.
3. Transfer the basket to Ninja Foodi Digital Air Fryer Oven and close the door.
4. Select "Air Fry" mode by rotating the dial.
5. Press the TIME/SLICES button and change the value to 8 minutes.
6. Press the TEMP/SHADE button and change the value to 400 °F.
7. Press Start/Stop to begin cooking.
8. Enjoy.

Seafood Casserole

Servings: 8
Cooking Time: 20 Minutes.

Ingredients:
- 8 ounces haddock, skinned and diced
- 1 pound scallops
- 1 pound large shrimp, peeled and deveined
- 3 to 4 garlic cloves, minced
- ½ cup heavy cream
- ½ cup Swiss cheese, shredded
- 2 tablespoons Parmesan, grated
- Paprika, to taste
- Sea salt and black pepper, to taste

Directions:
1. Grease the SearPlate with cooking spray.
2. Toss shrimp, scallops, and haddock chunks in the greased SearPlate.
3. Drizzle salt, black pepper, and minced garlic over the seafood mix.
4. Top this seafood with cream, Swiss cheese, paprika, and Parmesan cheese.
5. Transfer the dish to the Ninja Digital Air Fryer Oven and close its oven door.
6. Select "Bake" mode by rotating the dial.
7. Press the TIME/SLICES button and change the value to 20 minutes.
8. Press the TEMP/SHADE button and change the value to 375 °F.
9. Press Start/Stop to begin cooking.
10. Serve warm.

Air Fried Fish Cakes

Servings: 1
Cooking Time: 10 Minutes
Ingredients:
- ½ pound white fish, finely chopped
- 1/3 cup panko breadcrumbs
- 2 tablespoons cilantro, chopped
- 1 tablespoon chili sauce
- Cooking spray
- ½ egg
- 1 tablespoon mayonnaise
- 1/8 teaspoon ground pepper
- 1 pinch of salt

Directions:
1. Take a bowl and add all ingredients together until well combined.
2. Shape the mixture into cakes.
3. Grease the air fry basket using cooking spray.
4. Turn on your Ninja Foodi Digital Air Fryer Oven and rotate the knob to select "Air Fry".
5. Select the timer for about 10 minutes and temperature for 400 °F.
6. Let the fish cakes cook until they are golden brown.
7. Serve and enjoy!

Buttered Crab Shells

Servings: 4
Cooking Time: 20 Minutes
Ingredients:

- 4 soft crab shells, cleaned
- 1 cup buttermilk
- 3 eggs
- 2 cups panko breadcrumb
- 2 teaspoons seafood seasoning
- 1½ teaspoons lemon zest, grated
- 2 tablespoons butter, melted

Directions:

1. In a shallow bowl, place the buttermilk.
2. In a second bowl, whisk the eggs.
3. In a third bowl, mix together the breadcrumbs, seafood seasoning, and lemon zest.
4. Soak the crab shells into the buttermilk for about 10 minutes.
5. Now, dip the crab shells into beaten eggs and then, coat with the breadcrumb mixture.
6. Press AIR OVEN MODE button of Ninja Foodi Digital Air Fryer Oven and turn the dial to select "Air Fry" mode.
7. Press TIME/SLICES button and again turn the dial to set the cooking time to 10 minutes.
8. Now push TEMP/SHADE button and rotate the dial to set the temperature at 375 °F.
9. Press "Start/Stop" button to start.
10. When the unit beeps to show that it is preheated, open the oven door and grease the air fry basket.
11. Place the crab shells into the prepared air fry basket and insert in the oven.
12. When cooking time is completed, open the oven door and transfer the crab shells onto serving plates.
13. Drizzle crab shells with the melted butter and serve immediately.

Crab Cakes

Servings: 4
Cooking Time: 10 Minutes
Ingredients:

- ¼ cup red bell pepper, seeded and chopped finely
- 2 scallions, chopped finely
- 2 tablespoons mayonnaise
- 2 tablespoons breadcrumbs
- 1 tablespoon Dijon mustard
- 1 teaspoon old bay seasoning
- 8 ounces lump crabmeat, drained

Directions:

1. In a large bowl, add all the ingredients except crabmeat and mix until well combined.
2. Gently fold in the crabmeat.
3. Make 4 equal-sized patties from the mixture.
4. Arrange the patties onto the lightly greased SearPlate.

5. Press AIR OVEN MODE button of Ninja Foodi Digital Air Fryer Oven and turn the dial to select the "Air Fry" mode.
6. Press TIME/SLICES button and again turn the dial to set the cooking time to 10 minutes.
7. Now push TEMP/SHADE button and rotate the dial to set the temperature at 370 °F.
8. Press "Start/Stop" button to start.
9. When the unit beeps to show that it is preheated, open the oven door and insert the SearPlate in oven.
10. When cooking time is completed, open the oven door and serve hot.

Garlic Shrimp With Lemon

Servings: 1
Cooking Time: 12 Minutes
Ingredients:

- ½ pound raw shrimp
- 1/8 teaspoon garlic powder
- Salt and black pepper, to taste
- Vegetable oil, to coat shrimp
- Chili flakes
- Lemon wedges
- Parsley

Directions:

1. Take a bowl and coat the shrimp with vegetable oil.
2. Add garlic powder, pepper and salt and toss to coat well.
3. Now, transfer shrimp to a plate or air fry basket.
4. Turn on your Ninja Foodi Digital Air Fryer Oven and rotate the knob to select "Air Fry".
5. Select the timer for about 12 minutes and temperature for 400 °F.
6. Transfer shrimp to a bowl and add lemon wedges.
7. Sprinkle parsley and chili flakes evenly on top.
8. Serve and enjoy!

Baked Fish Fillet With Pepper

Servings: 1
Cooking Time: 30 Minutes
Ingredients:

- 8 oz frozen white fish fillet
- 1 tbsp fresh parsley, chopped
- 1 1/2 tbsp olive oil
- 1 tbsp lemon juice
- 1 tbsp roasted red bell pepper, diced
- 1/2 tsp Italian seasoning

Directions:

1. Place a fish fillet in a baking dish.
2. Drizzle oil and lemon juice over fish. Season with Italian seasoning.
3. Top with roasted pepper and parsley.
4. Select bake mode then set the temperature to 400 °F and time for 30 minutes. Press start.
5. Once the Ninja Foodi Digital Air Fryer Oven is preheated then place the baking dish into the oven.
6. Serve and enjoy.

Spiced Shrimp

Servings: 3
Cooking Time: 5 Minutes
Ingredients:
- 1 pound tiger shrimp
- 3 tablespoons olive oil
- 1 teaspoon old bay seasoning
- ½ teaspoon cayenne pepper
- ½ teaspoon smoked paprika
- Salt, as required

Directions:
1. In a large bowl, add all the ingredients and stir to combine.
2. Press AIR OVEN MODE button of Ninja Foodi Digital Air Fryer Oven and turn the dial to select "Air Fry" mode.
3. Press TIME/SLICES button and again turn the dial to set the cooking time to 5 minutes.
4. Now push TEMP/SHADE button and rotate the dial to set the temperature at 390 °F.
5. Press "Start/Stop" button to start.
6. When the unit beeps to show that it is preheated, open the oven door.
7. Arrange the shrimp into the greased air fry basket and insert in the oven.
8. When cooking time is completed, open the oven door and serve hot.

Rosemary Baked Salmon

Servings: 4
Cooking Time: 15 Minutes
Ingredients:
- 1 pound salmon, cut into 4 pieces
- ¼ teaspoon dried basil
- 1 tablespoon olive oil
- ½ tablespoon dried rosemary
- Salt and pepper to taste

Directions:
1. Place salmon pieces into the Air Fryer basket.
2. In a small bowl, mix olive oil, basil, and rosemary. Brush salmon with oil mixture. Place the wire rack inside
3. Select "AIR FRY" mode on your Ninja Foodi Digital Air Fryer Oven.
4. Set the temperature to 400 °F, and set time to 15 minutes.
5. Press "START/PAUSE" to begin preheating.
6. Once the Ninja Foodi Digital Air Fryer Oven is preheated, place the Air Crisp Basket on the wire rack and close the oven door to start cooking. Cook for 15 minutes.
7. Serve and enjoy.

Lemon Pepper Shrimp

Servings: 4
Cooking Time: 8 Minutes
Ingredients:
- 2 lemons, juiced
- ½ tablespoon lemon pepper

- 2 tablespoons olive oil
- ½ teaspoon paprika
- ½ teaspoon garlic powder
- 1½ pounds shrimp

Directions:
1. Take a bowl, add all the ingredients together and mix well.
2. Add shrimp and toss to coat well.
3. Turn on your Ninja Foodi Digital Air Fryer Oven and rotate the knob to select "Air Fry".
4. Select the timer for about 6 to 8 minutes and temperature for 400 °F.
5. Place shrimp in the air fry basket and cook until pink.
6. Serve and enjoy!

Tilapia With Herbs And Garlic

Servings: 1
Cooking Time: 10 Minutes
Ingredients:
- 1 teaspoon olive oil
- 1 teaspoon fresh chives, chopped
- 1 fresh tilapia fillet
- ½ teaspoon garlic, minced
- 1 teaspoon fresh parsley, chopped
- Fresh ground pepper, to taste
- Salt, to taste

Directions:
1. Take a small bowl and add everything except the tilapia fillets and stir together.
2. Dredge tilapia fillets in the prepared mixture.
3. Turn on your Ninja Foodi Digital Air Fryer Oven and rotate the knob to select "Air Fry".
4. Select the timer for about 10 minutes and temperature for 400 °F.
5. Grease the air fry basket using little olive oil and place the seasoned fillets.
6. Let it cook and then serve.

Basil Garlic Shrimp

Servings: 4
Cooking Time: 10 Minutes
Ingredients:
- 2 lbs shrimp, shelled & deveined
- 1 tbsp fresh lemon juice
- 1/3 cup dry white wine
- 2 tsp garlic, minced
- 1/2 cup basil, shredded
- 6 tbsp butter
- 2 tbsp sun-dried tomatoes, chopped
- 1 1/2 tbsp olive oil
- Pepper and salt to taste

Directions:
1. Season shrimp with pepper and salt.
2. Heat oil in a pan over high heat.
3. Add shrimp to the pan and sauté for 1 minute per side.

4. Transfer shrimp to the baking dish.
5. Select bake mode then set the temperature to 350 °F and time for 7 minutes. Press start.
6. Once the Ninja Foodi Digital Air Fryer Oven is preheated then place the baking dish into the oven.
7. Meanwhile, add garlic in the same pan and cook for 15 seconds, then stir in tomatoes, lemon juice, and wine, stir until liquid reduced by 2/3.
8. Add basil and butter and stir until butter is melted. Season with pepper and salt.
9. Pour sauce over shrimp and serve.

Beer-battered Fish

Servings: 4
Cooking Time: 15 Minutes.
Ingredients:
- 1 ½ cups all-purpose flour
- kosher salt, to taste
- ½ teaspoon Old Bay seasoning
- 1 bottle lager
- 1 large egg, beaten
- 2 pounds cod, cut into 12 pieces
- freshly ground black pepper
- vegetable oil for frying
- lemon wedges, for serving

Directions:
1. Mix flour with old bay, salt, egg, and beer in a bowl.
2. Rub the cod with black pepper and salt.
3. Coat the codfish with the beer batter and place it in the air fry basket.
4. Transfer the basket to Ninja Foodi Digital Air Fryer Oven and close the door.
5. Select "Air Fry" mode by rotating the dial.
6. Press the TIME/SLICES button and change the value to 15 minutes
7. Press the TEMP/SHADE button and change the value to 350 °F.
8. Press Start/Stop to begin cooking.
9. Serve warm.

Herb Salmon

Servings: 4
Cooking Time: 15 Minutes
Ingredients:
- 1 lbs salmon, cut into 4 pieces
- 1/4 tsp dried basil
- 1 tbsp olive oil
- 1/2 tbsp dried rosemary
- Pepper
- Salt

Directions:
1. Place salmon pieces in an air fryer basket.
2. In a small bowl, mix together olive oil, basil, and rosemary.
3. Brush salmon with oil mixture.
4. Place the basket in the oven.

5. Select air fry then set the temperature to 400 °F and time for 15 minutes. Press start.
6. Once the Ninja Foodi Digital Air Fryer Oven is preheated then place the basket into the top rails of the oven.
7. Serve and enjoy.

Spicy Shrimp

Servings: 4
Cooking Time: 8 Minutes
Ingredients:
- 1 lb shrimp, peeled and deveined
- 1 tbsp soy sauce
- 3 tbsp butter, melted
- 1 tsp garlic, chopped
- 1 tbsp chili paste

Directions:
1. Add shrimp into the baking dish.
2. In a bowl, mix together butter, soy sauce, chili paste, and garlic and pour over shrimp and mix well.
3. Select bake mode then set the temperature to 400 °F and time for 8 minutes. Press start.
4. Once the Ninja Foodi Digital Air Fryer Oven is preheated then place the baking dish into the oven.
5. Serve and enjoy.

Pesto Fish Fillets

Servings: 4
Cooking Time: 10 Minutes
Ingredients:
- 4 tilapia fillets
- 2 tbsp olive oil

For pesto:
- 2/3 cup basil
- 1/2 cup olive oil
- 2 tbsp parmesan cheese, shredded
- 4 tbsp pine nuts
- 2 garlic cloves
- Pepper
- Salt

Directions:
1. Select air fry mode set the temperature to 350 °F and set the timer to 10 minutes. Press the setting dial to preheat.
2. Brush fish fillets with oil and season with pepper and salt.
3. Arrange fish fillets in the air fryer basket.
4. Once the unit is preheated, open the door, and place the air fryer basket on the top level of the oven, and close the door.
5. Add all pesto ingredients into the blender and blend until smooth.
6. Pour pesto over fish fillets and serve.

Spicy Salmon

Servings: 2
Cooking Time: 11 Minutes
Ingredients:
- 1 teaspoon smoked paprika
- 1 teaspoon cayenne pepper
- 1 teaspoon onion powder
- 1 teaspoon garlic powder
- Salt and ground black pepper, as required
- 2 salmon fillets
- 2 teaspoons olive oil

Directions:
1. Add the spices in a bowl and mix well.
2. Drizzle the salmon fillets with oil and then rub with the spice mixture.
3. Press AIR OVEN MODE button of Ninja Foodi Digital Air Fryer Oven and turn the dial to select "Air Fry" mode.
4. Press TIME/SLICES button and again turn the dial to set the cooking time to 11 minutes.
5. Now push TEMP/SHADE button and rotate the dial to set the temperature at 390 °F.
6. Press "Start/Stop" button to start.
7. When the unit beeps to show that it is preheated, open the oven door.
8. Arrange the salmon fillets into the greased air fry basket and insert in the oven.
9. When cooking time is completed, open the oven door and serve hot.

Scallops With Capers Sauce

Servings: 2
Cooking Time: 6 Minutes
Ingredients:
- 10 sea scallops, cleaned and patted very dry
- Salt and ground black pepper, as required
- ¼ cup extra-virgin olive oil
- 2 tablespoons fresh parsley, finely chopped
- 2 teaspoons capers, finely chopped
- 1 teaspoon fresh lemon zest, finely grated
- ½ teaspoon garlic, finely chopped

Directions:
1. Season each scallop evenly with salt and black pepper.
2. Press AIR OVEN MODE button of Ninja Foodi Digital Air Fryer Oven and turn the dial to select "Air Fry" mode.
3. Press TIME/SLICES button and again turn the dial to set the cooking time to 6 minutes.
4. Now push TEMP/SHADE button and rotate the dial to set the temperature at 400 °F.
5. Press "Start/Stop" button to start.
6. When the unit beeps to show that it is preheated, open the oven door and grease the air fry basket.
7. Place the scallops into the prepared air fry basket and insert in the oven.
8. Meanwhile, for the sauce - in a bowl, mix the remaining ingredients.

9. When cooking time is completed, open the oven door and transfer the scallops onto serving plates.
10. Top with the sauce and serve immediately.

Shrimp Fajitas

Servings: 2
Cooking Time: 10 Minutes
Ingredients:
- ½ pound raw shrimp
- ½ small onion, sliced
- ½ tablespoon vegetable oil, divided
- ½ tablespoon fajita seasoning
- 1 red bell pepper, sliced
- 1 green bell pepper, sliced

Directions:
1. Take a bowl and season the vegetables. Add half of the oil and fajita seasoning.
2. Turn on your Ninja Foodi Digital Air Fryer Oven and rotate the knob to select "Air Fry".
3. Select the timer for 3 minutes and temperature for 375 °F.
4. Air fry the vegetables.
5. Now, meanwhile season the shrimp with rest of oil and fajita seasoning.
6. After 3 minutes add the seasoned shrimp to the side.
7. Now, air fry for another 6 minutes at the same temperature.
8. Serve and enjoy!

Sweet & Sour Herring

Servings: 2
Cooking Time: 12 Minutes
Ingredients:
- 2 herring fillets
- 1 garlic clove, minced
- 1 teaspoon fresh rosemary, minced
- 1 tablespoon butter, melted
- 1 tablespoon balsamic vinegar
- ¼ teaspoon maple syrup
- 1 teaspoon Sriracha

Directions:
1. In a large resalable bag, place all the ingredients and seal the bag. Shake the bag well to mix.
2. Place the bag in the refrigerator to marinate for at least 30 minutes. Remove the fish fillets from the bag and shake off the excess marinade.
3. Arrange the fish fillets onto the greased sheet pan in single layer.
4. Select "BAKE" mode on your Ninja Foodi Digital Air Fryer Oven.
5. Set the cooking time to 12 minutes and the temperature at 450 °F.
6. Press the "START/PAUSE" button to start.
7. Insert the sheet pan into the oven.
8. Flip the fillets once halfway through.

9. When the unit beeps to show that cooking time is completed, press the "Power" button to stop cooking and open the door.
10. Serve hot.

Salmon With Broccoli

Servings: 2
Cooking Time: 12 Minutes
Ingredients:
- 1½ cups small broccoli florets
- 2 tablespoons vegetable oil, divided
- Salt and ground black pepper, as required
- 1 (½-inch) piece fresh ginger, grated
- 1 tablespoon soy sauce
- 1 teaspoon rice vinegar
- 1 teaspoon light brown sugar
- ¼ teaspoon cornstarch
- 2 skin-on salmon fillets

Directions:
1. In a bowl, mix together the broccoli, 1 tablespoon of oil, salt, and black pepper.
2. In another bowl, mix well the ginger, soy sauce, vinegar, sugar, and cornstarch.
3. Coat the salmon fillets with remaining oil and then with the ginger mixture.
4. Press AIR OVEN MODE button of Ninja Foodi Digital Air Fryer Oven and turn the dial to select "Air Fry" mode.
5. Press TIME/SLICES button and again turn the dial to set the cooking time to 12 minutes.
6. Now push TEMP/SHADE button and rotate the dial to set the temperature at 375 °F.
7. Press "Start/Stop" button to start.
8. When the unit beeps to show that it is preheated, open the oven door.
9. Arrange the broccoli florets into the greased air fry basket and top with the salmon fillets.
10. Insert the basket in the oven.
11. When cooking time is completed, remove basket from oven and cool for 5 minutes before serving.

Air Fryer Trout

Servings: 4
Cooking Time: 16 Minutes
Ingredients:
- 1 lb trout fillets
- 1 tsp garlic powder
- 3 tbsp breadcrumbs
- 1 tbsp olive oil
- 1 tsp chili powder
- 1 tsp onion powder

Directions:
1. Select air fry mode set the temperature to 375 °F and set the timer to 16 minutes. Press the setting dial to preheat.
2. In a small bowl, mix breadcrumbs, garlic powder, onion powder, and chili powder.
3. Brush fish fillets with oil and coat with breadcrumbs.

4. Place coated fish fillets into the air fryer basket.
5. Once the unit is preheated, open the door, and place the air fryer basket on the top level of the oven, and close the door.
6. Serve and enjoy.

Parmesan Flounder

Servings: 4
Cooking Time: 20 Minutes.
Ingredients:
- ¼ cup olive oil
- 4 fillets flounder
- Kosher salt, to taste
- Freshly ground black pepper
- ½ cup Parmesan, grated
- ¼ cup bread crumbs
- 4 garlic cloves, minced
- Juice and zest of 1 lemon

Directions:
1. Mix parmesan, breadcrumbs, and all the ingredients in a bowl and coat the flounder well.
2. Place the fish in SearPlate.
3. Transfer the SearPlate to Ninja Foodi Digital Air Fryer Oven and close the door.
4. Select "Bake" mode by rotating the dial.
5. Press the TIME/SLICES button and change the value to 20 minutes.
6. Press the TEMP/SHADE button and change the value to 425 °F.
7. Press Start/Stop to begin cooking.
8. Serve warm.

Air-fried Flounder

Servings: 4
Cooking Time: 12 Minutes
Ingredients:
- 1 whole egg
- 1 cup dry breadcrumbs
- ¼ cup olive oil
- 3 flounder fillets
- 1 lemon, sliced

Directions:
1. In a shallow bowl, beat the egg.
2. In another bowl, add the breadcrumbs and oil and mix until a crumbly mixture is formed.
3. Dip flounder fillets into the beaten egg and then coat with the breadcrumb mixture.
4. Preheat your Ninja Foodi Digital Air Fryer Oven and turn the select the "AIR FRY" mode.
5. Press the Time button and again turn the dial to set the cooking time to 12 minutes.
6. Now push the Temp button and rotate the dial to set the temperature at 356 °F.
7. Press the "START/PAUSE" button to start.
8. When the unit beeps to show that it is preheated, open the door.

9. Arrange the flounder fillets in a greased "Air Crisp Basket" and insert it in the oven.

10. Garnish with the lemon slices and serve hot.

Flavorful Baked Shrimp

Servings: 4
Cooking Time: 15 Minutes
Ingredients:
- 1 lb shrimp, peel & devein
- 2 1/4 tsp dry mustard
- 2 tsp cumin
- 2 tsp paprika
- 2 tsp black pepper
- 4 tsp cayenne pepper
- 2 tsp garlic powder
- 2 tsp onion powder
- 1 tsp dried oregano
- 1 tsp dried thyme
- 1/2 cup butter, melted
- 3 tsp salt

Directions:
1. Add shrimp, butter, and remaining ingredients into the bowl and toss well.
2. Transfer shrimp mixture into the baking dish.
3. Select bake mode then set the temperature to 400 °F and time for 15 minutes. Press start.
4. Once the Ninja Foodi Digital Air Fryer Oven is preheated then place the baking dish into the oven.
5. Serve and enjoy.

Lobster Tail Casserole

Servings: 6
Cooking Time: 16 Minutes.
Ingredients:
- 1 pound salmon fillets, cut into 8 equal pieces
- 16 large sea scallops
- 16 large prawns, peeled and deveined
- 8 East Coast lobster tails split in half
- ⅓ cup butter
- ¼ cup white wine
- ¼ cup lemon juice
- 2 tablespoons chopped fresh tarragon
- 2 medium garlic cloves, minced
- ½ teaspoon paprika
- ¼ teaspoon ground cayenne pepper

Directions:
1. Whisk butter with lemon juice, wine, garlic, tarragon, paprika, salt, and cayenne pepper in a small saucepan.
2. Stir cook this mixture over medium heat for 1 minute.
3. Toss scallops, salmon fillet, and prawns in the SearPlate and pour the butter mixture on top.
4. Transfer the dish to Ninja Foodi Digital Air Fryer Oven and close the door.
5. Select "Bake" mode by rotating the dial.

6. Press the TIME/SLICES button and change the value to 15 minutes.
7. Press the TEMP/SHADE button and change the value to 450 °F.
8. Press Start/Stop to begin cooking.
9. Serve warm.

Tasty Crab Cakes

Servings: 4
Cooking Time: 15 Minutes
Ingredients:
- 1 egg
- 1 lb lump crab meat
- 1/4 tsp hot sauce
- 1 tsp lemon juice
- 1 1/2 tsp Worcestershire sauce
- 2 tsp Dijon mustard
- 1/4 cup mayonnaise
- 4 tbsp breadcrumbs
- 1 tbsp parsley, chopped
- 1 1/2 tsp old bay seasoning
- Pepper
- Salt

Directions:
1. Select air fry mode set the temperature to 375 °F and set the timer to 15 minutes. Press the setting dial to preheat.
2. In a bowl, mix crab meat with remaining ingredients until well combined.
3. Make patties from crabmeat mixture and place into the air fryer basket.
4. Once the unit is preheated, open the door, and place the air fryer basket on the top level of the oven, and close the door.
5. Serve and enjoy.

Buttered Trout

Servings: 2
Cooking Time: 10 Minutes
Ingredients:
- 2 trout fillets
- Salt and ground black pepper, as required
- 1 tablespoon butter, melted

Directions:
1. Season each trout fillet with salt and black pepper and then coat with the butter.
2. Arrange the trout fillets onto the greased SearPlate in single layer.
3. Press AIR OVEN MODE button of Ninja Foodi Digital Air Fryer Oven and turn the dial to select "Air Fry" mode.
4. Press TIME/SLICES button and again turn the dial set the cooking time to 10 minutes.
5. Now push TEMP/SHADE button and rotate the dial set the temperature at 360 °F.
6. Press "Start/Stop" button to start.
7. When the unit beeps to show that it is preheated, open the oven door.

8. Insert the SearPlate in oven.
9. Flip the fillets once halfway through.
10. When cooking time is completed, open the oven door and serve hot.

Blackened Fish Fillets

Servings: 4
Cooking Time: 10 Minutes
Ingredients:
- 4 mahi-mahi fish fillets
- 1/2 tsp cayenne
- 1 tbsp olive oil
- 1 tsp thyme
- 1 tsp oregano
- 1 1/2 tsp onion powder
- 2 tbsp butter
- 1 tsp smoked paprika
- 1 tsp garlic powder
- Pepper
- Salt

Directions:
1. Select air fry mode set the temperature to 380 °F and set the timer to 10 minutes. Press the setting dial to preheat.
2. In a small bowl, mix butter, onion powder, garlic powder, oil, paprika, thyme, oregano, cayenne, pepper, and salt.
3. Coat fish fillets with butter mixture.
4. Place fish fillets into the air fryer basket.
5. Once the unit is preheated, open the door, and place the air fryer basket on the top level of the oven, and close the door.
6. Serve and enjoy.

Lemon Herb Fish Fillets

Servings: 4
Cooking Time: 10 Minutes
Ingredients:
- 4 tilapia fillets
- 1 tsp lemon juice
- 1 tsp garlic powder
- 1 tsp dried oregano
- Pepper
- Salt

Directions:
1. Select air fry mode set the temperature to 400 °F and set the timer to 10 minutes. Press the setting dial to preheat.
2. In a small bowl, mix garlic powder, oregano, lemon juice, pepper, and salt.
3. Rub fish fillets with spice mixture and place into the air fryer basket.
4. Once the unit is preheated, open the door, and place the air fryer basket on the top level of the oven, and close the door.
5. Serve and enjoy.

Fish Casserole

Servings: 3
Cooking Time: 40 Minutes
Ingredients:
- ½ tablespoon unsalted butter, softened
- ¼ teaspoon salt
- 1 pound white fish fillet
- ¼ teaspoon pepper
- ½ sweet onion, thinly sliced
- 2 teaspoons extra-virgin olive oil, divided
- ¼ teaspoon dry thyme
- 1 pinch nutmeg
- 1 bread slice, crusts removed
- ¼ teaspoon paprika
- 1/8 teaspoon garlic powder
- ½ cup shredded Swiss cheese

Directions:
1. Turn on your Ninja Foodi Digital Air Fryer Oven and rotate the knob to select "Bake".
2. Preheat by selecting the timer for 3 minutes and temperature for 400 °F.
3. Arrange fish fillet on a dish and season with salt and pepper.
4. Take a pan and heat oil over medium-high heat. Add onion and cook until it starts to brown.
5. Stir in thyme and nutmeg.
6. Spread the onion mixture over fish.
7. In a food processor, add bread slice, paprika, garlic powder and a little oil.
8. Process until we have a moist mixture.
9. Sprinkle crumbs over the onion mixture.
10. Add cheese on top of casserole and place inside Ninja Foodi Digital Air Fryer Oven.
11. Select the timer for about 18 to 22 minutes and temperature for 400 °F.
12. Serve warm.

Broiled Scallops

Servings: 2
Cooking Time: 8 Minutes
Ingredients:
- 1 pound bay scallops
- 1 tablespoon lemon juice
- 1 tablespoon butter, melted
- ½ tablespoon garlic salt

Directions:
1. Turn on your Ninja Foodi Digital Air Fryer Oven and rotate the knob to select "Broil".
2. Rinse scallop and place in SearPlate.
3. Season with garlic salt, butter and lemon juice.
4. Select the timer for about 8 minutes and temperature for high.
5. Remove from oven and serve warm.

Air Fried Scallops

Servings: 4
Cooking Time: 4 Minutes
Ingredients:
- 16 scallops
- ¼ teaspoon garlic powder
- 1 teaspoon olive oil
- Salt and pepper to taste

Directions:
1. Add scallops and remaining ingredients into the mixing bowl and toss well. Add scallops to the Air Fryer basket.
2. Place the wire rack inside your Ninja Foodi Digital Air Fryer Oven.
3. Select "AIR FRY" mode, set the temperature to 390 °F, and set the time to 4 minutes.
4. Press "START/PAUSE" to begin preheating.
5. Once the Ninja Foodi Digital Air Fryer Oven is preheated, place the Air Crisp Basket on the wire rack and close the oven door to start cooking. Cook for 4 minutes.
6. Serve and enjoy.

Zesty Salmon

Servings: 3
Cooking Time: 8 Minutes
Ingredients:
- 1 ½ pounds salmon
- ½ teaspoon red chili powder
- Salt and black pepper, to taste
- 1 lemon, cut into slices
- 1 tablespoon fresh dill, chopped

Directions:
1. Season the salmon with chili powder, salt, and black pepper.
2. Select "AIR FRY" function on your Ninja Foodi Digital Air Fryer Oven.
3. Set the temperature at 375 °F and cooking time to 8 minutes.
4. Press the "START/PAUSE" button to start.
5. Arrange the salmon fillets into the greased Air Crisp Basket and insert them in the oven.
6. When cooking time is completed, open the door and serve hot with the garnishing of fresh dill.

Chili Garlic Salmon

Servings: 3
Cooking Time: 15 Minutes
Ingredients:
- 1 lb salmon fillets
- 2 tbsp butter, melted
- 1 garlic clove, minced
- 2 tsp honey
- 1 tsp lime zest
- 1 tsp chili powder
- 1 tsp cumin powder
- 2 tbsp lime juice

- 1/2 tsp salt

Directions:
1. In a saucepan, heat lime juice, garlic, honey, and salt over medium heat.
2. Remove pan from heat and add butter and stir well.
3. Brush salmon with lime mixture and season with chili powder, cumin, and lime zest.
4. Place salmon fillets in an air fryer basket.
5. Select air fry then set the temperature to 350 °F and time for 15 minutes. Press start.
6. Once the Ninja Foodi Digital Air Fryer Oven is preheated then place the basket into the top rails of the oven.
7. Serve and enjoy.

Nuts Crusted Salmon

Servings: 2
Cooking Time: 15 Minutes
Ingredients:
- 2 skinless salmon fillets
- Salt and ground black pepper, as required
- 3 tablespoons walnuts, chopped finely
- 3 tablespoons quick-cooking oats, crushed
- 2 tablespoons olive oil

Directions:
1. Rub the salmon fillets with salt and black pepper evenly.
2. In a bowl, mix together the walnuts, oats and oil.
3. Arrange the salmon fillets onto the greased SearPlate in a single layer.
4. Place the oat mixture over salmon fillets and gently press down.
5. Press AIR OVEN MODE button of Ninja Foodi Digital Air Fryer Oven and turn the dial to select the "Bake" mode.
6. Press TIME/SLICES button and again turn the dial to set the cooking time to 15 minutes.
7. Now push TEMP/SHADE button and rotate the dial to set the temperature at 400 °F.
8. Press "Start/Stop" button to start.
9. When the unit beeps to show that it is preheated, open the oven door.
10. Insert the SearPlate in oven.
11. When cooking time is completed, open the oven door and serve hot.

Seafood Medley Mix

Servings: 1
Cooking Time: 15 Minutes
Ingredients:
- ½ pound frozen seafood medley
- Oil or cooking spray
- Salt and black pepper, to taste

Directions:
1. Take an air fry basket and evenly spray with a cooking spray.
2. Put frozen seafood medley in the air fry basket.
3. Turn on your Ninja Foodi Digital Air Fryer Oven and rotate the knob to select "Air Fry".

4. Select the timer for 15 minutes and temperature for 400 °F.
5. Season the seafood medley with salt and pepper.
6. Serve and enjoy!

Tasty Sriracha Shrimp

Servings: 4
Cooking Time: 6 Minutes
Ingredients:
- 12 oz shrimp, peeled & deveined
- 1 1/2 tbsp butter, melted
- 2 tbsp sriracha sauce
- 1/2 lime juice
- 1 1/2 tbsp soy sauce
- 1 1/2 tbsp honey

Directions:
1. Select air fry mode set the temperature to 400 °F and set the timer to 6 minutes. Press the setting dial to preheat.
2. In a bowl, add shrimp and remaining ingredients and mix well. Cover and place in refrigerator for 30 minutes.
3. Add marinated shrimp into the air fryer basket.
4. Once the unit is preheated, open the door, and place the air fryer basket on the top level of the oven, and close the door.
5. Serve and enjoy.

Baked Sardines With Garlic And Oregano

Servings: 4
Cooking Time: 45 Minutes.
Ingredients:
- 2 pounds fresh sardines
- Salt and black pepper to taste
- 2 tablespoons Greek oregano
- 6 cloves garlic, thinly sliced
- ½ cup olive oil
- ½ cup freshly squeezed lemon juice
- ½ cup water

Directions:
1. Mix salt, black pepper, oregano, garlic, olive oil, lemon juice, and water in SearPlate.
2. Spread the sardines in the marinade and rub well.
3. Leave the sardines for 10 minutes to marinate.
4. Transfer the SearPlate to Ninja Foodi Digital Air Fryer Oven and close the door.
5. Select "Air Fry" mode by rotating the dial.
6. Press the TIME/SLICES button and change the value to 45 minutes.
7. Press the TEMP/SHADE button and change the value to 355 °F.
8. Press Start/Stop to begin cooking.
9. Serve warm.

Salmon Burgers

Servings: 6
Cooking Time: 22 Minutes

Ingredients:
- 3 large russet potatoes, peeled and cubed
- 1 cooked salmon fillet
- 1 egg
- ¾ cup frozen vegetables (of your choice), parboiled and drained
- 2 tablespoons fresh parsley, chopped
- 1 teaspoon fresh dill, chopped
- Salt and ground black pepper, as required
- 1 cup breadcrumbs
- ¼ cup olive oil
- Boiling water

Directions:
1. In a pan of boiling water, cook the potatoes for about 10 minutes.
2. Drain the potatoes well.
3. Transfer the potatoes into a bowl and mash with a potato masher.
4. Set aside to cool completely.
5. In another bowl, add the salmon and flake with a fork.
6. Add the cooked potatoes, egg, parboiled vegetables, parsley, dill, salt, and black pepper and mix until well combined.
7. Make 6 equal-sized patties from the mixture.
8. Coat patties with breadcrumb evenly and then drizzle with the oil evenly.
9. Press AIR OVEN MODE button of Ninja Foodi Digital Air Fryer Oven and turn the dial to select "Air Fry" mode.
10. Press TIME/SLICES button and again turn the dial to set the cooking time to 12 minutes.
11. Now push TEMP/SHADE button and rotate the dial to set the temperature at 355 °F.
12. Press "Start/Stop" button to start.
13. When the unit beeps to show that it is preheated, open the oven door.
14. Arrange the patties in greased air fry basket and insert in the oven.
15. Flip the patties once halfway through.
16. When cooking time is completed, open the oven door and serve hot.

Rum-glazed Shrimp

Servings: 4
Cooking Time: 5 Minutes.
Ingredients:
- 1 ½ pounds shrimp, peeled and deveined
- 3 tablespoons olive oil
- ⅓ cup sweet chili sauce
- ¼ cup soy sauce
- ¼ Captain Morgan Spiced Rum
- 2 garlic cloves, minced
- Juice of 1 lime
- ½ teaspoon crushed red pepper flakes
- 1 green onion, thinly sliced

Directions:

1. Mix shrimp with all the ingredients in a bowl.
2. Cover and marinate the shrimp for 30 minutes.
3. Spread the glazed shrimp in a SearPlate.
4. Transfer the SearPlate to Ninja Foodi Digital Air Fryer Oven and close the door.
5. Select "Bake" mode by rotating the dial.
6. Press the TIME/SLICES button and change the value to 5 minutes.
7. Press the TEMP/SHADE button and change the value to 375 °F.
8. Press Start/Stop to begin cooking.
9. Serve warm.

Fish Sticks

Servings: 4
Cooking Time: 12 Minutes
Ingredients:
- 4 fish fillets, tilapia
- 1- ½ cup all-purpose flour
- 3 large eggs, beaten
- 1 ⅓ cups Panko bread crumbs
- Salt, to taste

Directions:
1. Take a shallow bowl and put all-purpose flour in it.
2. In a separate bowl and whisk the egg in it.
3. Take a third bowl and mix bread crumbs with salt. Coat the fish with flour, and then dredge with egg wash.
4. Then coat it with Panko bread crumbs.
5. Now place fish in a crisper basket and insert it in your Ninja Foodi Digital Air Fryer Oven.
6. Select "AIR FRY" and adjust the temperature to 390 °F for 12 minutes.
7. Remember to flip the fish halfway through.
8. Remove the fish and then serve.

Lemon Dill Fish Fillets

Servings: 2
Cooking Time: 14 Minutes
Ingredients:
- 2 mahi-mahi fillets
- 1 tbsp olive oil
- 1 tbsp lemon juice
- 1 tbsp dill, chopped
- 2 lemon slices
- Pepper
- Salt

Directions:
1. Select air fry mode set the temperature to 400 °F and set the timer to 14 minutes. Press the setting dial to preheat.
2. In a small bowl, mix oil, lemon juice, dill, pepper, and salt.
3. Brush fish fillets with oil mixture and place them into the air fryer basket.
4. Place lemon slices on top of fish fillets.

5. Once the unit is preheated, open the door, and place the air fryer basket on the top level of the oven, and close the door.
6. Serve and enjoy.

Air Fried Shrimp

Servings: 3
Cooking Time: 7 Minutes
Ingredients:
- 4 tablespoons salted butter, melted
- 1 tablespoon fresh lemon juice
- 1 tablespoon garlic, minced
- 2 teaspoons red pepper flakes, crushed
- 1pound shrimp, peeled and deveined
- 2 tablespoons fresh basil, chopped
- 1 tablespoon fresh chives, chopped
- 2 tablespoons chicken broth

Directions:
1. In a 7-inch round baking pan, place butter, lemon juice, garlic, and red pepper flakes and mix well.
2. Select the "AIR FRY" function on your Ninja Food Digital Air Fryer Oven.
3. Set the temperature at 325 °F and cooking time to minutes.
4. Press the "START/PAUSE" button to start. Place the pan over a wire rack.
5. Insert the wire rack in the oven.
6. After 2 minutes of cooking in the pan, stir in the shrimp basil, chives, and broth.
7. When cooking time is completed, open the door and st the mixture.
8. Serve hot.

Shrimp Casserole

Servings: 4
Cooking Time: 12 Minutes
Ingredients:
- 1 lb shrimp, peeled and deveined
- 2 tbsp white wine
- 1 tbsp garlic, minced
- 1/2 cup breadcrumbs
- 1/4 cup butter, melted
- Pepper
- Salt

Directions:
1. Add shrimp into the bowl.
2. Pour remaining ingredients over shrimp and toss well.
3. Pour shrimp mixture into the greased baking dish.
4. Select bake mode then set the temperature to 400 °F a time for 12 minutes. Press start.
5. Once the Ninja Foodi Digital Air Fryer Oven preheated then place the baking dish into the oven.
6. Serve and enjoy.

Breaded Shrimp

Servings: 2
Cooking Time: 7 Minutes
Ingredients:

- ¼ teaspoon garlic powder
- ¼ teaspoon onion powder
- ¼ teaspoon salt
- ½ pound raw shrimp
- 1 egg
- 2 teaspoons flour
- ½ teaspoon corn starch
- 1 tablespoon water
- 6 tablespoons fine breadcrumbs
- 6 tablespoons panko breadcrumbs

Directions:
1. Take a small bowl, add flour, corn starch, garlic powder, onion powder and salt.
2. Add shrimp in the bowl and toss to coat well.
3. In a second bowl, whisk in the egg.
4. Mix the panko breadcrumbs and fine breadcrumbs together in another bowl.
5. Now, take seasoned shrimp, dip in the egg and place in the bread crumbs mixture.
6. Lightly grease the air fry basket.
7. Turn on your Ninja Foodi Digital Air Fryer Oven and rotate the knob to select "Air Fry".
8. Select the timer for about 7 minutes and temperature for 370 °F.
9. Place the coated shrimp to the air fry basket and let it cook.
10. Serve and enjoy!

Salmon & Asparagus Parcel

Servings: 2
Cooking Time: 13 Minutes
Ingredients:

- 2 salmon fillets
- 6 asparagus stalks
- ¼ cup white sauce
- 1 teaspoon oil
- ¼ cup champagne
- Salt and ground black pepper, as required

Directions:
1. In a bowl, mix together all the ingredients.
2. Divide the salmon mixture over 2 pieces of foil evenly.
3. Seal the foil around the salmon mixture to form the packet.
4. Press AIR OVEN MODE button of Ninja Foodi Digital Air Fryer Oven and turn the dial to select "Air Fry" mode.
5. Press TIME/SLICES button and again turn the dial to set the cooking time to 13 minutes.
6. Now push TEMP/SHADE button and rotate the dial to set the temperature at 355 °F.
7. Press "Start/Stop" button to start.

8. When the unit beeps to show that it is preheated, open the oven door.
9. Arrange the salmon parcels into the air fry basket and insert in the oven.
10. When cooking time is completed, open the oven door and serve hot.

Crispy Cod

Servings: 4
Cooking Time: 15 Minutes
Ingredients:

- 4 (¾-inch thick) cod fillets
- Salt, as required
- 2 tablespoons all-purpose flour
- 2 eggs
- ½ cup panko breadcrumbs
- 1 teaspoon fresh dill, minced
- ½ teaspoon dry mustard
- ½ teaspoon lemon zest, grated
- ½ teaspoon onion powder
- ½ teaspoon paprika
- Olive oil cooking spray

Directions:
1. Season the cod fillets with salt generously.
2. In a shallow bowl, place the flour.
3. Crack the eggs in a second bowl and beat well.
4. In a third bowl, mix together the panko, dill, lemon zest, mustard and spices.
5. Coat each cod fillet with the flour, then dip into beaten eggs and finally, coat with panko mixture.
6. Press AIR OVEN MODE button of Ninja Foodi Digital Air Fryer Oven and turn the dial to select "Air Fry" mode.
7. Press TIME/SLICES button and again turn the dial to set the cooking time to 15 minutes.
8. Now push TEMP/SHADE button and rotate the dial to set the temperature at 400 °F.
9. Press "Start/Stop" button to start.
10. When the unit beeps to show that it is preheated, open the oven door and grease the air fry basket.
11. Place the cod fillets into the prepared air fry basket and insert in the oven.
12. Flip the cod fillets once halfway through.
13. When cooking time is completed, open the oven door and serve hot.

Maple Bacon Salmon

Servings: 4
Cooking Time: 29 Minutes.
Ingredients:

- Salmon
- 1 lemon, sliced
- 1 skin-on salmon fillet
- 2 ½ teaspoons salt, black pepper, and garlic seasoning
- 1 tablespoon Dijon mustard
- ⅓ cup olive oil
- 2 tablespoons lemon juice

- 2 tablespoons maple syrup
- Chopped chives for garnish
- Candied Bacon
- 3 tablespoons maple syrup
- 1 tablespoon packed brown sugar
- ¼ teaspoon salt, black pepper and garlic seasoning

Directions:
1. Place lemon slices in the SearPlate and top them with salmon.
2. Drizzle salt, black pepper, and garlic seasoning on top.
3. Mix mustard, oil, maple syrup, lemon juice, salt, black pepper, and seasoning in a bowl.
4. Pour this sauce over the salmon.
5. Transfer the SearPlate to Ninja Foodi Digital Air Fryer Oven and close the door.
6. Select "Air Fry" mode by rotating the dial.
7. Press the TIME/SLICES button and change the value to 25 minutes.
8. Press the TEMP/SHADE button and change the value to 350 °F.
9. Press Start/Stop to begin cooking.
10. Meanwhile, mix brown sugar, salt, black pepper, and garlic seasoning in a bowl.
11. Sauté bacon in a skillet until crispy and pour the sugar syrup on top.
12. Cook for 4 minutes until the liquid is absorbed.
13. Allow the bacon to cool and then crumble it.
14. Garnish the salmon with crumbled bacon and chopped chives.
15. Serve warm.

Salmon With Veggies

Servings: 2
Cooking Time: 10 Minutes
Ingredients:
- 2 salmon fillets
- 1/2 cup roasted red peppers, sliced
- 1 cup mushrooms, sliced
- 1 tbsp butter, melted
- 1/2 tsp dill weed
- 1 tbsp lemon juice
- Pepper
- Salt

Directions:
1. Select air fry mode set the temperature to 400 °F and set the timer to 10 minutes. Press the setting dial to preheat.
2. In a small bowl, mix butter, lemon juice, dill, pepper, and salt.
3. Brush fish fillets with butter mixture and place them into the air fryer basket.
4. Add mushrooms and roasted peppers around the fish fillets.
5. Once the unit is preheated, open the door, and place the air fryer basket on the top level of the oven, and close the door.
6. Serve and enjoy.

Cod Burgers

Servings: 4
Cooking Time: 7 Minutes
Ingredients:
- ½ pound cod fillets
- ½ teaspoon fresh lime zest, grated finely
- ½ egg
- ½ teaspoon red chili paste
- Salt, to taste
- ½ tablespoon fresh lime juice
- 3 tablespoons coconut, grated and divided
- 1 small scallion, chopped finely
- 1 tablespoon fresh parsley, chopped

Directions:
1. In a food processor, add cod filets, lime zest, egg, chil paste, salt and lime juice and pulse until smooth.
2. Transfer the cod mixture into a bowl.
3. Add 1½ tablespoons coconut, scallion and parsley and mix until well combined.
4. Make 4 equal-sized patties from the mixture.
5. In a shallow dish, place the remaining coconut.
6. Coat the patties in coconut evenly.
7. Press AIR OVEN MODE button of Ninja Foodi Digita Air Fryer Oven and turn the dial to select "Air Fry" mode.
8. Press TIME/SLICES button and again turn the dial t set the cooking time to 7 minutes.
9. Now push TEMP/SHADE button and rotate the dial t set the temperature at 375 °F.
10. Press "Start/Stop" button to start.
11. When the unit beeps to show that it is preheated, ope the oven door.
12. Arrange the patties into the greased air fry basket an insert in the oven.
13. When cooking time is completed, open the oven doc and serve hot.

Cod With Sauce

Servings: 2
Cooking Time: 15 Minutes
Ingredients:
- 2 cod fillets
- Salt and ground black pepper, as required
- ¼ teaspoon sesame oil
- 1 cup water
- 5 little squares rock sugar
- 5 tablespoons light soy sauce
- 1 teaspoon dark soy sauce
- 2 scallions (green part), sliced
- ¼ cup fresh cilantro, chopped
- 3 tablespoons olive oil
- 5 ginger slices

Directions:
1. Season each cod fillet evenly with salt, and black pepp and drizzle with sesame oil.
2. Set aside at room temperature for about 15-20 minutes.

3. Press AIR OVEN MODE button of Ninja Foodi Digital Air Fryer Oven and turn the dial to select "Air Fry" mode.

4. Press TIME/SLICES button and again turn the dial to set the cooking time to 12 minutes.

5. Now push TEMP/SHADE button and rotate the dial to set the temperature at 355 °F.

6. Press "Start/Stop" button to start.

7. When the unit beeps to show that it is preheated, open the oven door.

8. Arrange the cod fillets into the greased air fry basket and insert in the oven.

9. Meanwhile, in a small pan, add the water and bring it to a boil.

10. Add the rock sugar and both soy sauces and cook until sugar is dissolved, stirring continuously.

11. Remove from the heat and set aside.

12. Remove the cod fillets from oven and transfer onto serving plates.

13. Top each fillet with scallion and cilantro.

14. In a small frying pan, heat the olive oil over medium heat and sauté the ginger slices for about 2-3 minutes.

15. Remove the frying pan from heat and discard the ginger slices.

16. When cooking time is completed, open the oven door and transfer the cod fillets onto serving plates.

17. Carefully pour the hot oil evenly over cod fillets.

18. Top with the sauce mixture and serve.

Tangy Sea Bass

Servings: 2
Cooking Time: 12 Minutes
Ingredients:
- 2 sea bass fillets
- 1 garlic clove, minced
- 1 teaspoon fresh dill, minced
- 1 tablespoon olive oil
- 1 tablespoon balsamic vinegar
- Salt and black pepper, to taste

Directions:
1. In a large resealable bag, add all the ingredients. Seal the bag and shake well to mix.

2. Refrigerate to marinate for at least 30 minutes.

3. Remove the fish fillets from bag and shake off the excess marinade.

4. Arrange the fish fillets onto the greased sheet pan in a single layer.

5. Select "BAKE" function on your Ninja Foodi Digital Air Fryer Oven.

6. Set the temperature at 450 °F. and the cooking time to 12 minutes.

7. Press the "START/PAUSE" button to start.

8. Insert the sheet pan into the oven.

9. When cooking time is completed, open the oven door. Flip the fish fillets once halfway through.

10. When cooking time is completed, open the door and serve hot.

Prawns In Butter Sauce

Servings: 2
Cooking Time: 6 Minutes
Ingredients:
- ½ pound large prawns, peeled and deveined
- 1 large garlic clove, minced
- 1 tablespoon butter, melted
- 1 teaspoon fresh lemon zest, grated

Directions:
1. In a bowl, add all the ingredients and toss to coat well.

2. Set aside at room temperature for about 30 minutes.

3. Arrange the prawn mixture into a SearPlate.

4. Press AIR OVEN MODE button of Ninja Foodi Digital Air Fryer Oven and turn the dial to select "Bake" mode.

5. Press TIME/SLICES button and again turn the dial to set the cooking time to 6 minutes.

6. Now push TEMP/SHADE button and rotate the dial to set the temperature at 450 °F.

7. Press "Start/Stop" button to start.

8. When the unit beeps to show that it is preheated, open the oven door.

9. Insert the SearPlate in the oven. Close the oven and let it cook.

10. When cooking time is completed, open the oven door and serve immediately.

Fish In Yogurt Marinade

Servings: 2
Cooking Time: 10 Minutes.
Ingredients:
- 1 cup plain Greek yogurt
- Finely grated zest of 1 lemon
- 1 tablespoon lemon juice
- 1 tablespoon finely minced garlic
- 3 tablespoons fresh oregano leaves
- 1 teaspoon ground cumin
- ¼ teaspoon ground allspice
- ½ teaspoon salt
- ½ teaspoon freshly ground black pepper
- 1½ pounds perch filets

Directions:
1. Mix lemon zest, yogurt, garlic, cumin, oregano, black pepper, salt, and all spices in SearPlate.

2. Add fish to this marinade, mix well to coat then cover it with a plastic wrap.

3. Marinate for 15 minutes in the refrigerator, then uncover.

4. Transfer the SearPlate to Ninja Foodi Digital Air Fryer Oven and close the door.

5. Select "Bake" mode by rotating the dial.

6. Press the TIME/SLICES button and change the value to 10 minutes.

7. Press the TEMP/SHADE button and change the value to 450 °F.

8. Press Start/Stop to begin cooking.

9. Serve warm.

Sweet & Spicy Salmon

Servings: 4
Cooking Time: 8 Minutes
Ingredients:

- 4 salmon fillets
- 1 tsp smoked paprika
- 1 tsp chili powder
- 4 tbsp honey
- 1/2 tsp red pepper flakes, crushed
- 1/2 tsp garlic powder
- Pepper
- Salt

Directions:

1. Select air fry mode set the temperature to 390 °F and set the timer to 8 minutes. Press the setting dial to preheat.
2. In a small bowl, mix honey, chili powder, paprika, garlic powder, red pepper flakes, pepper, and salt.
3. Brush fish fillets with honey mixture and place into the air fryer basket.
4. Once the unit is preheated, open the door, and place the air fryer basket on the top level of the oven, and close the door.
5. Serve and enjoy.

Italian Salmon

Servings: 5
Cooking Time: 20 Minutes
Ingredients:

- 1 3/4 lbs salmon fillet
- 1 tbsp fresh dill, chopped
- 1/4 cup capers
- 1/3 cup artichoke hearts
- 1/3 cup basil pesto
- 1/4 cup sun-dried tomatoes, drained
- 1/4 cup olives, pitted and chopped
- 1 tsp paprika
- 1/4 tsp salt

Directions:

1. Spray sheet pan with cooking spray.
2. Arrange salmon fillet on a greased sheet pan. Season with paprika and salt.
3. Add remaining ingredients on top of salmon.
4. Select bake mode then set the temperature to 400 °F and time for 20 minutes. Press start.
5. Once the Ninja Foodi Digital Air Fryer Oven is preheated then place the sheet pan into the oven.
6. Serve and enjoy.

Lobster Tails With Lemon-garlic Butter

Servings: 1
Cooking Time: 10 Minutes
Ingredients:

- 2 tablespoons butter
- ½ teaspoon lemon zest
- 1 lobster tail
- ½ clove garlic, grated
- ½ teaspoon parsley, chopped
- Salt, to taste
- Fresh ground black pepper, to taste

Directions:

1. Cut the lobster tail lengthwise through the center of the hard top shell.
2. Cut to the bottom of the shell and spread the tail halves apart.
3. Place the lobster tail in the air fry basket.
4. Take a saucepan and melt butter on medium heat.
5. Add garlic and lemon zest and cook for 30 seconds.
6. Now, pour the butter mixture onto lobster tail.
7. Turn on your Ninja Foodi Digital Air Fryer Oven and rotate the knob to select "Air Fry".
8. Select the timer for about 5 to 7 minutes and temperature for 380 °F.
9. Let it cook and serve with parsley as topping.

Dehydrated Recipes

Lemon Slices

Servings: 4
Cooking Time: 10 Hours
Ingredients:
* 4 lemons, wash and cut into 1/4-inch thick slices
Directions:
1. Arrange lemon slices in an air fryer basket and place the basket in the oven.
2. Select dehydrate then set the temperature to 125 °F and time to 10 hours. Press start.
3. Store in a container.

Nutritious Almonds

Servings: 4
Cooking Time: 12 Hours
Ingredients:
* 1 cup almonds, soaked in water for overnight
* 1/4 tsp cayenne
* 1/2 tbsp olive oil
Directions:
1. Toss almonds with oil and cayenne.
2. Spread almonds in an air fryer basket and place the basket in the oven.
3. Select dehydrate then set the temperature to 125 °F and time to 12 hours. Press start.
4. Store in a container.

Sweet Mango Slices

Servings: 2
Cooking Time: 12 Hours
Ingredients:
* 2 mangoes, peel and cut into 1/4-inch thick slices
* 1/2 tbsp honey
* 2 tbsp lime juice
Directions:
1. In a bowl, mix together lime juice and honey.
2. Add mango slices and coat well.
3. Arrange mango slices in an air fryer basket and place the basket in the oven.
4. Select dehydrate then set the temperature to 135 °F and time to 12 hours. Press start.
5. Store in a container.

Dehydrated Raspberries

Servings: 4
Cooking Time: 12 Hours
Ingredients:
* 2 cups fresh raspberries, wash and pat dry with a paper towel
Directions:
1. Select dehydrate mode, set temperature to 135 °F, and set timer to 12 hours.

2. Place raspberries in the air fryer basket and place basket into top rails of the oven. Close door.

Pear Slices

Servings: 4
Cooking Time: 5 Hours
Ingredients:
* 2 pears, cut into 1/4-inch thick slices
Directions:
1. Select dehydrate mode, set temperature to 160 °F, and set timer to 5 hours.
2. Place pear slices in the air fryer basket and place basket into top rails of the oven. Close door.

Mushroom Slices

Servings: 4
Cooking Time: 5 Hours
Ingredients:
* 1 cup mushrooms, clean & cut into 1/8-inch thick slices
* 1/4 tbsp fresh lemon juice
* Salt
Directions:
1. Add sliced mushrooms, lemon juice, and salt into the bowl and toss well.
2. Arrange mushroom slices in an air fryer basket and place the basket in the oven.
3. Select dehydrate then set the temperature to 160 °F and time to 5 hours. Press start.
4. Store in a container.

Beet Slices

Servings: 2
Cooking Time: 10 Hours
Ingredients:
* 1 beet, sliced thinly
* Salt
Directions:
1. Select dehydrate mode, set temperature to 135 °F, and set timer to 10 hours.
2. Place beet slices in the air fryer basket and sprinkle with salt.
3. Place basket into top rails of the oven. Close door.

Pork Jerky

Servings: 4
Cooking Time: 5 Hours
Ingredients:
* 1 lb pork lean meat, sliced thinly
* 1 tsp chili powder
* 1 tsp smoked paprika
* 1/2 tsp garlic powder
* Pepper
* Salt
Directions:

1. Add paprika, garlic powder, chili powder, pepper, and salt in a bowl and mix well.
2. Add the sliced meat and mix well.
3. Cover and place in the refrigerator overnight.
4. Arrange meat slices in an air fryer basket and place the basket in the oven.
5. Select dehydrate then set the temperature to 160 °F and time to 5 hours. Press start.
6. Store in a container.

Green Bean Chips

Servings: 2
Cooking Time: 8 Hours
Ingredients:
- 25 green beans
- 1 tbsp olive oil
- 2 tbsp nutritional yeast
- Salt

Directions:
1. In a bowl, toss green beans with the remaining ingredients.
2. Arrange green beans in an air fryer basket and place the basket in the oven.
3. Select dehydrate then set the temperature to 135 °F and time to 8 hours. Press start.
4. Store in a container.

Apple Slices

Servings: 4
Cooking Time: 8 Hours
Ingredients:
- 2 apple, cored and cut into 1/8-inch thick slices
- 1 tsp cinnamon

Directions:
1. Select dehydrate mode, set temperature to 145 °F, and set timer to 8 hours.
2. Place apple slices in the air fryer basket and sprinkle cinnamon on top of apple slices.
3. Place basket into top rails of the oven. Close door.

Tomato Slices

Servings: 4
Cooking Time: 12 Hours
Ingredients:
- 4 tomatoes, sliced thinly
- Pinch of cayenne
- Pepper
- Salt

Directions:
1. Arrange tomato slices in an air fryer basket and season with cayenne, pepper, and salt, and place the basket in the oven.
2. Select dehydrate then set the temperature to 135 °F and time to 12 hours. Press start.
3. Store in a container.

Eggplant Slices

Servings: 2
Cooking Time: 6 Hours
Ingredients:
- 1 medium eggplant, sliced 1/4-inch thick
- 1/4 tsp garlic powder
- 1 1/2 tsp paprika
- Pinch of cayenne

Directions:
1. Add eggplant slices, cayenne, garlic powder, and paprika into the bowl and toss well.
2. Arrange eggplant slices in an air fryer basket and place the basket in the oven.
3. Select dehydrate then set the temperature to 140 °F and time to 6 hours. Press start.
4. Store in a container.

Dried Pineapple Pieces

Servings: 2
Cooking Time: 12 Hours
Ingredients:
- 1 cup pineapple chunks

Directions:
1. Arrange pineapple chunks in an air fryer basket and place the basket in the oven.
2. Select dehydrate then set the temperature to 135 °F and time to 12 hours. Press start.
3. Store in an air-tight container.

Mango Slices

Servings: 4
Cooking Time: 12 Hours
Ingredients:
- 2 mangoes, peel, and cut into 1/4-inch thick slices

Directions:
1. Select dehydrate mode, set temperature to 135 °F, and set timer to 12 hours.
2. Place mango slices in the air fryer basket and place basket into top rails of the oven. Close door.

Kiwi Slices

Servings: 4
Cooking Time: 12 Hours
Ingredients:
- 2 kiwis, peeled & cut into 1/4-inch thick slices

Directions:
1. Select dehydrate mode, set temperature to 135 °F, and set timer to 12 hours.
2. Place kiwi slices in the air fryer basket and place basket into top rails of the oven. Close door.

Brussels Sprout Chips

Servings: 4
Cooking Time: 10 Hours
Ingredients:
- 1 lb Brussels sprouts, cut the stem, and separate leaves
- 2 tbsp sriracha
- 1 tsp soy sauce
- Pinch of salt

Directions:
1. In a mixing bowl, toss Brussels sprouts with soy sauce, sriracha, and salt.
2. Select dehydrate mode, set temperature to 115 °F, and set timer to 10 hours.
3. Place Brussels sprouts in the air fryer basket and place basket into top rails of the oven. Close door.

Sweet Potato Slices

Servings: 3
Cooking Time: 12 Hours
Ingredients:
- 1 sweet potato, sliced thinly
- 3 tbsp olive oil
- 1/2 tsp chili powder
- 1 tsp salt

Directions:
1. Add sweet potato slices into the large bowl.
2. Mix together chili powder, oil, and salt and pour over sweet potato slices and mix well.
3. Arrange sweet potato slices in an air fryer basket and place the basket in the oven.
4. Select dehydrate then set the temperature to 125 °F and time to 12 hours. Press start.
5. Store in a container.

Parsnips Slices

Servings: 3
Cooking Time: 10 Hours
Ingredients:
- 2 parsnips, peel & thinly sliced

Directions:
1. Arrange parsnips slices in an air fryer basket and place the basket in the oven.
2. Select dehydrate then set the temperature to 115 °F and time to 10 hours. Press start.
3. Store in a container.

Beef Jerky

Servings: 4
Cooking Time: 8 Hours
Ingredients:
- 1 lb flank steak, cut into thin slices
- 1 1/2 tbsp ranch seasoning
- 1/2 cup Worcestershire sauce
- 1/4 tsp cayenne
- 1 tsp liquid smoke
- 1 tbsp chili flakes
- 1/2 cup soy sauce

Directions:
1. Add all ingredients into the large bowl and mix well.
2. Cover and place in the refrigerator overnight.
3. Arrange meat slices in an air fryer basket and place the basket in the oven.
4. Select dehydrate then set the temperature to 145 °F and time to 8 hours. Press start.
5. Store in a container.

Strawberry Slices

Servings: 3
Cooking Time: 12 Hours
Ingredients:
- 1 cup strawberries, cut into 1/8-inch thick slices

Directions:
1. Arrange strawberry slices in an air fryer basket and place the basket in the oven.
2. Select dehydrate then set the temperature to 130 °F and time to 12 hours. Press start.
3. Store in a container.

Chicken Jerky

Servings: 4
Cooking Time: 7 Hours
Ingredients:
- 1 1/2 lb chicken tenders, boneless & cut into 1/4-inch slices
- 1/2 tsp garlic powder
- 1 tsp lemon juice
- 1/2 cup soy sauce
- 1/4 tsp ground ginger
- 1/4 tsp black pepper

Directions:
1. Mix all ingredients except chicken into the zip-lock bag.
2. Add chicken slices, seal bag, and place in the refrigerator for 1 hour.
3. Select dehydrate mode, set temperature to 145 °F, and set timer to 7 hours.
4. Place chicken slices in the air fryer basket and place basket into top rails of the oven. Close door.

Cauliflower Florets

Servings: 2
Cooking Time: 8 Hours
Ingredients:
- 2 cups cauliflower florets, chopped
- 1/4 tsp ground cumin
- 1/2 tsp chili powder
- 1/2 tbsp paprika
- 1 1/2 tbsp olive oil

Directions:
1. Add cauliflower into the large bowl.
2. Add remaining ingredients over the cauliflower and toss well.

3. Arrange cauliflower florets in an air fryer basket and place the basket in the oven.

4. Select dehydrate then set the temperature to 130 °F and time to 8 hours. Press start.

5. Store in a container.

Dehydrated Chickpeas

Servings: 4
Cooking Time: 10 Hours
Ingredients:
- 14 oz can chickpeas, drained and rinsed
- Salt

Directions:
1. Select dehydrate mode, set temperature to 135 °F, and set timer to 10 hours.
2. Place chickpeas in the air fryer basket and season with salt.
3. Place basket into top rails of the oven. Close door.

Zucchini Chips

Servings: 4
Cooking Time: 10 Hours

Ingredients:
- 4 cups zucchini slices
- 3 tbsp BBQ sauce

Directions:
1. Add zucchini slices into the bowl. Pour BBQ sauce over zucchini slices and mix well.
2. Arrange zucchini slices in an air fryer basket and place the basket in the oven.
3. Select dehydrate then set the temperature to 135 °F and time to 10 hours. Press start.
4. Store in a container.

Dehydrated Pineapple

Servings: 2
Cooking Time: 12 Hours
Ingredients:
- 1 cup pineapple chunks

Directions:
1. Select dehydrate mode, set temperature to 135 °F, and set timer to 12 hours.
2. Place pineapple chunks in the air fryer basket and place basket into top rails of the oven. Close door.

Vegetables & Sides Recipes

Feta And Vegetable Bake

Servings: 4
Cooking Time: 30 Minutes.
Ingredients:
- ½ cup brown rice, cooked
- 5 ounces feta cheese, cubed
- 2 tablespoons olive oil
- 2 tablespoons basil, dried
- 2 tablespoons parsley, dried
- 1 garlic clove
- 1 onion, julienned
- 1 bell pepper, red, julienned
- 2 good handful cherry tomatoes
- 1 jalapeño, chopped
- 1 handful olives, sliced
- 10 tablespoons water

Directions:
1. Spread the cheese in a SearPlate and drizzle half of the herbs on top.
2. Toss remaining vegetables with rice and water, spread over the cheese.
3. Add remaining herbs on top and spread them evenly.

4. Transfer the pan to Ninja Foodi Digital Air Fryer Oven and close the door.
5. Select "Bake" mode by rotating the dial.
6. Press the TEMP/SHADE button and change the value 350 °F.
7. Press the TIME/SLICES button and change the value 30 minutes, then press Start/Stop to begin cooking.
8. Serve warm.

Broccoli Casserole

Servings: 6
Cooking Time: 45 Minutes.
Ingredients:
- 1 cup mayonnaise
- 10 ½ ounces cream of celery soup
- 2 large eggs, beaten
- 20 ounces chopped broccoli
- 2 tablespoons onion, minced
- 1 cup Cheddar cheese, grated
- 1 tablespoon Worcestershire sauce
- 1 teaspoon seasoned salt
- Black pepper, to taste
- 2 tablespoons butter

Directions:
1. Whisk mayonnaise with eggs, condensed soup in a large bowl.
2. Stir in salt, black pepper, Worcestershire sauce, and cheddar cheese.
3. Spread broccoli and onion in a greased casserole dish.
4. Top the veggies with the mayonnaise mixture.
5. Transfer this broccoli casserole to Ninja Foodi Digital Air Fryer Oven and close its oven door.
6. Rotate the Ninja Foodi dial to select the "Bake" mode.
7. Press the TIME/SLICES button and again use the dial to set the cooking time to 45 minutes.
8. Now Press the TEMP/SHADE button and rotate the dial to set the temperature at 350 °F.
9. Slice and serve warm.

Vegetable Casserole

Servings: 6
Cooking Time: 42 Minutes.
Ingredients:
- 2 cups peas
- 8 ounces mushrooms, sliced
- 4 tablespoons all-purpose flour
- 1 ½ cups celery, sliced
- 1 ½ cups carrots, sliced
- ½ teaspoon mustard powder
- 2 cups milk
- Salt and black pepper, to taste
- 7 tablespoons butter
- 1 cup breadcrumbs
- ½ cup Parmesan cheese, grated

Directions:
1. Grease and rub a casserole dish with butter and keep it aside.
2. Add carrots, onion, and celery to a saucepan, then fill it with water.
3. Cover this pot and cook for 10 minutes, then stir in peas.
4. Cook for 4 minutes, then strain the vegetables.
5. Now melt 1 tablespoon of butter in the same saucepan and toss in mushrooms to sauté.
6. Once the mushrooms are soft, transfer them to the vegetables.
7. Prepare the sauce by melting 4 tablespoons of butter in a suitable saucepan.
8. Stir in mustard and flour, then stir cook for 2 minutes.
9. Gradually pour in the milk and stir cook until thickened, then add salt and black pepper.
10. Add vegetables and mushrooms to the flour milk mixture and mix well.
11. Spread this vegetable blend in the casserole dish evenly.
12. Toss the breadcrumbs with the remaining butter and spread it on top of vegetables.
13. Top this casserole dish with cheese.
14. Transfer the dish to Ninja Foodi Digital Air Fryer Oven and close the door.
15. Select "Air Fry" mode by rotating the dial.

16. Press the TIME/SLICES button and change the value to 25 minutes.
17. Press the TEMP/SHADE button and change the value to 350 °F.
18. Press Start/Stop to begin cooking.
19. Serve warm.

Potato Croquettes

Servings: 6
Cooking Time: 1 Hour
Ingredients:
- 2 cups sweet potatoes, mashed
- 2 cups quinoa, cooked
- ¼ cup celery, diced
- ¼ cup scallions, chopped
- ¼ cup parsley, chopped
- ¼ cup flour
- 2 teaspoon Italian seasoning
- 2 garlic cloves, minced
- Salt and pepper to taste
- Cooking spray

Directions:
1. Spray sheet pan with cooking spray and set aside.
2. Add all ingredients into the large bowl and mix well. Make 1-inch round croquettes from the mixture and place them on a sheet pan.
3. Place the wire rack inside your Ninja Foodi Digital Air Fryer Oven.
4. Select "BAKE" mode set the temperature to 375 °F, and set time to 60 minutes
5. Press "START/PAUSE" to begin preheating.
6. Once the Ninja Foodi Digital Air Fryer Oven is preheated, place a sheet pan on a wire rack and close the oven door to start cooking.
7. Cook for an hour.
8. Serve and enjoy.

Sour Green Beans

Servings: 2
Cooking Time: 20 Minutes
Ingredients:
- 1 bag frozen cut green beans
- ¼ cup nutritional yeast
- 3 tablespoons balsamic vinegar
- Salt and ground black pepper, to taste

Directions:
1. In a bowl, add the green beans, nutritional yeast, vinegar, salt, and black pepper and toss to coat well.
2. Select the "AIR FRY" function and set the temperature at 400 °F on your Ninja Foodi Digital Air Fryer Oven.
3. Set the cooking time to 20 minutes.
4. Press the "START/PAUSE" button to start. When the unit beeps to show that it is preheated, open the door.
5. Arrange the green beans into the greased Air Crisp Basket and insert them in the oven.

6. When cooking time is completed, open the door and serve hot.

Roasted Vegetables

Servings: 6
Cooking Time: 15 Minutes.
Ingredients:
- 2 medium bell peppers cored, chopped
- 2 medium carrots, peeled and sliced
- 1 small zucchini, ends trimmed, sliced
- 1 medium broccoli, florets
- ½ red onion, peeled and diced
- 2 tablespoons olive oil
- 1 ½ teaspoons Italian seasoning
- 2 garlic cloves, minced
- Salt and freshly ground black pepper
- 1 cup grape tomatoes
- 1 tablespoon fresh lemon juice

Directions:
1. Toss all the veggies with olive oil, Italian seasoning, salt, black pepper, and garlic in a large salad bowl.
2. Spread this broccoli-zucchini mixture in the SearPlate.
3. Transfer the SearPlate to Ninja Foodi Digital Air Fryer Oven and close the door.
4. Select "Bake" mode by rotating the dial.
5. Press the TIME/SLICES button and change the value to 15 minutes.
6. Press the TEMP/SHADE button and change the value to 400 °F.
7. Press Start/Stop to begin cooking.
8. Serve warm with lemon juice on top.
9. Enjoy.

Blue Cheese Soufflés

Servings: 4
Cooking Time: 17 Minutes.
Ingredients:
- 2 ounces unsalted butter
- 1 ounce breadcrumbs
- 1 ounce plain flour
- 1 pinch English mustard powder
- 1 pinch cayenne pepper
- 10 ounces semi-skimmed milk
- 3 ounces blue murder cheese
- 1 fresh thyme sprig, chopped
- 4 medium eggs, separated

Directions:
1. Grease four ramekins with butter and sprinkle with breadcrumbs.
2. Melt butter in a suitable saucepan, stir in flour, cayenne, and mustard powder.
3. Then mix well and cook for 1 minute, then slowly pour in the milk.
4. Mix well until smooth, then boil the sauce. Cook for 2 minutes.

5. Stir in cheese, and mix well until melted.
6. Add black pepper, salt, and egg yolks.
7. Beat egg whites in a bowl with a mixer until they make stiff peaks.
8. Add egg whites to the cheese sauce, then mix well.
9. Divide the mixture into the ramekins and transfer to Ninja Foodi Digital Air Fryer Oven, then close its door.
10. Select the "Bake" mode by rotating the dial.
11. Press the TIME/SLICES button and change the value to 14 minutes.
12. Press the TEMP/SHADE button and change the value to 350 °F.
13. Press Start/Stop to begin cooking.
14. Serve warm.

Herbed Bell Peppers

Servings: 4
Cooking Time: 8 Minutes
Ingredients:
- 1½ pounds mixed bell peppers, seeded and sliced
- 1 small onion, sliced
- ½ teaspoon dried thyme, crushed
- ½ teaspoon dried savory, crushed
- Salt and ground black pepper, as required
- 2 tablespoons butter, melted

Directions:
1. In a bowl, add the bell peppers, onion, herbs, salt and black pepper and toss to coat well.
2. Press AIR OVEN MODE button of Ninja Foodi Digital Air Fryer Oven and turn the dial to select "Air Fry" mode.
3. Press TIME/SLICES button and again turn the dial to set the cooking time to 8 minutes.
4. Now push TEMP/SHADE button and rotate the dial to set the temperature at 360 °F.
5. Press "Start/Stop" button to start.
6. When the unit beeps to show that it is preheated, open the oven door.
7. Arrange the bell peppers into the air fry basket and insert in the oven.
8. When cooking time is completed, open the oven door and transfer the bell peppers into a bowl.
9. Drizzle with butter and serve immediately.

Tofu With Broccoli

Servings: 2
Cooking Time: 15 Minutes
Ingredients:
- 8 ounces block firm tofu, pressed and cubed
- 1 small head broccoli, cut into florets
- 1 tablespoon canola oil
- 1 tablespoon nutritional yeast
- ¼ teaspoon dried parsley
- Salt and ground black pepper, as required

Directions:
1. In a bowl, mix together the tofu, broccoli and the remaining ingredients.

2. Press AIR OVEN MODE button of Ninja Foodi Digital Air Fryer Oven and turn the dial to select "Air Fry" mode.
3. Press TIME/SLICES button and again turn the dial to set the cooking time to 15 minutes.
4. Now push TEMP/SHADE button and rotate the dial to set the temperature at 390 °F.
5. Press "Start/Stop" button to start.
6. When the unit beeps to show that it is preheated, open the oven door.
7. Arrange the tofu mixture into the greased air fry basket and insert in the oven.
8. Flip the tofu mixture once halfway through.
9. When cooking time is completed, open the oven door and serve hot.

Parmesan Broccoli

Servings: 8
Cooking Time: 15 Minutes
Ingredients:
- 2 pounds broccoli, cut into 1-inch florets
- 2 tablespoons butter
- Salt and ground black pepper, as required
- ¼ cup Parmesan cheese, grated

Directions:
1. In a pan of boiling water, add the broccoli and cook for about 3-4 minutes.
2. Drain the broccoli well.
3. In a bowl, place the broccoli, cauliflower, oil, salt, and black pepper and toss to coat well.
4. Press AIR OVEN MODE button of Ninja Foodi Digital Air Fryer Oven and turn the dial to select "Air Fry" mode.
5. Press TIME/SLICES button and again turn the dial to set the cooking time to 15 minutes.
6. Now push TEMP/SHADE button and rotate the dial to set the temperature at 400 °F.
7. Press "Start/Stop" button to start.
8. When the unit beeps to show that it is preheated, open the oven door.
9. Arrange the broccoli mixture in air fry basket and insert in the oven.
10. Toss the broccoli mixture once halfway through.
11. When cooking time is completed, open the oven door and transfer the veggie mixture into a large bowl.
12. Immediately stir in the cheese and serve immediately.

Broiled Lemon Pepper Sprouts

Servings: 4
Cooking Time: 5 Minutes
Ingredients:
- 2 teaspoons lemon pepper seasoning
- 2 tablespoons olive oil
- 1 pound Brussels sprouts, sliced
- Salt to taste

Directions:
1. Take your Brussels and coat them with oil.
2. Season the sprouts with salt and lemon pepper.

3. Spread the prepared Brussels over the Cooking basket.
4. Set the temperature to 350 °F and timer at 5 minutes on the "AIR ROAST" function on your Ninja Foodi Digital Air Fryer Oven.
5. Let it cook, serve, and enjoy!

Air Fried Okra

Servings: 1
Cooking Time: 12 Minutes
Ingredients:
- ½ pound okra, ends trimmed and sliced
- ½ teaspoon ground coriander
- ½ teaspoon ground cumin
- 1 teaspoon olive oil
- ½ teaspoon mango powder
- ½ teaspoon chili powder
- ⅛ teaspoon pepper
- ¼ teaspoon salt

Directions:
1. Add all ingredients into the large bowl and toss them well.
2. Transfer okra mixture into the Air Fryer basket. Place the wire rack inside your Ninja Foodi Digital Air Fryer Oven.
3. Select "AIR FRY" mode set the temperature to 350 °F, and set time to 12 minutes.
4. Press "START/PAUSE" to begin preheating.
5. Once the Ninja Foodi Digital Air Fryer Oven is preheated, place the Air Crisp basket on the wire rack and close the oven door to start cooking. Cook for 12 minutes.
6. Serve and enjoy.

Succotash

Servings: 5
Cooking Time: 10 Minutes
Ingredients:
- Cooking oil spray
- 10 cups fresh corn kernels
- 2 ½ cups cherry tomatoes, halved
- 8 garlic cloves, minced
- 2 small onions, chopped
- 2 cups frozen lima beans
- 8 tablespoons unsalted butter, cut into small cubes
- Kosher salt and black pepper, to taste
- Thinly sliced fresh basil for garnish

Directions:
1. Lightly coat the sheet pans with cooking spray.
2. Divide the corn, cherry tomatoes, garlic, onions, lima beans, and butter cubes between the two pans. Season with salt and pepper and thoroughly mix to combine.
3. Install the wire racks inside your Ninja Foodi Digital Air Fryer Oven.
4. Select "AIR ROAST," temperature to 350 °F, and set the time to 20 minutes.
5. Press START/PAUSE to begin preheating.

6. When the unit has preheated, place a sheet pan on each wire rack. Close the oven door to begin cooking.

7. After 10 minutes, open the oven and stir the vegetables. Close the oven door to continue cooking.

Roasted Green Beans

Servings: 2
Cooking Time: 20 Minutes
Ingredients:
- 4 slices prosciutto
- ¼ pound green beans, ends trimmed
- 1 small yellow onion, sliced
- 1 tablespoon canola oil

Directions:
1. Preheat your Ninja Foodi Digital Air Fryer Oven to 350 °F for few minutes.
2. In a ninja oven basket and put prosciutto and BAKE it for 5 minutes at 390 °F.
3. Take a bowl and mix the remaining ingredients.
4. Take out the prosciutto from the oven.
5. Put the vegetables in an oven basket, and Air Fry them for15 more minutes.
6. Crumble the prosciutto and sprinkle it on top of roasted green beans.
7. Enjoy.

Green Tomatoes

Servings: 4
Cooking Time: 7 Minutes
Ingredients:
- 3 green tomatoes
- ½ teaspoon salt
- ½ cup flour
- 2 eggs
- 1/3 cup cornmeal
- 1/3 cup breadcrumbs
- 1/8 teaspoon paprika

Directions:
1. Slice the green tomatoes into ¼-inch slices and generously coat with salt. Allow for at least 5 minutes of resting time.
2. Put the flour in one bowl, the egg (whisked) in the second, and the cornmeal, breadcrumbs, and paprika in the third bowl to make a breading station.
3. Using a paper towel, pat green tomato slices dry.
4. Dip each tomato slice into the flour, then the egg, and finally the cornmeal mixture, making sure the tomato slices are completely covered.
5. Place them in air fry basket in a single layer.
6. Turn on Ninja Foodi Digital Air Fryer Oven and rotate the knob to select "Air Fry".
7. Select the timer for 9 minutes and the temperature for 380 °F.
8. Cook for 7-9 minutes, flipping and spritzing with oil halfway through.

Potato Casserole

Servings: 6
Cooking Time: 50 Minutes
Ingredients:
- 2 eggs
- 1 cup cheddar cheese, shredded
- 10 potatoes, peeled, halved & boiled
- 3 tbsp butter
- 1 cup sour cream
- 8 oz cream cheese, softened
- Pepper
- Salt

Directions:
1. Mash the potatoes using masher until smooth.
2. Add remaining ingredients into the mashed potatoes and stir well to combine.
3. Pour potato mixture into the greased baking dish.
4. Select bake mode then set the temperature to 325 °F and time for 50 minutes. Press start.
5. Once the Ninja Foodi Digital Air Fryer Oven is preheated then place the baking dish into the oven.
6. Serve and enjoy.

Vegetable Nachos

Servings: 3
Cooking Time: 5 Minutes
Ingredients:
- 8 ounces Tortilla chips
- ½ cup Grilled chicken
- 1 can Black beans, drained, rinsed
- 1 cup White queso
- ½ cup Grape tomatoes, halved
- 1/3 cup Green onion, diced

Directions:
1. Use foil to line the air fry basket.
2. Using a nonstick spray, coat the surface.
3. Assemble the nachos by layering the chips, chicken, and beans on top.
4. Place a layer of queso on top.
5. Add tomatoes and onions to the top.
6. Turn on Ninja Foodi Digital Air Fryer Oven and rotate the knob to select "Air Fry".
7. Select the timer for 5 minutes and the temperature for 355 °F.
8. Remove from Ninja Foodi Digital Air Fryer Oven serve.

Sweet & Spicy Parsnips

Servings: 5
Cooking Time: 44 Minutes
Ingredients:
- 1 ½ pound parsnip, peeled and cut into chunks
- 1 tablespoon butter, melted
- 2 tablespoons honey
- 1 tablespoon dried parsley flakes, crushed

- ¼ teaspoon red pepper flakes, crushed
- Salt and ground black pepper, to taste

Directions:

1. In a large bowl, mix the parsnips and butter.
2. Select the "AIR FRY" function and the temperature at 355 °F on your Ninja Foodi Digital Air Fryer Oven.
3. Set the cooking time to 44 minutes.
4. Press the "START/PAUSE" button to start.
5. Arrange the squash chunks into the greased Air Crisp Basket and insert them in the oven. Meanwhile, in another large bowl, mix the remaining ingredients.
6. After 40 minutes of cooking, press the "START/PAUSE" button to pause the unit. Transfer the parsnip chunks into the bowl of honey mixture and toss to coat well.
7. Again, arrange the parsnip chunks into the Air Crisp Basket and insert them in the oven. When cooking time is completed, open the door and serve hot.

Stuffed Eggplants

Servings: 4
Cooking Time: 11 Minutes

Ingredients:

- 4 small eggplants, halved lengthwise
- 1 teaspoon fresh lime juice
- 1 teaspoon vegetable oil
- 1 small onion, chopped
- ¼ teaspoon garlic, chopped
- ½ of small tomato, chopped
- Salt and ground black pepper, as required
- 1 tablespoon cottage cheese, chopped
- ¼ of green bell pepper, seeded and chopped
- 1 tablespoon tomato paste
- 1 tablespoon fresh cilantro, chopped

Directions:

1. Carefully cut a slice from one side of each eggplant lengthwise.
2. With a small spoon, scoop out the flesh from each eggplant, leaving a thick shell.
3. Transfer the eggplant flesh into a bowl.
4. Drizzle the eggplants with lime juice evenly.
5. Press AIR OVEN MODE button of Ninja Foodi Digital Air Fryer Oven and turn the dial to select "Air Fry" mode.
6. Press TIME/SLICES button and again turn the dial to set the cooking time to 3 minutes.
7. Now push TEMP/SHADE button and rotate the dial to set the temperature at 320 °F.
8. Press "Start/Stop" button to start.
9. When the unit beeps to show that it is preheated, open the oven door.
10. Arrange the hollowed eggplants into the greased air fry basket and insert in the oven.
11. Meanwhile, in a skillet, heat the oil over medium heat and sauté the onion and garlic for about 2 minutes.
12. Add the eggplant flesh, tomato, salt, and black pepper and sauté for about 2 minutes.

13. Stir in the cheese, bell pepper, tomato paste, and cilantro and cook for about 1 minute.
14. Remove the pan of the veggie mixture from heat.
15. When the cooking time is completed, open the oven door and arrange the cooked eggplants onto a plate.
16. Stuff each eggplant with the veggie mixture.
17. Close each with its cut part.
18. Again arrange the eggplants shells into the greased air fry basket and insert into the oven.
19. Press AIR OVEN MODE button of Ninja Foodi Digital Air Fryer Oven and turn the dial to select "Air Fry" mode.
20. Press TIME/SLICES button and again turn the dial to set the cooking time to 8 minutes.
21. Now push TEMP/SHADE button and rotate the dial to set the temperature at 320 °F.
22. Press "Start/Stop" button to start.
23. When cooking time is completed, open the oven door and transfer the eggplants onto serving plates.
24. Serve hot.

Roast Cauliflower And Broccoli

Servings: 4
Cooking Time: 10 Minutes.

Ingredients:

- ½ pound broccoli, florets
- ½ pound cauliflower, florets
- 1 tablespoon olive oil
- Black pepper, to taste
- Salt, to taste
- ⅓ cup water

Directions:

1. Toss all the veggies with seasoning in a large bowl.
2. Spread these vegetables in the air fry basket.
3. Transfer the basket to Ninja Foodi Digital Air Fryer Oven and close the door.
4. Select "Air Fry" mode by rotating the dial.
5. Press the TIME/SLICES button and change the value to 10 minutes.
6. Press the TEMP/SHADE button and change the value to 400 °F.
7. Press Start/Stop to begin cooking.
8. Serve warm.

Fried Tortellini

Servings: 8
Cooking Time: 10 Minutes.

Ingredients:

- 1 package cheese tortellini
- 1 cup Panko breadcrumbs
- ⅓ cup Parmesan, grated
- 1 teaspoon dried oregano
- ½ teaspoon garlic powder
- ½ teaspoon crushed red pepper flakes
- Kosher salt, to taste
- Freshly ground black pepper, to taste
- 1 cup all-purpose flour

- 2 large eggs

Directions:

1. Boil tortellini according to salted boiling water according to package's instructions, then drain.
2. Mix panko with garlic powder, black pepper, salt, red pepper flakes, oregano, Parmesan in a small bowl.
3. Beat eggs in one bowl and spread flour on a plate.
4. Coat the tortellini with the flour, dip into the eggs and then coat with the panko mixture.
5. Spread the tortellini in the air fry basket and spray them with cooking oil.
6. Transfer the basket to Ninja Foodi Digital Air Fryer Oven and close the door.
7. Select "Air Fry" mode by rotating the dial.
8. Press the TIME/SLICES button and change the value to 10 minutes.
9. Press the TEMP/SHADE button and change the value to 400 °F.
10. Press Start/Stop to begin cooking.

Vegan Cakes

Servings: 8
Cooking Time: 15 Minutes.

Ingredients:

- 4 potatoes, diced and boiled
- 1 bunch green onions
- 1 lime, zest, and juice
- 1½-inch knob of fresh ginger
- 1 tablespoon tamari
- 4 tablespoons red curry paste
- 4 sheets nori
- 1 can heart of palm, drained
- ¾ cup canned artichoke hearts, drained
- Black pepper, to taste
- Salt, to taste

Directions:

1. Add potatoes, green onions, lime zest, juice, and the rest of the ingredients to a food processor.
2. Press the pulse button and blend until smooth.
3. Make 8 small patties out of this mixture.
4. Place the patties in the air fry basket.
5. Transfer the basket to Ninja Foodi Digital Air Fryer Oven and close the door.
6. Select "Air Fry" mode by rotating the dial.
7. Press the TIME/SLICES button and change the value to 15 minutes.
8. Press the TEMP/SHADE button and change the value to 400 °F.
9. Press Start/Stop to begin cooking.
10. Serve warm.

Cheesy Zucchini Casserole

Servings: 6
Cooking Time: 45 Minutes

Ingredients:

- 2 egg whites

- 4 small zucchinis, diced
- 3 cups spinach
- 1 tsp dried basil
- 1/2 tsp pepper
- 2 tsp garlic powder
- 1/4 cup breadcrumbs
- 1/4 cup parmesan cheese, grated
- 1/4 cup feta cheese, crumbled
- 2 tbsp olive oil
- 1/2 tsp kosher salt

Directions:

1. Heat oil in a pan over medium heat.
2. Add zucchini, and spinach and cook for 5 minutes.
3. Transfer mixture into the mixing bowl.
4. Add remaining ingredients to the mixing bowl and mix well.
5. Pour mixture into the greased baking dish.
6. Select bake mode then set the temperature to 400 °F and time for 40 minutes. Press start.
7. Once the Ninja Foodi Digital Air Fryer Oven is preheated then place the baking dish into the oven.
8. Serve and enjoy.

Soy Sauce Green Beans

Servings: 2
Cooking Time: 10 Minutes

Ingredients:

- 8 ounces fresh green beans, trimmed and cut in half
- 1 tablespoon soy sauce
- 1 teaspoon sesame oil

Directions:

1. In a bowl, mix together the green beans, soy sauce and sesame oil.
2. Press AIR OVEN MODE button of Ninja Foodi Digital Air Fryer Oven and turn the dial to select "Air Fry" mode.
3. Press TIME/SLICES button and again turn the dial to set the cooking time to 10 minutes.
4. Now push TEMP/SHADE button and rotate the dial to set the temperature at 390 °F.
5. Press "Start/Stop" button to start.
6. When the unit beeps to show that it is preheated, open the oven door.
7. Arrange the green beans in air fry basket and insert to the oven.
8. When cooking time is completed, open the oven door and serve hot.

Stuffed Peppers

Servings: 6
Cooking Time: 15 Minutes

Ingredients:

- 6 green bell peppers
- 1 pound lean ground beef
- 1 tablespoon olive oil
- ¼ cup green onion, diced
- ¼ cup fresh parsley

- ½ teaspoon ground sage
- ½ teaspoon garlic salt
- 1 cup rice, cooked
- 1 cup marinara sauce to taste
- ¼ cup mozzarella cheese, shredded

Directions:

1. Cook the ground beef in a medium sized skillet until it is well done.
2. Return the beef to the pan after draining it.
3. Combine the olive oil, green onion, parsley, sage, and salt in a large mixing bowl and add to the skillet with beef.
4. Add the cooked rice and marinara sauce in the skillet and stir this rice-beef mixture thoroughly.
5. Remove the tops off each pepper and discard the seeds.
6. Scoop the mixture into each pepper and place it in the air fry basket.
7. Turn on Ninja Foodi Digital Air Fryer Oven and rotate the knob to select "Air Fry".
8. Select the timer for 10 minutes and temperature for 355 °F.
9. Dish out to serve and enjoy.

Baked Sweet Potatoes & Apple

Servings: 2
Cooking Time: 30 Minutes
Ingredients:

- 2 large sweet potatoes, diced
- 2 large apples, diced
- 2 tbsp honey
- 1 tbsp olive oil

Directions:

1. In a large bowl, add sweet potatoes, oil, and apples and toss well.
2. Spread sweet potatoes mixture onto the sheet pan.
3. Select bake mode then set the temperature to 400 °F and time for 30 minutes. Press start.
4. Once the Ninja Foodi Digital Air Fryer Oven is preheated then place the sheet pan into the oven.
5. Drizzle with honey and serve.

Healthy Green Beans

Servings: 2
Cooking Time: 10 Minutes
Ingredients:

- 2 cups green beans
- 1/8 tsp ground allspice
- 2 tbsp olive oil
- 1/2 tsp salt

Directions:

1. Add all ingredients into the mixing bowl and toss well.
2. Arrange green beans in an air fryer basket.
3. Select air fry then set the temperature to 370 °F and time for 10 minutes. Press start.
4. Once the Ninja Foodi Digital Air Fryer Oven is preheated then place the basket into the top rails of the oven.
5. Serve and enjoy.

Beans & Veggie Burgers

Servings: 4
Cooking Time: 22 Minutes
Ingredients:

- 1 cup cooked black beans
- 2 cups boiled potatoes, peeled, and mashed
- 1 cup fresh spinach, chopped
- 1 cup fresh mushrooms, chopped
- 2 teaspoons Chile lime seasoning
- Olive oil cooking spray

Directions:

1. In a large bowl, add the beans, potatoes, spinach, mushrooms, and seasoning and with your hands, mix until well combined.
2. Make 4 equal-sized patties from the mixture.
3. Spray the patties with cooking spray evenly.
4. Press AIR OVEN MODE button of Ninja Foodi Digital Air Fryer Oven and turn the dial to select "Air Fry" mode.
5. Press TIME/SLICES button and again turn the dial to set the cooking time to 22 minutes.
6. Now push TEMP/SHADE button and rotate the dial to set the temperature at 370 °F.
7. Press "Start/Stop" button to start.
8. When the unit beeps to show that it is preheated, open the oven door.
9. Arrange the patties in the greased air fry basket and insert in the oven.
10. Flip the patties once after 12 minutes.
11. When cooking time is completed, open the oven door and remove the air fry basket from the oven.

Veggies Stuffed Bell Peppers

Servings: 6
Cooking Time: 25 Minutes
Ingredients:

- 6 large bell peppers
- 1 bread roll, finely chopped
- 1 carrot, peeled and finely chopped
- 1 onion, finely chopped
- 1 potato, peeled and finely chopped
- ½ cup fresh peas, shelled
- 2 garlic cloves, minced
- 2 teaspoons fresh parsley, chopped
- Salt and ground black pepper, as required
- ⅓ cup cheddar cheese, grated

Directions:

1. Remove the tops of each bell pepper and discard the seeds.
2. Chop the bell pepper tops finely.
3. In a bowl, place bell pepper tops, bread loaf, vegetables, garlic, parsley, salt and black pepper and mix well.
4. Stuff each bell pepper with the vegetable mixture.
5. Press AIR OVEN MODE button of Ninja Foodi Digital Air Fryer Oven and turn the dial to select "Air Fry" mode.

6. Press TIME/SLICES button and again turn the dial to set the cooking time to 25 minutes.
7. Now push TEMP/SHADE button and rotate the dial to set the temperature at 330 °F.
8. Press "Start/Stop" button to start.
9. When the unit beeps to show that it is preheated, open the oven door.
10. Arrange the bell peppers into the greased air fry basket and insert in the oven.
11. After 20 minutes, sprinkle each bell pepper with cheddar cheese.
12. When cooking time is completed, open the oven door and transfer the bell peppers onto serving plates.
13. Serve hot.

Cauliflower Tots

Servings: 4
Cooking Time: 10 Minutes
Ingredients:
- Cooking spray
- 450g cauliflower tots

Directions:
1. Using nonstick cooking spray, coat the air fry basket.
2. Place as many cauliflower tots as you can in the air fry basket, ensuring sure they do not touch, and air fry in batches if needed.
3. Turn on Ninja Foodi Digital Air Fryer Oven and rotate the knob to select "Air Fry".
4. Select the timer for 6 minutes and the temperature for 400 °F.
5. Pull the basket out, flip the tots, and cook for another 3 minutes, or until browned and cooked through.
6. Remove from Ninja Foodi Digital Air Fryer Oven to serve.

Cauliflower In Buffalo Sauce

Servings: 4
Cooking Time: 12 Minutes
Ingredients:
- 1 large head cauliflower, cut into bite-size florets
- 1 tablespoon olive oil
- 2 teaspoons garlic powder
- Salt and ground black pepper, as required
- ⅔ cup warm buffalo sauce

Directions:
1. In a large bowl, add cauliflower florets, olive oil, garlic powder, salt and pepper and toss to coat.
2. Press AIR OVEN MODE button of Ninja Foodi Digital Air Fryer Oven and turn the dial to select "Air Fry" mode.
3. Press TIME/SLICES button and again turn the dial to set the cooking time to 12 minutes.
4. Now push TEMP/SHADE button and rotate the dial to set the temperature at 375 °F.
5. Press "Start/Stop" button to start.
6. When the unit beeps to show that it is preheated, open the oven door.

7. Arrange the cauliflower florets in the air fry basket and insert in the oven.
8. After 7 minutes of cooking, coat the cauliflower florets with buffalo sauce.
9. When cooking time is completed, open the oven door and serve hot.

Broccoli With Cauliflower

Servings: 4
Cooking Time: 20 Minutes
Ingredients:
- 1½ cups broccoli, cut into 1-inch pieces
- 1½ cups cauliflower, cut into 1-inch pieces
- 1 tablespoon olive oil
- Salt, as required

Directions:
1. In a bowl, add the vegetables, oil, and salt and toss to coat well.
2. Press AIR OVEN MODE button of Ninja Foodi Digital Air Fryer Oven and turn the dial to select "Air Fry" mode.
3. Press TIME/SLICES button and again turn the dial to set the cooking time to 20 minutes.
4. Now push TEMP/SHADE button and rotate the dial to set the temperature at 375 °F.
5. Press "Start/Stop" button to start.
6. When the unit beeps to show that it is preheated, open the oven door.
7. Arrange the veggie mixture into the greased air fry basket and insert in the oven.
8. When cooking time is completed, open the oven door and serve hot.

Caramelized Baby Carrots

Servings: 4
Cooking Time: 15 Minutes
Ingredients:
- ½ cup butter, melted
- ½ cup brown sugar
- 1 pound bag baby carrots

Directions:
1. In a bowl, mix together the butter, brown sugar and carrots.
2. Press AIR OVEN MODE button of Ninja Foodi Digital Air Fryer Oven and turn the dial to select "Air Fry" mode.
3. Press TIME/SLICES button and again turn the dial to set the cooking time to 15 minutes.
4. Now push TEMP/SHADE button and rotate the dial to set the temperature at 400 °F.
5. Press "Start/Stop" button to start.
6. When the unit beeps to show that it is preheated, open the oven door.
7. Arrange the carrots in a greased air fry basket and insert in the oven.
8. When cooking time is completed, open the oven door and serve warm.

Brussels Sprouts Gratin

Servings: 6
Cooking Time: 35 Minutes.
Ingredients:

- 1 pound Brussels sprouts
- 1 garlic clove, cut in half
- 3 tablespoons butter, divided
- 2 tablespoons shallots, minced
- 2 tablespoons all-purpose flour
- Kosher salt, to taste
- Freshly ground black pepper
- 1 dash ground nutmeg
- 1 cup milk
- ½ cup fontina cheese, shredded
- 1 strip of bacon, cooked and crumbled
- ½ cup fine bread crumbs

Directions:

1. Trim the Brussels sprouts and remove their outer leaves.
2. Slice the sprouts into quarters, then rinse them under cold water.
3. Grease a gratin dish with cooking spray and rub it with garlic halves.
4. Boil salted water in a suitable pan, then add Brussels sprouts.
5. Cook the sprouts for 3 minutes, then immediately drain.
6. Place a suitable saucepan over medium-low heat and melt 2 tablespoons of butter in it.
7. Toss in shallots and sauté until soft, then stir in flour, nutmeg, ½ teaspoons of salt, and black pepper.
8. Stir cook for 2 minutes, then gradually add milk and a half and half cream.
9. Mix well and add bacon along with shredded cheese.
10. Fold in Brussels sprouts and transfer this mixture to the SearPlate.
11. Toss breadcrumbs with 1 tablespoon butter and spread over.
12. Transfer the gratin on wire rack in Ninja Foodi Digital Air Fryer Oven and close the door.
13. Select "Bake" mode by rotating the dial.
14. Press the TIME/SLICES button and change the value to 25 minutes.
15. Press the TEMP/SHADE button and change the value to 350 °F.
16. Press Start/Stop to begin cooking.
17. Enjoy!

Broiled Broccoli

Servings: 4
Cooking Time: 20 Minutes
Ingredients:

- 2 heads of broccoli, diced into large chunks
- 1½ teaspoons olive oil
- Salt and pepper, to taste

Directions:

1. Slice your broccoli into large chunks. Left the stems long to make sure they would not break apart.
2. Sprinkle the broccoli with 1 tablespoon of olive oil in a large mixing bowl and season to taste with salt and pepper. Toss everything together to make sure the broccoli is well-coated.
3. Place the broccoli on the SearPlate in a single layer.
4. Turn on Ninja Foodi Digital Air Fryer Oven and rotate the knob to select "Broil".
5. Select the timer for 15 minutes and temperature to low.
6. Serve and enjoy.

Tofu In Sweet & Sour Sauce

Servings: 4
Cooking Time: 20 Minutes
Ingredients:
For Tofu:

- 1 block firm tofu, pressed and cubed
- ½ cup arrowroot flour
- ½ teaspoon sesame oil

For Sauce:

- 4 tablespoons low-sodium soy sauce
- 1½ tablespoons rice vinegar
- 1½ tablespoons chili sauce
- 1 tablespoon agave nectar
- 2 large garlic cloves, minced
- 1 teaspoon fresh ginger, peeled and grated
- 2 scallions (green part), chopped

Directions:

1. In a bowl, mix together the tofu, arrowroot flour, and sesame oil.
2. Press AIR OVEN MODE button of Ninja Foodi Digital Air Fryer Oven and turn the dial to select "Air Fry" mode.
3. Press TIME/SLICES button and again turn the dial to set the cooking time to 20 minutes.
4. Now push TEMP/SHADE button and rotate the dial to set the temperature at 360 °F.
5. Press "Start/Stop" button to start.
6. When the unit beeps to show that it is preheated, open the oven door.
7. Arrange the tofu cubes in greased air fry basket and insert in the oven.
8. Flip the tofu cubes once halfway through.
9. Meanwhile, for the sauce - in a bowl, add all the ingredients except scallions and beat until well combined.
10. When cooking time is completed, open the oven door and remove the tofu.
11. Transfer the tofu into a skillet with sauce over medium heat and cook for about 3 minutes, stirring occasionally.
12. Garnish with scallions and serve hot.

Broccoli & Rice

Servings: 8
Cooking Time: 20 Minutes
Ingredients:
- 16 oz frozen broccoli florets
- 1 1/2 cups cooked brown rice
- 1 large onion, chopped
- 4 tbsp parmesan cheese, grated
- 10.5 oz condensed cheddar cheese soup
- 1/3 cup milk
- 1 tbsp butter

Directions:
1. Melt butter in a pan over medium heat.
2. Add onion and cook until tender.
3. Add broccoli and cook until broccoli is tender.
4. Stir in rice, soup, and milk and cook until hot.
5. Stir in cheese and pour the mixture into the baking dish.
6. Select bake mode then set the temperature to 350 °F and time for 20 minutes. Press start.
7. Once the Ninja Foodi Digital Air Fryer Oven is preheated then place the baking dish into the oven.
8. Serve and enjoy.

Vegetable Mix

Servings: 7
Cooking Time: 10 Minutes
Ingredients:
- 4 pounces mushrooms, sliced
- ¼ pound green beans, ends trimmed
- 1 yellow summer squash, sliced
- 2 carrots chopped
- 1 zucchini, sliced
- 1 red bell pepper, seeded and sliced
- ½ sweet onion, sliced
- 1 tablespoon olive oil
- Salt and black pepper to taste

Directions:
1. Toss the red bell pepper, green beans, carrots, zucchini, summer squash, mushrooms, and onion in a large bowl.
2. Stir in black pepper, salt, and olive oil to season the veggies.
3. Spread these vegetables in a baking pan evenly. Transfer these veggies to the Ninja Foodi Digital Air Fryer Oven and close its door.
4. Select the "BAKE" Mode using the function keys on your Ninja Foodi Digital Air Fryer Oven.
5. Set the cooking time to 10 minutes and temperature to 350 °F then press "START/PAUSE" to initiate preheating.
6. Serve warm.

Baked Vegetables

Servings: 4
Cooking Time: 35 Minutes
Ingredients:
- 3 cups Brussels sprouts, cut in half

- 2 zucchini, cut into 1/2-inch slices
- 2 bell peppers, cut into 2-inch chunks
- 8 oz mushrooms, cut in half
- 1 onion, cut into wedges
- 2 tbsp vinegar
- 1/4 cup olive oil
- 1/2 tsp salt

Directions:
1. Add vegetables into the zip-lock bag. Mix together vinegar, oil, and salt and pour over vegetables.
2. Seal zip-lock bag and shake well and place it in the refrigerator for 1 hour.
3. Spread vegetables on a sheet pan.
4. Select bake mode then set the temperature to 375 °F and time for 35 minutes. Press start.
5. Once the Ninja Foodi Digital Air Fryer Oven i preheated then place the sheet pan into the oven.
6. Serve and enjoy.

Sweet Potato Fries

Servings: 4
Cooking Time: 30 Minutes
Ingredients:
- 4 sweet potatoes, cut it into wedges
- 2 tablespoons of olive oil
- salt, to taste

Directions:
1. Soak the potato slices in cold water for 30 minutes.
2. Pat dry potato slices and let them get dry. Season ther with salt and oil.
3. Layer it in a baking sheet and BAKE in your Ninj Foodi Digital Air Fryer Oven for 30 minutes at 390 °F.
4. Serve and enjoy.

Veggie Rice

Servings: 2
Cooking Time: 18 Minutes
Ingredients:
- 2 cups cooked white rice
- 1 tablespoon vegetable oil
- 2 teaspoons sesame oil, toasted and divided
- 1 tablespoon water
- Salt and ground white pepper, as required
- 1 large egg, lightly beaten
- ½ cup frozen peas, thawed
- ½ cup frozen carrots, thawed
- 1 teaspoon soy sauce
- 1 teaspoon Sriracha sauce
- ½ teaspoon sesame seeds, toasted

Directions:
1. In a large bowl, add the rice, vegetable oil, one teaspoo of sesame oil, water, salt, and white pepper and mix well.
2. Transfer rice mixture into a lightly greased SearPlate.
3. Press AIR OVEN MODE button of Ninja Foodi Digit Air Fryer Oven and turn the dial to select "Air Fry" mode.

4. Press TIME/SLICES button and again turn the dial to set the cooking time to 18 minutes.
5. Now push TEMP/SHADE button and rotate the dial to set the temperature at 380 °F.
6. Press "Start/Stop" button to start.
7. When the unit beeps to show that it is preheated, open the oven door.
8. Insert the SearPlate in the oven.
9. While cooking, stir the mixture once after 12 minutes.
10. After 12 minutes of cooking, press "Start/Stop" to pause cooking.
11. Remove the pan from oven and place the beaten egg over rice.
12. Again, insert the pan in the oven and press "Start/Stop" to resume cooking.
13. After 16 minutes of cooking, press "Start/Stop" to pause cooking.
14. Remove the SearPlate from and stir in the peas and carrots.
15. Again, insert the SearPlate in the oven and press "Start/Stop" to resume cooking.
16. Meanwhile, in a bowl, mix together the soy sauce, Sriracha sauce, sesame seeds and the remaining sesame oil.
17. When cooking time is completed, open the oven door and transfer the rice mixture into a serving bowl.
18. Drizzle with the sauce mixture and serve.

Veggie Patties

Servings: 2
Cooking Time: 15 Minutes
Ingredients:
- 1 egg
- 1 zucchini, grated & squeezed
- 1/4 cup parmesan cheese, grated
- 1 carrot, grated & squeezed
- 1/4 cup breadcrumbs
- Pepper
- Salt

Directions:
1. Add all ingredients into the bowl and mix until well combined.
2. Make patties from the mixture and place them in an air fryer basket.
3. Select air fry then set the temperature to 400 °F and time for 15 minutes. Press start.
4. Once the Ninja Foodi Digital Air Fryer Oven is preheated then place the basket into the top rails of the oven.
5. Serve and enjoy.

Vinegar Green Beans

Servings: 2
Cooking Time: 20 Minutes
Ingredients:
- 1 bag frozen cut green beans
- 1/4 cup nutritional yeast
- 3 tablespoons balsamic vinegar

- Salt and ground black pepper, as required

Directions:
1. In a bowl, add the green beans, nutritional yeast, vinegar, salt, and black pepper and toss to coat well.
2. Press AIR OVEN MODE button of Ninja Foodi Digital Air Fryer Oven and turn the dial to select "Air Fry" mode.
3. Press TIME/SLICES button and again turn the dial to set the cooking time to 20 minutes.
4. Now push TEMP/SHADE button and rotate the dial to set the temperature at 400 °F.
5. Press "Start/Stop" button to start.
6. When the unit beeps to show that it is preheated, open the oven door.
7. Arrange the green beans into the greased air fry basket and insert in the oven.
8. When cooking time is completed, open the oven door and serve hot.

Cheesy Kale

Servings: 3
Cooking Time: 15 Minutes
Ingredients:
- 1 pound fresh kale, tough ribs removed and chopped
- 3 tablespoons olive oil
- Salt and ground black pepper, as required
- 1 cup goat cheese, crumbled
- 1 teaspoon fresh lemon juice

Directions:
1. In a bowl, add the kale, oil, salt, and black pepper and mix well.
2. Press AIR OVEN MODE button of Ninja Foodi Digital Air Fryer Oven and turn the dial to select "Air Fry" mode.
3. Press TIME/SLICES button and again turn the dial to set the cooking time to 15 minutes.
4. Now push TEMP/SHADE button and rotate the dial to set the temperature at 340 °F.
5. Press "Start/Stop" button to start.
6. When the unit beeps to show that it is preheated, open the oven door and grease the air fry basket.
7. Arrange the kale into air fry basket and insert in the oven.
8. When cooking time is completed, open the oven door and immediately transfer the kale mixture into a bowl.
9. Stir in the cheese and lemon juice and serve hot.

Sweet & Tangy Mushrooms

Servings: 4
Cooking Time: 23minutes
Ingredients:
- ¼ cup soy sauce
- ¼ cup honey
- ¼ cup balsamic vinegar
- 2 garlic cloves, chopped finely
- ½ teaspoon red pepper flakes, crushed
- 18 ounces cremini mushrooms, halved

Directions:

1. In a bowl, place the soy sauce, honey, vinegar, garlic, and red pepper flakes and mix well. Set aside.
2. Place the mushroom into the greased sheet pan in a single layer.
3. Select "BAKE" mode and set the cooking time to 15 minutes on your Ninja Foodi Digital Air Fryer Oven.
4. Set the temperature at 350 °F.
5. Press the "START/PAUSE" button to start.
6. When the unit beeps to show that it is preheated, open the door. Insert the sheet pan into the oven.
7. After 8 minutes of cooking, place the honey mixture in a sheet pan and toss to coat well.
8. When the unit beeps to show that cooking time is completed, press the "Power" button to stop cooking and open the door.
9. Serve hot.

Pita Bread Pizza

Servings: 1
Cooking Time: 5 Minutes
Ingredients:
- 2 tablespoons marinara sauce
- 1 whole-wheat pita bread
- ½ cup fresh baby spinach leaves
- ½ of small plum tomato, cut into 4 slices
- ½ of garlic clove, sliced thinly
- ½ ounce part-skim mozzarella cheese, shredded
- ½ tablespoon Parmigiano-Reggiano cheese, shredded

Directions:
1. Arrange the pita bread onto a plate.
2. Spread marinara sauce over 1 side of each pita bread evenly.
3. Top with the spinach leaves, followed by tomato slices, garlic, and cheeses.
4. Press AIR OVEN MODE button of Ninja Foodi Digital Air Fryer Oven and turn the dial to select "Air Fry" mode.
5. Press TIME/SLICES button and again turn the dial to set the cooking time to 5 minutes.
6. Now push TEMP/SHADE button and rotate the dial to set the temperature at 350 °F.
7. Press "Start/Stop" button to start.
8. When the unit beeps to show that it is preheated, open the oven door.
9. Arrange the pita bread into the greased air fry basket and insert in the oven.
10. When cooking time is completed, open the oven door and transfer the pizza onto a serving plate.
11. Set aside to cool slightly.
12. Serve warm.

Sweet Potato Casserole

Servings: 6
Cooking Time: 35 Minutes.
Ingredients:
- 3 cups sweet potatoes, mashed and cooled
- 1 ½ cups brown sugar, packed
- 2 large eggs, beaten
- 1 teaspoon vanilla extract
- ½ cup milk
- ¾ cup butter, melted
- ⅓ cup flour
- 4 ounces pecans, chopped

Directions:
1. Mix the sweet potato mash with vanilla extract, milk, eggs, 1 cup of brown sugar, and ½ cup of melted butter in a large bowl.
2. Spread this sweet potato mixture in SearPlate.
3. Now whisk remaining sugar and butter with flour in a separate bowl.
4. Fold in pecan, then top the sweet potatoes mixed with this pecan mixture.
5. Transfer the dish to Ninja Foodi Digital Air Fryer Oven and close the door.
6. Select "Bake" mode by rotating the dial.
7. Press the TIME/SLICES button and change the value to 35 minutes.
8. Press the TEMP/SHADE button and change the value to 350 °F.
9. Press Start/Stop to begin cooking.
10. Slice and serve!

Parmesan Carrot

Servings: 2
Cooking Time: 20 Minutes
Ingredients:
- 3 carrots
- 1 tablespoon olive oil
- 1 clove garlic, crushed
- 2 tablespoons parmesan cheese, grated
- ¼ teaspoon red pepper, crushed

Directions:
1. Stir in the crushed garlic with olive oil.
2. Carrots should be washed and dried. Cut the tops in half and remove the tops. Then, to make flat surfaces, cut each half in half.
3. Toss the carrot fries with the garlic and olive oil mixture.
4. Combine the parmesan, red pepper, and black pepper in a mixing bowl. Half of the mixture should be sprinkled over the carrot fries that have been coated.
5. Toss in the remaining parmesan mixture and repeat.
6. Arrange the carrot fries in an equal layer in an air fry basket or on a SearPlate.
7. Turn on Ninja Foodi Digital Air Fryer Oven and rotate the knob to select "Air Fry".
8. Select the timer for 20 minutes and the temperature for 350 °F.
9. Remove from Ninja Foodi Digital Air Fryer Oven serve.

Baked Eggplant

Servings: 6
Cooking Time: 35 Minutes
Ingredients:

- 1 medium eggplant, sliced
- 1 tbsp olive oil
- 4 garlic cloves, minced
- 1/4 tsp pepper
- 3 oz parmesan cheese, grated
- 3 medium zucchini, sliced
- 1 cup cherry tomatoes, halved
- 1/4 tsp salt

Directions:

1. In a bowl, add tomatoes, eggplant, zucchini, olive oil, garlic, cheese, pepper, and salt toss well until combined.
2. Transfer eggplant mixture into the baking dish.
3. Select bake mode then set the temperature to 350 °F and time for 35 minutes. Press start.
4. Once the Ninja Foodi Digital Air Fryer Oven is preheated then place the baking dish into the oven.
5. Serve and enjoy.

Eggplant Parmesan

Servings: 2
Cooking Time: 20 Minutes
Ingredients:

- 1 medium eggplant
- 2 eggs, beaten
- 1/4 cup panko breadcrumbs
- 1 cup mozzarella cheese
- 2 cups marinara sauce
- Olive oil spray
- 2 tablespoons parmesan cheese

Directions:

1. Peel the eggplant and cut it into 1/4-inch slices.
2. In a shallow plate, place the breadcrumbs.
3. Whisk the eggs in a small bowl.
4. Dip the eggplant slices in the egg mixture gently. After that, cover both sides in breadcrumbs.
5. Fill your air fry basket with eggplant in a single layer. Using an olive oil spray, coat the tops of the slices.
6. Turn on Ninja Foodi Digital Air Fryer Oven and rotate the knob to select "Air Roast".
7. Select the timer for 12 minutes and the temperature for 400 °F.
8. Flip your eggplant slices after 8 minutes and drizzle the tops with olive oil.
9. Cook for another 4 minutes after spraying the tops of your eggplant.
10. Spread marinara sauce evenly over the top of your eggplant rounds and sprinkle with mozzarella and parmesan cheese.
11. Rotate the knob to select "Air Fry".
12. Set the time for 3 minutes and temperature for 350 °F.
13. Dish out to serve hot.

Spicy Potato

Servings: 4
Cooking Time: 25 Minutes
Ingredients:

- 2 cups water
- 6 russet potatoes, peeled and cubed
- 1/2 tablespoon extra-virgin olive oil
- 1/2 of onion, chopped
- 1 tablespoon fresh rosemary, chopped
- 1 garlic clove, minced
- 1 jalapeño pepper, chopped
- 1/2 teaspoon garam masala powder
- 1/4 teaspoon ground cumin
- 1/4 teaspoon red chili powder
- Salt and ground black pepper, as required

Directions:

1. In a large bowl, add the water and potatoes and set aside for about 30 minutes.
2. Drain well and pat dry with the paper towels.
3. In a bowl, add the potatoes and oil and toss to coat well.
4. Press AIR OVEN MODE button of Ninja Foodi Digital Air Fryer Oven and turn the dial to select "Air Fry" mode.
5. Press TIME/SLICES button and again turn the dial to set the cooking time to 5 minutes.
6. Now push TEMP/SHADE button and rotate the dial to set the temperature at 330 °F.
7. Press "Start/Stop" button to start.
8. When the unit beeps to show that it is preheated, open the oven door.
9. Arrange the potato cubes in air fry basket and insert in the oven.
10. Remove from oven and transfer the potatoes into a bowl.
11. Add the remaining ingredients and toss to coat well.
12. Press AIR OVEN MODE button of Ninja Foodi Digital Air Fryer Oven and turn the dial to select "Air Fry" mode.
13. Press TIME/SLICES button and again turn the dial to set the cooking time to 20 minutes.
14. Now push TEMP/SHADE button and rotate the dial to set the temperature at 390 °F.
15. Press "Start/Stop" button to start.
16. When the unit beeps to show that it is preheated, open the oven door.
17. Arrange the potato mixture in air fry basket and insert in the oven.
18. When cooking time is completed, open the oven door and serve hot.

Stuffed Zucchini

Servings: 4
Cooking Time: 35 Minutes
Ingredients:
- 2 zucchinis, cut in half lengthwise
- ½ teaspoon garlic powder
- Salt, as required
- 1 teaspoon olive oil
- 4 ounces fresh mushrooms, chopped
- 4 ounces carrots, peeled and shredded
- 3 ounces onion, chopped
- 4 ounces goat cheese, crumbled
- 12 fresh basil leaves
- ½ teaspoon onion powder

Directions:
1. Carefully, scoop the flesh from the middle of each zucchini half.
2. Season each zucchini half with a little garlic powder and salt.
3. Arrange the zucchini halves into the greased SearPlate.
4. Place the oat mixture over salmon fillets and gently, press down.
5. Press AIR OVEN MODE button of Ninja Foodi Digital Air Fryer Oven and turn the dial to select the "Bake" mode.
6. Press TIME/SLICES button and again turn the dial to set the cooking time to 20 minutes.
7. Now push TEMP/SHADE button and rotate the dial to set the temperature at 450 °F.
8. Press "Start/Stop" button to start.
9. When the unit beeps to show that it is preheated, open the oven door.
10. Insert the SearPlate in oven.
11. Meanwhile, in a skillet, heat the oil over medium heat and cook the mushrooms, carrots, onions, onion powder and salt and cook for about 5-6 minutes.
12. Remove from the heat and set aside.
13. Remove the SearPlate from oven and set aside.
14. Stuff each zucchini half with veggie mixture and top with basil leaves, followed by the cheese.
15. Press AIR OVEN MODE button of Ninja Foodi Digital Air Fryer Oven and turn the dial to select the "Bake" mode.
16. Press TIME/SLICES button and again turn the dial to set the cooking time to 15 minutes.
17. Now push TEMP/SHADE button and rotate the dial to set the temperature at 450 °F.
18. Press "Start/Stop" button to start.
19. When the unit beeps to show that it is preheated, open the oven door.
20. Insert the SearPlate in oven.
21. When cooking time is completed, open the oven door and transfer the zucchini halves onto a platter.
22. Serve warm.

Curried Cauliflower Florets

Servings: 4
Cooking Time: 15 Minutes
Ingredients:
- 2 lbs cauliflower, cut into florets
- 1 1/2 tsp curry powder
- 1 tbsp olive oil
- 1 tsp kosher salt

Directions:
1. Toss cauliflower florets in a large bowl with olive oil.
2. Sprinkle cauliflower florets with curry powder and salt.
3. Spread cauliflower florets onto the sheet pan.
4. Select bake mode then set the temperature to 425 °F and time for 15 minutes. Press start.
5. Once the Ninja Foodi Digital Air Fryer Oven is preheated then place the sheet pan into the oven.
6. Serve and enjoy.

Creamy Spinach Bake

Servings: 6
Cooking Time: 10 Minutes
Ingredients:
- 10 oz spinach, chopped
- 1/4 cup parmesan cheese, shredded
- 1/2 onion, chopped
- 2 tsp garlic powder
- 1 cup cheddar cheese, shredded
- 1/2 cup mayonnaise
- 2/3 cup Greek yogurt

Directions:
1. Add all ingredients into the large bowl and mix until well combined.
2. Pour into the greased baking dish.
3. Select bake mode then set the temperature to 400 °F and time for 10 minutes. Press start.
4. Once the Ninja Foodi Digital Air Fryer Oven is preheated then place the baking dish into the oven.
5. Serve and enjoy.

Wine Braised Mushrooms

Servings: 6
Cooking Time: 32 Minutes
Ingredients:
- 1 tablespoon butter
- 2 teaspoons Herbs de Provence
- ½ teaspoon garlic powder
- 2 pounds fresh mushrooms, quartered
- 2 tablespoons white wine

Directions:
1. In a frying pan, mix together the butter, Herbs de Provence, and garlic powder over medium-low heat and stir fry for about 2 minutes.
2. Stir in the mushrooms and remove from the heat.
3. Transfer the mushroom mixture into a SearPlate.
4. Press AIR OVEN MODE button of Ninja Foodi Digital Air Fryer Oven and turn the dial to select "Air Fry" mode.
5. Press TIME/SLICES button and again turn the dial set the cooking time to 30 minutes.

6. Now push TEMP/SHADE button and rotate the dial to set the temperature at 320 °F.
7. Press "Start/Stop" button to start.
8. When the unit beeps to show that it is preheated, open the oven door.
9. Insert the SearPlate in the oven.
10. After 25 minutes of cooking, stir the wine into mushroom mixture.
11. When cooking time is completed, open the oven door and serve hot.

Baked Olives

Servings: 4
Cooking Time: 5 Minutes
Ingredients:
- 2 cups olives
- 2 tsp garlic, minced
- 2 tbsp olive oil
- 1/4 tsp chili flakes
- Pepper
- Salt

Directions:
1. Add olives and remaining ingredients into the bowl and mix well.
2. Add olives to the air fryer basket.
3. Select air fry then set the temperature to 300 °F and time for 5 minutes. Press start.
4. Once the Ninja Foodi Digital Air Fryer Oven is preheated then place the basket into the top rails of the oven.
5. Serve and enjoy.

Tomato Zucchini Bake

Servings: 6
Cooking Time: 30 Minutes
Ingredients:
- 3 tomatoes, sliced
- 4 medium zucchinis, sliced
- 1 cup parmesan cheese, shredded
- 1 tbsp olive oil
- Pepper
- Salt

Directions:
1. Arrange sliced tomatoes and zucchinis in the baking dish.
2. Drizzle with olive oil and season with pepper and salt.
3. Sprinkle parmesan cheese on top of vegetables.
4. Select bake mode then set the temperature to 350 °F and time for 30 minutes. Press start.
5. Once the Ninja Foodi Digital Air Fryer Oven is preheated then place the baking dish into the oven.
6. Serve and enjoy.

Cheesy Green Bean Casserole

Servings: 6
Cooking Time: 35 Minutes.
Ingredients:
- 4 cups green beans, cooked and chopped
- 3 tablespoons butter
- 8 ounces mushrooms, sliced
- ¼ cup onion, chopped
- 2 tablespoons flour
- 1 teaspoon salt
- ¼ teaspoon ground black pepper
- 1 ½ cups milk
- 2 cups cheddar cheese, shredded
- 2 tablespoons sour cream
- 1 cup soft breadcrumbs
- 2 tablespoons butter, melted
- ¼ cup Parmesan cheese, grated
- 1 cup French fried onions

Directions:
1. Add butter to a suitable saucepan and melt it over medium-low heat.
2. Toss in onion and mushrooms, then sauté until soft.
3. Stir in flour, salt, and black pepper. Mix well, then slowly pour in the milk.
4. Stir in sour cream, green beans, and cheddar cheese, then cook until it thickens.
5. Transfer this green bean mixture to a SearPlate and spread it evenly.
6. Toss breadcrumbs with fried onion and butter.
7. Top the mixture with this bread crumbs mixture.
8. Transfer the dish to Ninja Foodi Digital Air Fryer Oven and close the door.
9. Select "Bake" mode by rotating the dial.
10. Press the TIME/SLICES button and change the value to 25 minutes.
11. Press the TEMP/SHADE button and change the value to 350 °F.
12. Press Start/Stop to begin cooking.
13. Serve and enjoy!

Baked Potato

Servings: 4
Cooking Time: 45 Minutes
Ingredients:
- 4 russet potatoes
- 1½ tablespoons olive oil
- 1½ tablespoons sea salt

Directions:
1. Poke each potato, massage it all over with olive oil and sea salt.
2. Place the potato in the SearPlate.
3. Turn on Ninja Foodi Digital Air Fryer Oven and rotate the knob to select "Bake".
4. Select the timer for 40 minutes and the temperature for 350 °F.
5. Remove the baked potatoes from the Ninja Foodi, split them in half, and top them with chosen toppings!

Herb Potatoes

Servings: 2
Cooking Time: 25 Minutes
Ingredients:
- 3/4 lb potatoes, diced into 1-inch pieces
- 1/4 tsp garlic powder
- 1/4 tsp mixed herbs
- 1/4 tsp pepper
- 1/4 tsp salt

Directions:
1. Add potatoes, mixed herbs, garlic powder, pepper, and salt in a bowl and toss well.
2. Spread potatoes in an air fryer basket.
3. Select air fry then set the temperature to 400 °F and time to 25 minutes. Press start.
4. Once the Ninja Foodi Digital Air Fryer Oven is preheated then place the air fryer basket into the top rails of the oven.
5. Stir potatoes halfway through.
6. Serve and enjoy.

Quinoa Burgers

Servings: 4
Cooking Time: 10 Minutes
Ingredients:
- ½ cup cooked and cooled quinoa
- 1 cup rolled oats
- 2 eggs, lightly beaten
- ¼ cup white onion, minced
- ¼ cup feta cheese, crumbled
- Salt and ground black pepper, as required
- Olive oil cooking spray

Directions:
1. In a large bowl, add all ingredients and mix until well combined.
2. Make 4 equal-sized patties from the mixture.
3. Lightly spray the patties with cooking spray.
4. Press AIR OVEN MODE button of Ninja Foodi Digital Air Fryer Oven and turn the dial to select "Air Fry" mode.
5. Press TIME/SLICES button and again turn the dial to set the cooking time to 10 minutes.
6. Now push TEMP/SHADE button and rotate the dial to set the temperature at 400 °F.
7. Press "Start/Stop" button to start.
8. When the unit beeps to show that it is preheated, open the oven door.
9. Arrange the patties into the greased air fry basket and insert in the oven.
10. Flip the patties once halfway through.
11. When cooking time is completed, open the oven door and transfer the patties onto a platter.
12. Serve warm.

Asparagus With Garlic And Parmesan

Servings: 4
Cooking Time: 10 Minutes
Ingredients:
- 1 bundle asparagus
- 1 teaspoon olive oil
- 1/8 teaspoon garlic salt
- 1 tablespoon parmesan cheese
- Pepper to taste

Directions:
1. Clean the asparagus and dry it. To remove the woody stalks, cut 1 inch off the bottom.
2. In a SearPlate, arrange asparagus in a single layer and spray with oil.
3. On top of the asparagus, evenly sprinkle garlic salt. Season with salt and pepper, then sprinkle with Parmesan cheese.
4. Turn on Ninja Foodi Digital Air Fryer Oven and rotate the knob to select "Air Fry".
5. Select the timer for 10 minutes and the temperature for 350 °F.
6. Enjoy right away.

Spicy Brussels Sprouts

Servings: 6
Cooking Time: 30 Minutes
Ingredients:
- 2 cups Brussels sprouts, halved
- 1/4 tsp garlic powder
- 1/4 cup olive oil
- 1/4 tsp cayenne
- 1/4 tsp chili powder
- 1/4 tsp salt

Directions:
1. Add all ingredients into the large bowl and toss well.
2. Transfer Brussels sprouts on a sheet pan.
3. Select bake mode then set the temperature to 400 °F and time for 30 minutes. Press start.
4. Once the Ninja Foodi Digital Air Fryer Oven preheated then place the baking dish into the oven.
5. Stir Brussels sprouts halfway through.
6. Serve and enjoy.

Creamy Cauliflower Hummus

Servings: 8
Cooking Time: 35 Minutes
Ingredients:
- 1 cauliflower head, cut into florets
- 2 tbsp fresh lime juice
- 1 tsp garlic, chopped
- 1/3 cup tahini
- 3 tbsp olive oil
- Pepper
- Salt

Directions:
1. Spread cauliflower onto the sheet pan.
2. Select bake mode then set the temperature to 400 °F and time for 35 minutes. Press start.
3. Once the Ninja Foodi Digital Air Fryer Oven is preheated then place the sheet pan into the oven.
4. Transfer cauliflower into the food processor. Add remaining ingredients and process until smooth.
5. Serve and enjoy.

Dessert Recipes

Chocolate Oatmeal Cookies

Servings: 36
Cooking Time: 10 Minutes
Ingredients:
- 3 cups quick-cooking oatmeal
- 1½ cups all-purpose flour
- ½ cup cream
- ¼ cup cocoa powder
- ¾ cup white sugar
- 1 package instant chocolate pudding mix
- 1 teaspoon baking soda
- 1 teaspoon salt
- 1 cup butter, softened
- ¾ cup brown sugar
- 2 eggs
- 1 teaspoon vanilla extract
- 2 cups chocolate chips
- Cooking spray

Directions:
1. Using parchment paper, line the air fry basket.
2. Using nonstick cooking spray, coat the air fry basket.
3. Combine the oats, flour, cocoa powder, pudding mix, baking soda, and salt in a mixing dish. Set aside.
4. Mix cream, butter, brown sugar, and white sugar in a separate bowl using an electric mixer.
5. Combine the eggs and vanilla essence in a mixing bowl. Mix in the oatmeal mixture thoroughly. Mix the chocolate chips and walnuts in a bowl.
6. Using a large cookie scoop, drop dough into the air fry basket; level out and leave about 1 inch between each cookie.
7. Turn on Ninja Foodi Digital Air Fryer Oven and rotate the knob to select "Air Fry".
8. Select the timer for 10 minutes and the temperature for 350 °F.
9. Before serving, cool on a wire rack.

Air Fried Churros

Servings: 8
Cooking Time: 12 Minutes.
Ingredients:
- 1 cup water
- ⅓ cup butter, cut into cubes
- 2 tablespoons granulated sugar
- ¼ teaspoon salt
- 1 cup all-purpose flour
- 2 large eggs
- 1 teaspoon vanilla extract
- oil spray
- Cinnamon Coating:
- ½ cup granulated sugar
- ¾ teaspoons ground cinnamon

Directions:
1. Grease the SearPlate with cooking spray.
2. Warm water with butter, salt, and sugar in a suitable saucepan until it boils.
3. Now reduce its heat, then slowly stir in flour and mix well until smooth.
4. Remove the mixture from the heat and leave it for 4 minutes to cool.
5. Add vanilla extract and eggs, then beat the mixture until it comes together as a batter.
6. Transfer this churro mixture to a piping bag with star-shaped tips and pipe the batter on the prepared SearPlate to get 4-inch churros using this batter.
7. Refrigerate these churros for 1 hour, then transfer them to the Air fry sheet.

8. Transfer the SearPlate into Ninja Foodi Digital Air Fryer Oven and close the door.
9. Select "Air Fry" mode by rotating the dial.
10. Press the TEMP/SHADE button and change the value to 375 °F.
11. Press the TIME/SLICES button and change the value to 12 minutes, then press Start/Stop to begin cooking.
12. Meanwhile, mix granulated sugar with cinnamon in a bowl.
13. Drizzle this mixture over the air fried churros.
14. Serve.

Cinnamon Rolls

Servings: 6
Cooking Time: 30 Minutes
Ingredients:
- 2 tablespoons butter, melted
- 1/3 cup packed brown sugar
- ½ teaspoon ground cinnamon
- Salt, to taste
- All-purpose flour for surface
- 1 tube refrigerated crescent rolls
- 56g cream cheese, softened
- ½ cup powdered sugar
- 1 tablespoon whole milk

Directions:
1. Combine butter, brown sugar, cinnamon, and a large pinch of salt in a medium mixing bowl until smooth and fluffy.
2. Roll out crescent rolls in one piece on a lightly floured surface. Fold in half by pinching the seams together. Make a medium rectangle out of the dough.
3. Cover the dough with butter mixture, leaving a ¼-inch border. Roll the dough, starting at one edge and cutting crosswise into 6 pieces.
4. Line bottom of air fry basket with parchment paper and brush with butter.
5. Place the pieces cut-side up in the prepared air fry basket, equally spaced.
6. Turn on Ninja Foodi Digital Air Fryer Oven and rotate the knob to select "Broil".
7. Select the timer for 15 minutes and the temperature for low.
8. Allow cooling for two minutes before serving.

Fried Oreo

Servings: 8
Cooking Time: 5 Minutes
Ingredients:
- 8 Oreo cookies
- 1 package of Pillsbury crescents rolls

Directions:
1. On a cutting board or counter, spread out the crescent dough.
2. Press down into each perforated line with your finger to make one large sheet.

3. Cut the dough into eighths.
4. In the center of each crescent roll square, place one Oreo cookie and roll each corner up.
5. Bunch up the remaining crescent roll to completely cover the Oreo cookie.
6. Place the Oreos in an even row in the SearPlate.
7. Turn on Ninja Foodi Digital Air Fryer Oven and rotate the knob to select "Bake".
8. Select the timer for 5 minutes and the temperature for 320 °F.
9. Allow cooling for two minutes before serving.

Butter Cake

Servings: 6
Cooking Time: 15 Minutes
Ingredients:
- 3 ounces butter, softened
- ½ cup caster sugar
- 1 egg
- 1⅓ cups plain flour, sifted
- Pinch of salt
- ½ cup milk
- 1 tablespoon icing sugar

Directions:
1. In a bowl, add the butter and sugar and whisk until light and creamy.
2. Add the egg and whisk until smooth and fluffy.
3. Add the flour and salt and mix well alternately with the milk.
4. Grease a small Bundt cake pan.
5. Place mixture evenly into the prepared cake pan.
6. Press AIR OVEN MODE button of Ninja Foodi Digital Air Fryer Oven and turn the dial to select "Air Fry" mode.
7. Press TIME/SLICES button and again turn the dial to set the cooking time to 15 minutes.
8. Now push TEMP/SHADE button and rotate the dial to set the temperature at 350 °F.
9. Press "Start/Stop" button to start.
10. When the unit beeps to show that it is preheated, open the oven door.
11. Arrange the pan into the air fry basket and insert in the oven.
12. When cooking time is completed, open the oven door and place the cake pan onto a wire rack to cool for about 1 minutes.
13. Carefully invert the cake onto the wire rack to completely cool before slicing.
14. Dust the cake with icing sugar and cut into desired size slices.

Strawberry Cupcakes

Servings: 10
Cooking Time: 8 Minutes
Ingredients:
For Cupcakes:
- ½ cup caster sugar
- 7 tablespoons butter
- 2 eggs
- ½ teaspoon vanilla essence
- ⅞ cup self-rising flour
For Frosting:
- 1 cup icing sugar
- 3 ½ tablespoons butter
- 1 tablespoon whipped cream
- ¼ cup fresh strawberries, sliced
- ½ teaspoon pink food color

Directions:
1. In a bowl, add the butter and sugar and beat until fluffy and light. Add the eggs, one at a time, and beat until well combined.
2. Stir in the vanilla extract. Gradually add the flour, beating continuously until well combined.
3. Place the mixture into ten silicone cups.
4. Select the "AIR FRY" function and the temperature at 340 °F.
5. Set the cooking time to 8 minutes. Press the "START/PAUSE" button to start.
6. Arrange the silicone cups into the Air Crisp Basket and insert them in the oven.
7. When cooking time is completed, open the door and place the silicon cups onto a wire rack to cool for about 10 minutes.
8. Place the muffins on a wire rack to cool before frosting completely. For the frosting - in a bowl, add the icing sugar and butter and whisk until fluffy and light.
9. Add the whipped cream, strawberry puree, and color. Mix until well combined.
10. Fill the pastry bag with frosting and decorate the cupcakes.

Apple Pastries

Servings: 6
Cooking Time: 10 Minutes
Ingredients:
- ½ of large apple, peeled, cored and chopped
- 1 teaspoon fresh orange zest, grated finely
- ½ tablespoon white sugar
- ½ teaspoon ground cinnamon
- 7 ounces prepared frozen puff pastry
Directions:
1. In a bowl, mix together all ingredients except puff pastry.
2. Cut the pastry in 16 squares.
3. Place about a teaspoon of the apple mixture in the center of each square.

4. Fold each square into a triangle and press the edges slightly with wet fingers.
5. Then with a fork, press the edges firmly.
6. Press AIR OVEN MODE button of Ninja Foodi Digital Air Fryer Oven and turn the dial to select "Air Fry" mode.
7. Press TIME/SLICES button and again turn the dial to set the cooking time to 10 minutes.
8. Now push TEMP/SHADE button and rotate the dial to set the temperature at 390 °F.
9. Press "Start/Stop" button to start.
10. When the unit beeps to show that it is preheated, open the oven door.
11. Arrange the pastries in the greased air fry basket and insert in the oven.
12. When cooking time is completed, open the oven door and transfer the pastries onto a platter.
13. Serve warm.

Fudge Brownies

Servings: 8
Cooking Time: 20 Minutes
Ingredients:
- 1 cup sugar
- ½ cup butter, melted
- ½ cup flour
- ⅓ cup cocoa powder
- 1 teaspoon baking powder
- 2 eggs
- 1 teaspoon vanilla extract
Directions:
1. Grease the SearPlate.
2. In a large bowl, add the sugar and butter and whisk until light and fluffy.
3. Add the remaining ingredients and mix until well combined.
4. Place mixture into the prepared pan and with the back of a spatula, smooth the top surface.
5. Press AIR OVEN MODE button of Ninja Foodi Digital Air Fryer Oven and turn the dial to select "Air Fry" mode.
6. Press TIME/SLICES button and again turn the dial to set the cooking time to 20 minutes.
7. Now push TEMP/SHADE button and rotate the dial to set the temperature at 350 °F.
8. Press "Start/Stop" button to start.
9. When the unit beeps to show that it is preheated, open the oven door.
10. Insert the SearPlate in the oven.
11. When cooking time is completed, open the oven door and place the SearPlate onto a wire rack to cool completely.
12. Cut into 8 equal-sized squares and serve.

Chocolate Chip Cookie

Servings: 6
Cooking Time: 12 Minutes.
Ingredients:

- ½ cup butter, softened
- ½ cup sugar
- ½ cup brown sugar
- 1 egg
- 1 teaspoon vanilla
- ½ teaspoon baking soda
- ¼ teaspoon salt
- 1 ½ cups all-purpose flour
- 1 cup chocolate chips

Directions:

1. Grease the SearPlate with cooking spray.
2. Beat butter with sugar and brown sugar in a mixing bowl.
3. Stir in vanilla, egg, salt, flour, and baking soda, then mix well.
4. Fold in chocolate chips, then knead this dough a bit.
5. Spread the prepared dough in the prepared SearPlate evenly.
6. Transfer the SearPlate into Ninja Foodi Digital Air Fryer Oven and close the door.
7. Select "Bake" mode by rotating the dial.
8. Press the TIME/SLICES button and change the value to 12 minutes.
9. Press the TEMP/SHADE button and change the value to 400 °F.
10. Press Start/Stop to begin cooking.
11. Serve oven fresh.

Choco Chip Bars

Servings: 12
Cooking Time: 30 Minutes
Ingredients:

- 2 eggs, lightly beaten
- 1 1/2 cups chocolate chips
- 1/2 tsp baking soda
- 1 1/2 cup all-purpose flour
- 1 tsp vanilla
- 1/2 cup sugar
- 1/2 cup brown sugar
- 1 stick butter

Directions:

1. In a large bowl, beat butter with sugar, vanilla, and brown sugar until fluffy.
2. Add eggs and vanilla and beat well.
3. Mix together flour and baking soda and add into the egg mixture and mix until just combined. Add 1 cup chocolate chips and fold well.
4. Pour batter into the greased baking dish. Sprinkle remaining chocolate chips on top.
5. Select bake mode then set the temperature to 350 °F and time for 30 minutes. Press start.

6. Once the Ninja Foodi Digital Air Fryer Oven is preheated then place the baking dish into the oven.
7. Slice and serve.

Blueberry Hand Pies

Servings: 8
Cooking Time: 20 Minutes
Ingredients:

- 1 cup blueberries
- 2½ tablespoons caster sugar
- 1 teaspoon lemon juice
- 1 pinch salt
- 320g refrigerated pie crust
- Water

Directions:

1. Combine the blueberries, sugar, lemon juice, and salt in a medium mixing bowl.
2. Roll out the piecrusts and cut out 6-8 separate circles.
3. In the center of each circle, place roughly 1 spoonful of the blueberry filling.
4. Wet the edges of the dough and fold it over the filling to create a half-moon shape.
5. Gently crimp the piecrust's edges together with a fork. Then, on the top of the hand pies, cut three slits.
6. Spray cooking oil over the hand pies.
7. Place them onto the SearPlate.
8. Turn on Ninja Foodi Digital Air Fryer Oven and rotate the knob to select "Bake".
9. Select the timer for 20 minutes and the temperature for 350 °F.
10. When the unit beeps to signify it has preheated, open the oven door and insert the SearPlate in the oven.
11. Allow cooling for two minutes before serving.

Tasty Banana Brownies

Servings: 12
Cooking Time: 20 Minutes
Ingredients:

- 1 egg
- 1 cup all-purpose flour
- 4 oz white chocolate chips
- 1/4 cup butter
- 1 tsp vanilla
- 1/2 cup sugar
- 2 bananas, mashed
- 1/4 tsp salt

Directions:

1. Add chocolate chips and butter into the microwave-safe bowl and microwave for 30 seconds or until chocolate melted.
2. In a bowl, whisk egg, vanilla, sugar, and salt.
3. Add bananas, flour, and melted choco butter mixture and mix until well combined.
4. Pour batter into the greased baking dish.
5. Select bake mode then set the temperature to 350 °F and time for 20 minutes. Press start.

6. Once the Ninja Foodi Digital Air Fryer Oven is preheated then place the baking dish into the oven.
7. Slice and serve.

Vanilla Cupcake

Servings: 12
Cooking Time: 20 Minutes
Ingredients:
- 3 eggs
- ½ cup butter
- ¼ cup milk
- 1 teaspoon vanilla
- 2/ 3 cup sugar
- 1 ½ teaspoon baking powder
- 1 ½ cups all-purpose flour
- ¼ teaspoon salt

Directions:
1. Line the muffin pan with cupcake liners and set it aside.
2. In a bowl, mix flour, salt, and baking powder and set aside.
3. In a separate bowl, beat the sugar and butter until fluffy. Add eggs one by one and beat until well combined.
4. Add flour mixture and beat until well combined. Add milk, vanilla, and remaining flour mixture and beat until fully incorporated.
5. Pour mixture into the prepared muffin pan. Place the wire rack inside.
6. Select "BAKE" mode, set the temperature to 350 °F, and set time to 20 minutes.
7. Press "START/PAUSE" to begin preheating.
8. Once the Ninja Foodi Digital Air Fryer Oven is preheated, place the muffin pan on the wire rack and close the oven door to start cooking. Cook for 20 minutes.
9. Serve and enjoy.

Brownie Bars

Servings: 8
Cooking Time: 28 Minutes.
Ingredients:
Brownie:
- ½ cup butter, cubed
- 1 ounce unsweetened chocolate
- 2 large eggs, beaten
- 1 teaspoon vanilla extract
- 1 cup sugar
- 1 cup all-purpose flour
- 1 teaspoon baking powder
- 1 cup walnuts, chopped
Filling:
- 6 ounces cream cheese softened
- ½ cup sugar
- ¼ cup butter, softened
- 2 tablespoons all-purpose flour
- 1 large egg, beaten
- ½ teaspoon vanilla extract

Topping:
- 1 cup chocolate chips
- 1 cup walnuts, chopped
- 2 cups mini marshmallows
Frosting:
- ¼ cup butter
- ¼ cup milk
- 2 ounces cream cheese
- 1 ounce unsweetened chocolate
- 3 cups confectioners' sugar
- 1 teaspoon vanilla extract

Directions:
1. In a small bowl, add and whisk all the ingredients for filling until smooth.
2. Melt butter with chocolate in a large saucepan over medium heat.
3. Mix well, then remove the melted chocolate from the heat.
4. Now stir in vanilla, eggs, baking powder, flour, sugar, and nuts then mix well.
5. Spread this chocolate batter in the SearPlate.
6. Drizzle nuts, marshmallows, and chocolate chips over the batter.
7. Transfer the SearPlate to Ninja Foodi Digital Air Fryer Oven and close the door.
8. Select "Air Fry" mode by rotating the dial.
9. Press the TIME/SLICES button and change the value to 28 minutes.
10. Press the TEMP/SHADE button and change the value to 350 °F.
11. Press Start/Stop to begin cooking.
12. Meanwhile, prepare the frosting by heating butter with cream cheese, chocolate and milk in a suitable saucepan over medium heat.
13. Mix well, then remove it from the heat.
14. Stir in vanilla and sugar, then mix well.
15. Pour this frosting over the brownie.
16. Allow the brownie to cool then slice into bars.
17. Serve.

Blueberry Muffins

Servings: 6
Cooking Time: 12 Minutes
Ingredients:
- 1 egg, beaten
- 1 ripe banana, peeled and mashed
- 1¼ cups almond flour
- 2 tablespoons granulated sugar
- ½ teaspoon baking powder
- 1 tablespoon coconut oil, melted
- ⅛ cup maple syrup
- 1 teaspoon apple cider vinegar
- 1 teaspoon vanilla extract
- 1 teaspoon lemon zest, grated
- Pinch of ground cinnamon

125

- ½ cup fresh blueberries

Directions:

1. In a large bowl, add all the ingredients except for blueberries and mix until well combined.

2. Gently fold in the blueberries.

3. Grease a 6-cup muffin pan.

4. Place the mixture into prepared muffin cups about ¾ full.

5. Press AIR OVEN MODE button of Ninja Foodi Digital Air Fryer Oven and turn the dial to select "Bake" mode.

6. Press TIME/SLICES button and again turn the dial to set the cooking time to 12 minutes.

7. Now push TEMP/SHADE button and rotate the dial to set the temperature at 375 °F.

8. Press "Start/Stop" button to start.

9. When the unit beeps to show that it is preheated, open the oven door.

10. Arrange the muffin pan over the wire rack and insert in the oven.

11. When cooking time is completed, open the oven door and place the muffin molds onto a wire rack to cool for about 10 minutes.

12. Carefully invert the muffins onto the wire rack to completely cool before serving.

Chocolate Bites

Servings: 8
Cooking Time: 13 Minutes

Ingredients:

- 2 cups plain flour
- 2 tablespoons cocoa powder
- ½ cup icing sugar
- Pinch of ground cinnamon
- 1 teaspoon vanilla extract
- ¾ cup chilled butter
- ¼ cup chocolate, chopped into 8 chunks

Directions:

1. In a bowl, mix together the flour, icing sugar, cocoa powder, cinnamon and vanilla extract.

2. With a pastry cutter, cut the butter and mix till a smooth dough forms.

3. Divide the dough into 8 equal-sized balls.

4. Press 1 chocolate chunk in the center of each ball and cover with the dough completely.

5. Place the balls into the SearPlate.

6. Press AIR OVEN MODE button of Ninja Foodi Digital Air Fryer Oven and turn the dial to select the "Air Fry" mode.

7. Press TIME/SLICES button and again turn the dial to set the cooking time to 8 minutes.

8. Now push TEMP/SHADE button and rotate the dial to set the temperature at 355 °F.

9. Press "Start/Stop" button to start.

10. When the unit beeps to show that it is preheated, open the oven door.

11. Insert the SearPlate in the oven.

12. After 8 minutes of cooking, set the temperature at 320 °F for 5 minutes.

13. When cooking time is completed, open the oven door and place the SearPlate onto the wire rack to cool completely before serving.

Peanut Brittle Bars

Servings: 6
Cooking Time: 28 Minutes.

Ingredients:

- 1-½ cups all-purpose flour
- ½ cup whole wheat flour
- 1 cup packed brown sugar
- 1 teaspoon baking soda
- ¼ teaspoon salt
- 1 cup butter
- Topping
- 1 cup milk chocolate chips
- 2 cups salted peanuts
- 12 ¼ ounces caramel ice cream topping
- 3 tablespoons all-purpose flour

Directions:

1. Mix flours with salt, baking soda, and brown sugar in a large bowl.

2. Spread the batter in a greased SearPlate.

3. Transfer the SearPlate to Ninja Foodi Digital Air Frye Oven and close the door.

4. Select "Bake" mode by rotating the dial.

5. Press the TIME/SLICES button and change the value t 12 minutes.

6. Press the TEMP/SHADE button and change the value t 350 °F.

7. Press Start/Stop to begin cooking.

8. Spread chocolate chips and peanuts on top.

9. Mix flour with caramels topping in a bowl and sprea on top.

10. Bake again for 16 minutes.

11. Serve.

Chocolate Mousse

Servings: 4
Cooking Time: 20 Minutes

Ingredients:

- ½ cup water
- ⅓ cup Dutch process cocoa
- 1 teaspoon instant espresso granules
- 4 ounces bittersweet chocolate, chopped
- 1 ounce unsweetened chocolate, chopped
- 1 tablespoon brandy
- ½ teaspoon vanilla extract
- 2 eggs
- 2 egg whites
- ⅓ cup sugar
- Dash of salt
- 1 ½ cups whipped topping

Directions:
1. Boil ½ cup water in a saucepan then stir in cocoa, espresso, chocolate and remove from the heat.
2. Mix well until chocolate is melted then whisk in brandy, vanilla, sugar and salt.
3. Beat eggs and fold in the mousse batter.
4. Separately beat egg whites in a bowl until foamy.
5. Add egg whites to the chocolate mousse and mix evenly.
6. Pour this mousse batter into 4 ramekins.
7. Put the ramekins in the Ninja Foodi Digital Air Fryer Oven.
8. Set the "BAKE" mode using the dial.
9. Press the Temp button and use the dial to 350 °F.
10. Press the Time button and use the dial to 15-20 minutes.
11. Allow the mousse to cool then garnish with whipped topping.
12. Serve.

Cherry Jam Tarts

Servings: 6
Cooking Time: 40 Minutes.
Ingredients:
- 2 sheets shortcrust pastry
For the frangipane:
- 4 ounces butter softened
- 4 ounces golden caster sugar
- 1 egg
- 1 tablespoon plain flour
- 4 ounces ground almonds
- 3 ounces cherry jam
For the icing:
- 1 cup icing sugar
- 12 glacé cherries
Directions:
1. Grease the 12 cups of the muffin tray with butter.
2. Roll the puff pastry into a 10 cm sheet, then cut 12 rounds out of it.
3. Place these rounds into each muffin cup and press them into these cups.
4. Transfer the muffin tray to the refrigerator and leave it for 20 minutes.
5. Add dried beans or pulses into each tart crust to add weight.
6. Transfer the muffin tray on wire rack in Ninja Foodi Digital Air Fryer Oven and close the door.
7. Select "Bake" mode by rotating the dial.
8. Press the TIME/SLICES button and change the value to 10 minutes.
9. Press the TEMP/SHADE button and change the value to 350 °F.
10. Press Start/Stop to begin cooking.
11. Now remove the dried beans from the crust and bake again for 10 minutes in Ninja Foodi Digital Air Fryer Oven.
12. Meanwhile, prepare the filling beat, beat butter with sugar and egg until fluffy.
13. Stir in flour and almonds ground, then mix well.

14. Divide this filling in the baked crusts and top them with a tablespoon of cherry jam.
15. Now again, place the muffin tray in Ninja Foodi Digital Air Fryer Oven.
16. Continue cooking on the "Bake" mode for 20 minutes at 350 °F.
17. Whisk the icing sugar with 2 tablespoons water and top the baked tarts with sugar mixture.
18. Serve.

Broiled Bananas With Cream

Servings: 3
Cooking Time: 10 Minutes
Ingredients:
- 3 large bananas, ripe
- 2 tablespoons dark brown sugar
- ⅔ cup heavy cream
- 1 pinch flaky salt
Directions:
1. Slice the bananas thickly.
2. Arrange in the SearPlate, gently overlapping.
3. Sprinkle the brown sugar evenly on top, followed by the cream and then the salt.
4. Turn on Ninja Foodi Digital Air Fryer Oven and rotate the knob to select "Broil".
5. Select the unit for 7 minutes at high.
6. When the unit beeps to signify it has preheated, open the oven door and insert the SearPlate.
7. Close the oven and cook until the cream has thickened, browned, and become spotty.
8. Allow cooling for two minutes before serving.

Chocolate Chip Cookies

Servings: 4
Cooking Time: 45 Minutes
Ingredients:
- ½ cup butter, melted
- ¼ cup packed brown sugar
- ¼ cup granulated sugar
- 1 large egg
- 1 teaspoon pure vanilla extract
- 1½ cups all-purpose flour
- ½ teaspoon baking soda
- ½ teaspoon kosher salt
- ½ teaspoon chocolate chips
Directions:
1. Whisk together melted butter and sugars in a medium mixing bowl. Whisk in the egg and vanilla extract until fully combined.
2. Combine the flour, baking soda, and salt.
3. Scoop dough onto the SearPlate with a large cookie scoop, leaving 2 inches between each cookie, and press to flatten slightly.
4. Turn on Ninja Foodi Digital Air Fryer Oven and rotate the knob to select "Air Fry".

5. Select the timer for 8 minutes and the temperature for 350 °F.

6. When the unit beeps to signify it has preheated, open the oven door and insert the SearPlate in the oven.

7. Allow cooling for two minutes before serving.

Chocolate Cake

Servings: 4
Cooking Time: 10 Minutes
Ingredients:
- 3 ½ oz butter, melted
- 3 ½ tablespoon sugar
- 1 ½ tablespoon self-rising flour
- 3 ½ oz dark chocolate, melted
- 2 eggs

Directions:
1. Grease 4 ramekins with butter.
2. Preheat Ninja Foodi Digital Air Fryer Oven on "BAKE" function at 375 °F.
3. Beat the eggs and sugar until frothy.
4. Stir in butter and chocolate; gently fold in the flour. Divide the mixture between the ramekins and bake for 10 minutes.
5. Let cool for 2 minutes before turning the cakes upside down onto serving plates.

Roasted Bananas

Servings: 1
Cooking Time: 7 Minutes
Ingredients:
- 1 banana, sliced
- Avocado oil for cooking spray

Directions:
1. Using parchment paper, line the air fry basket.
2. Place banana slices in the air fry basket, making sure they do not touch.
3. Mist banana slices with avocado oil.
4. Turn on Ninja Foodi Digital Air Fryer Oven and rotate the knob to select "Air Roast".
5. Select the timer for 5 minutes and the temperature for 370 °F.
6. Remove the banana slices from the basket and carefully flip them.
7. Cook for another 3 minutes, or until the banana slices are browning and caramelized. Remove from the basket with care.
8. Allow cooling for two minutes before serving.

Pineapple Cake

Servings: 9
Cooking Time: 40 Minutes
Ingredients:
- 1 egg
- 10 oz can crushed pineapple
- 1/2 tsp vanilla
- 1/2 tsp baking soda

- 1 cup of sugar
- 1 cup all-purpose flour
- Pinch of salt

Directions:
1. In a bowl, mix together egg, crushed pineapple, vanilla, baking soda, sugar, flour, and salt until well combined.
2. Pour batter into the greased baking pan.
3. Select bake mode then set the temperature to 350 °F and time for 40 minutes. Press start.
4. Once the Ninja Foodi Digital Air Fryer Oven is preheated then place the baking dish into the oven.
5. Slice and serve.

Cherry Clafoutis

Servings: 4
Cooking Time: 25 Minutes
Ingredients:
- 1½ cups fresh cherries, pitted
- 3 tablespoons vodka
- ¼ cup flour
- 2 tablespoons sugar
- Pinch of salt
- ½ cup sour cream
- 1 egg
- 1 tablespoon butter
- ¼ cup powdered sugar

Directions:
1. In a bowl, mix together the cherries and vodka.
2. In another bowl, mix together the flour, sugar, and salt.
3. Add the sour cream, and egg and mix until a smooth dough forms.
4. Grease a cake pan.
5. Place flour mixture evenly into the prepared cake pan.
6. Spread cherry mixture over the dough.
7. Place butter on top in the form of dots.
8. Press AIR OVEN MODE button of Ninja Foodi Digital Air Fryer Oven and turn the dial to select "Air Fry" mode.
9. Press TIME/SLICES button and again turn the dial set the cooking time to 25 minutes.
10. Now push TEMP/SHADE button and rotate the dial set the temperature at 355 °F.
11. Press "Start/Stop" button to start.
12. When the unit beeps to show that it is preheated, open the oven door.
13. Arrange the pan on wire rack and insert in the oven.
14. When cooking time is completed, open the oven door and place the pan onto a wire rack to cool for about 10-1 minutes before serving.
15. Now, invert the Clafoutis onto a platter and sprink with powdered sugar.
16. Cut the Clafoutis into desired sized slices and ser warm.

Walnut Brownies

Servings: 4
Cooking Time: 22 Minutes
Ingredients:
- ½ cup chocolate, roughly chopped
- ⅓ cup butter
- 5 tablespoons sugar
- 1 egg, beaten
- 1 teaspoon vanilla extract
- Pinch of salt
- 5 tablespoons self-rising flour
- ¼ cup walnuts, chopped

Directions:
1. In a microwave-safe bowl, add the chocolate and butter. Microwave on high heat for about 2 minutes, stirring after every 30 seconds.
2. Remove from microwave and set aside to cool.
3. In another bowl, add the sugar, egg, vanilla extract, and salt and whisk until creamy and light.
4. Add the chocolate mixture and whisk until well combined.
5. Add the flour, and walnuts and mix until well combined.
6. Line the SearPlate with a greased parchment paper.
7. Place mixture into the prepared SearPlate and with the back of spatula, smooth the top surface.
8. Press AIR OVEN MODE button of Ninja Foodi Digital Air Fryer Oven and turn the dial to select "Air Fry" mode.
9. Press TIME/SLICES button and again turn the dial to set the cooking time to 20 minutes.
10. Now push TEMP/SHADE button and rotate the dial to set the temperature at 355 °F.
11. Press "Start/Stop" button to start.
12. When the unit beeps to show that it is preheated, open the oven door.
13. Insert the SearPlate in the oven.
14. When cooking time is completed, open the oven door and place the SearPlate onto a wire rack to cool completely.
15. Cut into 4 equal-sized squares and serve.

Rice Pudding

Servings: 6
Cooking Time: 15 Minutes
Ingredients:
- 1 cup of milk
- ¾ cup of Arborio rice
- ¾ cup of granulated sugar
- 1 can of unsweetened full-fat coconut oil
- 1 cup of water
- ½ teaspoon of vanilla extract

Directions:
1. Rinse the rice well
2. Put the rice in the Air Crisp pan; add water, milk, vanilla, coconut milk.
3. Place the pan in the Ninja Foodi Digital Air Fryer Oven
4. Set the "AIR FRY "mode

5. Cook for 15 minutes at 400 °F
6. Serve immediately

Nutella Banana Muffins

Servings: 12
Cooking Time: 25 Minutes
Ingredients:
- 1⅔ cups plain flour
- 1 teaspoon baking soda
- 1 teaspoon baking powder
- 1 teaspoon ground cinnamon
- ¼ teaspoon salt
- 4 ripe bananas, peeled and mashed
- 2 eggs
- ½ cup brown sugar
- 1 teaspoon vanilla essence
- 3 tablespoons milk
- 1 tablespoon Nutella
- ¼ cup walnuts

Directions:
1. Grease 12 muffin molds. Set aside.
2. In a large bowl, put together the flour, baking soda, baking powder, cinnamon, and salt.
3. In another bowl, mix together the remaining ingredients except walnuts.
4. Add the banana mixture into flour mixture and mix until just combined.
5. Fold in the walnuts.
6. Place the mixture into the prepared muffin molds.
7. Press AIR OVEN MODE button of Ninja Foodi Digital Air Fryer Oven and turn the dial to select "Air Fry" mode.
8. Press TIME/SLICES button and again turn the dial to set the cooking time to 25 minutes.
9. Now push TEMP/SHADE button and rotate the dial to set the temperature at 250 °F.
10. Press "Start/Stop" button to start.
11. When the unit beeps to show that it is preheated, open the oven door.
12. Arrange the muffin molds on wire rack and insert in the oven.
13. When cooking time is completed, open the oven door and place the muffin molds on a wire rack to cool for about 10 minutes.
14. Carefully, invert the muffins onto the wire rack to completely cool before serving.

Creamy Lime Mousse

Servings: 2
Cooking Time: 12 Minutes
Ingredients:
For Mousse:
- 4 pounces cream cheese, softened
- ½ cup heavy cream
- 2 tablespoons fresh lime juice
- 2 tablespoons maple syrup
- A Pinch of salt

For Topping:
- 2 tablespoons heavy whipping cream

Directions:
1. In a bowl, add all the ingredients and mix until well combined.
2. Transfer the mixture into 2 ramekins.
3. Select "BAKE" mode and the cooking time to 12 minutes.
4. Set the temperature at 350 °F.
5. Press the "START/PAUSE" button to start.
6. Arrange the ramekins over the wire rack and insert them in the oven. When the unit beeps to show that cooking time is completed, press the "Power" button to stop cooking and open the door.
7. Remove from oven and set the ramekins aside to cool.
8. Refrigerate the ramekins for at least 3 hours before serving.

Nutella Banana Pastries

Servings: 4
Cooking Time: 12 Minutes
Ingredients:
- 1 puff pastry sheet
- ½ cup Nutella
- 2 bananas, peeled and sliced

Directions:
1. Cut the pastry sheet into 4 equal-sized squares.
2. Spread the Nutella on each square of pastry evenly.
3. Divide the banana slices over Nutella.
4. Fold each square into a triangle and with wet fingers, slightly press the edges.
5. Then with a fork, press the edges firmly.
6. Press AIR OVEN MODE button of Ninja Foodi Digital Air Fryer Oven and turn the dial to select "Air Fry" mode.
7. Press TIME/SLICES button and again turn the dial to set the cooking time to 12 minutes.
8. Now push TEMP/SHADE button and rotate the dial to set the temperature at 375 °F.
9. Press "Start/Stop" button to start.
10. When the unit beeps to show that it is preheated, open the oven door.
11. Arrange the pastries into the greased air fry basket and insert in the oven.
12. When cooking time is completed, open the oven door and serve warm.

Chocolate Muffins

Servings: 9
Cooking Time: 20 Minutes
Ingredients:
- 1 egg
- 1 tsp baking soda
- 1/2 cup cocoa powder
- 1 cup of chocolate chips
- 1 cup of sugar
- 2 cups all-purpose flour

- 1/2 cup olive oil
- 1 tsp vanilla
- 1/2 cup milk
- 1 cup Greek yogurt

Directions:
1. In a large bowl, mix flour, baking soda, cocoa powder, chocolate chips, and sugar.
2. In a mixing bowl, whisk the egg with oil, vanilla, milk, and yogurt. Add flour and mix until well combined.
3. Pour batter into the greased muffin pan.
4. Select bake mode then set the temperature to 400 °F and time for 20 minutes. Press start.
5. Once the Ninja Foodi Digital Air Fryer Oven is preheated then place the muffin pan into the oven.
6. Serve and enjoy.

Plum Crisp

Servings: 2
Cooking Time: 40 Minutes
Ingredients:
- 1 ½ cups plums, pitted and sliced
- ¼ cup sugar, divided
- 1 ½ teaspoons cornstarch
- 3 tablespoons flour
- ¼ teaspoon ground cinnamon
- Pinch of salt
- 1 ½ tablespoon cold butter, chopped
- 3 tablespoons rolled oats

Directions:
1. In a bowl, place plum slices, 1 teaspoon of sugar, and cornstarch and toss to coat well.
2. Divide the plum mixture into lightly greased 2 ramekins. In a bowl, mix the flour, remaining sugar, cinnamon, and salt.
3. With a pastry blender, cut in bitterer until a crumbly mixture form. Add the oats and gently stir to combine.
4. Place the oat mixture over plum slices into each ramekin.
5. Select "BAKE" mode and the cooking time to 40 minutes.
6. Set the temperature at 350 °F. Press the "START/PAUSE" button to start.
7. Arrange the ramekins over the wire rack and insert them in the oven.
8. When the unit beeps to show that cooking time is completed, press the "Power" button to stop cooking and open the door.
9. Remove from Ninja Foodi Digital Air Fryer Oven and place the ramekins onto a wire rack to cool for about 10 minutes.
10. Serve warm.

Raisin Bread Pudding

Servings: 3
Cooking Time: 12 Minutes
Ingredients:
- 1 cup milk
- 1 egg
- 1 tablespoon brown sugar
- ½ teaspoon ground cinnamon
- ¼ teaspoon vanilla extract
- 2 tablespoons raisins, soaked in hot water for 15 minutes
- 2 bread slices, cut into small cubes
- 1 tablespoon sugar

Directions:
1. In a bowl, mix together the milk, egg, brown sugar, cinnamon, and vanilla extract.
2. Stir in the raisins.
3. In the SearPlate, spread the bread cubes and top evenly with the milk mixture.
4. Refrigerate for about 15-20 minutes.
5. Press AIR OVEN MODE button of Ninja Foodi Digital Air Fryer Oven and turn the dial to select "Air Fry" mode.
6. Press TIME/SLICES button and again turn the dial to set the cooking time to 12 minutes.
7. Now push TEMP/SHADE button and rotate the dial to set the temperature at 375 °F.
8. Press "Start/Stop" button to start.
9. When the unit beeps to show that it is preheated, open the oven door.
10. Insert the SearPlate in the oven.
11. When cooking time is completed, open the oven door and place the SearPlate aside to cool slightly.
12. Serve warm.

Easy Peach Cobbler

Servings: 8
Cooking Time: 50 Minutes
Ingredients:
- 1/2 cup butter, melted
- 30 oz can peaches, sliced with syrup
- 15 oz yellow cake mix

Directions:
1. Add half cake mix into the greased baking dish.
2. Pour peaches over cake mix and stir gently.
3. Sprinkle the remaining cake mix on top of peaches and stir gently again. Drizzle with melted butter.
4. Select bake mode then set the temperature to 350 °F and time for 50 minutes. Press start.
5. Once the Ninja Foodi Digital Air Fryer Oven is preheated then place the baking dish into the oven.
6. Serve and enjoy.

Nutella Brownies

Servings: 6
Cooking Time: 30 Minutes
Ingredients:
- 2 eggs
- 1/2 cup all-purpose flour
- 1 1/4 cup Nutella
- 1/4 cup cashews, chopped

Directions:
1. In a bowl, mix together eggs, flour, and Nutella until just combined.
2. Pour mixture into the greased baking pan and spread evenly. Sprinkle chopped cashews on top.
3. Select bake mode then set the temperature to 350 °F and time for 30 minutes. Press start.
4. Once the Ninja Foodi Digital Air Fryer Oven is preheated then place the baking dish into the oven.
5. Slice and serve.

Cranberry-apple Pie

Servings: 8
Cooking Time: 45 Minutes.
Ingredients:
- 2 ½ cups all-purpose flour
- 1 tablespoon sugar
- ¾ teaspoon salt
- ½ cup cold unsalted butter, cubed
- ⅓ cup cold shortening
- 7 tablespoons ice water

Filling:
- ½ cup dried currants or raisins
- 2 tablespoons dark rum
- 1 cup fresh cranberries, divided
- ¾ cup sugar, divided
- 6 baking apples, peeled and cut into slices
- 2 tablespoons tapioca
- 1 tablespoon lemon juice
- 2 teaspoons grated lemon zest
- ½ teaspoon ground cinnamon
- Egg Wash
- 2 teaspoons sugar
- Dash ground cinnamon
- 1 large egg
- 1 tablespoon milk

Directions:
1. Mix flour with butter, salt, and sugar in a bowl.
2. Stir in water and mix well until smooth.
3. Divide the prepared dough into two halves and spread each into a ⅛-inch-thick round.
4. Blend cranberries with sugar in a food processor.
5. Transfer to a bowl and stir in remaining filling ingredients.
6. Spread one dough round on the SearPlate.
7. Spread the prepared filling in the crust.
8. Slice the other dough round into strips and make a crisscross pattern on top.
9. Brush the pie with egg and milk mixture, then drizzle sugar and cinnamon top.

10. Transfer the SearPlate into Ninja Foodi Digital Air Fryer Oven and close the door.
11. Select "Bake" mode by rotating the dial.
12. Press the TIME/SLICES button and change the value to 45 minutes.
13. Press the TEMP/SHADE button and change the value to 325 °F.
14. Press Start/Stop to begin cooking.
15. Cool on a wire rack for 30 minutes.
16. Serve.

Cannoli

Servings: 4
Cooking Time: 12 Minutes.
Ingredients:
Filling:
- 1 container ricotta
- ½ cup mascarpone cheese
- ½ cup powdered sugar, divided
- ¾ cup heavy cream
- 1 teaspoon vanilla extract
- 1 teaspoon orange zest
- ¼ teaspoon kosher salt
- ½ cup mini chocolate chips, for garnish
Shells:
- 2 cups all-purpose flour
- ¼ cup granulated sugar
- 1 teaspoon kosher salt
- ½ teaspoon cinnamon
- 4 tablespoons cold butter, cut into cubes
- 6 tablespoons white wine
- 1 large egg
- 1 egg white for brushing
- Vegetable oil for frying
Directions:
1. For the filling, beat all the ingredients in a mixer and fold in whipped cream.
2. Cover and refrigerate this filling for 1 hour.
3. Mix all the shell ingredients in a bowl until smooth.
4. Cover this dough and refrigerate for 1 hour.
5. Roll the prepared dough into a ⅛-inch-thick sheet.
6. Cut 4 small circles out of the prepared dough and wrap it around the cannoli molds.
7. Brush the prepared dough with egg whites to seal the edges.
8. Place the shells in the air fry basket.
9. Transfer the basket to Ninja Foodi Digital Air Fryer Oven and close the door.
10. Select "Air Fry" mode by rotating the dial.
11. Press the TIME/SLICES button and change the value to 12 minutes.
12. Press the TEMP/SHADE button and change the value to 350 °F.
13. Press Start/Stop to begin cooking.

14. Place filling in a pastry bag fitted with an open star tip. Pipe filling into shells, then dip ends in mini chocolate chips.
15. Transfer the prepared filling to a piping bag.
16. Pipe the filling into the cannoli shells.
17. Serve.

Caramel Apple Pie

Servings: 6
Cooking Time: 48 Minutes.
Ingredients:
Topping:
- ¼ cup all-purpose flour
- ⅓ cup packed brown sugar
- 2 tablespoons butter, softened
- ½ teaspoon ground cinnamon
Pie:
- 6 cups sliced peeled tart apples
- 1 tablespoon lemon juice
- ½ cup sugar
- 3 tablespoons all-purpose flour
- ½ teaspoon ground cinnamon
- 1 unbaked pastry shell
- 28 caramels
- 1 can evaporated milk
Directions:
1. Mix flour with cinnamon, butter, and brown sugar.
2. Spread this mixture in the SearPlate.
3. Transfer the SearPlate to Ninja Foodi Digital Air Fryer Oven and close the door.
4. Select "Bake" mode by rotating the dial.
5. Press the TIME/SLICES button and change the value to 8 minutes.
6. Press the TEMP/SHADE button and change the value to 350 °F.
7. Press Start/Stop to begin cooking.
8. Meanwhile, mix apple with lemon juice, cinnamon, flour, and sugar.
9. Spread the filling in the baked crust and return to the air fryer oven.
10. Bake again for 35 minutes in the oven.
11. Mix caramels with milk in a pan and cook until melted.
12. Spread the caramel on top of the pie and bake for minutes.
13. Serve.

Banana Pancakes Dippers

Servings: 2
Cooking Time: 15 Minutes
Ingredients:
- 1½ cups all-purpose flour
- 3 bananas, halved and sliced lengthwise
- 1 tablespoon baking powder
- 1 tablespoon packed brown sugar
- 1 teaspoon salt
- ¾ cup whole milk

- ½ cup sour cream
- 2 large eggs
- 1 teaspoon vanilla extract

Directions:

1. Combine flour, baking powder, brown sugar, and salt in bowl.
2. Mix the milk and sour cream in a separate bowl, then add the eggs one at a time. Pour in the vanilla extract.
3. Combine the wet and dry ingredients until just mixed.
4. Grease the SearPlate with cooking spray and line it with parchment paper.
5. Place bananas on SearPlate in a single layer on parchment paper after dipping them in pancake batter.
6. Turn on Ninja Foodi Digital Air Fryer Oven and rotate the knob to select "Air Roast".
7. Select the timer for 16 minutes and the temperature to 375 °F.
8. Allow cooling for two minutes before serving.

Vanilla Soufflé

Servings: 6
Cooking Time: 23 Minutes
Ingredients:

- ¼ cup butter, softened
- ¼ cup all-purpose flour
- ½ cup plus 2 tablespoons sugar, divided
- 1 cup milk
- 3 teaspoons vanilla extract, divided
- 4 egg yolks
- 5 egg whites
- 1 teaspoon cream of tartar
- 2 tablespoons powdered sugar plus extra for dusting

Directions:

1. In a bowl, add the butter, and flour and mix until a smooth paste forms.
2. In a medium pan, mix together ½ cup of sugar and milk over medium-low heat and cook for about 3 minutes or until the sugar is dissolved, stirring continuously.
3. Add the flour mixture, whisking continuously and simmer for about 3-4 minutes or until mixture becomes thick.
4. Remove from the heat and stir in 1 teaspoon of vanilla extract.
5. Set aside for about 10 minutes to cool.
6. In a bowl, add the egg yolks and 1 teaspoon of vanilla extract and mix well.
7. Add the egg yolk mixture into milk mixture and mix until well combined.
8. In another bowl, add the egg whites, cream of tartar, remaining sugar, and vanilla extract and with a wire whisk, beat until stiff peaks form.
9. Fold the egg white mixture into milk mixture.
10. Grease 6 ramekins and sprinkle each with a pinch of sugar.
11. Place mixture into the prepared ramekins and with the back of a spoon, smooth the top surface.

12. Press AIR OVEN MODE button of Ninja Foodi Digital Air Fryer Oven and turn the dial to select "Air Fry" mode.
13. Press TIME/SLICES button and again turn the dial to set the cooking time to 16 minutes.
14. Now push TEMP/SHADE button and rotate the dial to set the temperature at 330 °F.
15. Press "Start/Stop" button to start.
16. When the unit beeps to show that it is preheated, open the oven door.
17. Arrange the ramekins on wire rack and insert in the oven.
18. When cooking time is completed, open the oven door and place the ramekins onto a wire rack to cool slightly.
19. Sprinkle with the powdered sugar and serve warm.

Easy Carrot Cake

Servings: 6
Cooking Time: 20 Minutes
Ingredients:

- 1 egg
- 1 cup all-purpose flour
- 1 tsp vanilla
- 1/2 cup sugar
- 1/2 tbsp olive oil
- 1 1/2 tsp baking powder
- 1/4 tsp nutmeg
- 1 tsp cinnamon
- 3/4 cup grated carrots
- 1/4 cup applesauce
- 1/4 tsp salt

Directions:

1. Add all ingredients into the mixing bowl and mix until well combined.
2. Pour batter into the greased cake pan.
3. Select bake mode then set the temperature to 350 °F and time for 20 minutes. Press start.
4. Once the Ninja Foodi Digital Air Fryer Oven is preheated then place the cake pan into the oven.
5. Slice and serve.

Brownie Muffins

Servings: 12
Cooking Time: 10 Minutes
Ingredients:

- 1 package Betty Crocker fudge brownie mix
- ¼ cup walnuts, chopped
- 1 egg
- ⅓ cup vegetable oil
- 2 teaspoons water

Directions:

1. Grease 12 muffin molds. Set aside.
2. In a bowl, mix together all the ingredients.
3. Place the mixture into the prepared muffin molds.
4. Press AIR OVEN MODE button of Ninja Foodi Digital Air Fryer Oven and turn the dial to select "Air Fry" mode.

5. Press TIME/SLICES button and again turn the dial to set the cooking time to 10 minutes.

6. Now push TEMP/SHADE button and rotate the dial to set the temperature at 300 °F.

7. Press "Start/Stop" button to start.

8. When the unit beeps to show that it is preheated, open the oven door.

9. Arrange the muffin molds into the air fry basket and insert in the oven.

10. When cooking time is completed, open the oven door and place the muffin molds onto a wire rack to cool for about 10 minutes.

11. Carefully invert the muffins onto the wire rack to completely cool before serving.

Air Fried Doughnuts

Servings: 8
Cooking Time: 6 Minutes.

Ingredients:

- Cooking spray
- ½ cup milk
- ¼ cup/1 teaspoon granulated sugar
- 2 ¼ teaspoons active dry yeast
- 2 cups all-purpose flour
- ½ teaspoon kosher salt
- 4 tablespoons melted butter
- 1 large egg
- 1 teaspoon pure vanilla extract

Directions:

1. Warm up the milk in a suitable saucepan, then add yeast and 1 teaspoon of sugar.

2. Mix well and leave this milk for 8 minutes.

3. Add flour, salt, butter, egg, vanilla, and ¼ cup of sugar to the warm milk.

4. Mix well and knead over a floured surface until smooth.

5. Place this dough in a lightly greased bowl and brush it with cooking oil.

6. Cover the prepared dough and leave it in a warm place for 1 hour.

7. Punch the raised dough, then roll into ½-inch-thick rectangle.

8. Cut 3 circles out of this dough sheet using a biscuit cutter.

9. Now cut the rounds from the center to make a hole.

10. Place the doughnuts in the air fry basket.

11. Transfer the basket to Ninja Foodi Digital Air Fryer Oven and close the door.

12. Select "Air Fry" mode by rotating the dial.

13. Press the TIME/SLICES button and change the value to 6 minutes.

14. Press the TEMP/SHADE button and change the value to 375 °F.

15. Press Start/Stop to begin cooking.

16. Cook the doughnuts in batches to avoid overcrowding.

17. Serve fresh.

Blueberry Cobbler

Servings: 6
Cooking Time: 20 Minutes

Ingredients:

For Filling:

- 2½ cups fresh blueberries
- 1 teaspoon vanilla extract
- 1 teaspoon fresh lemon juice
- 1 cup sugar
- 1 teaspoon flour
- 1 tablespoon butter, melted

For Topping:

- 1¾ cups all-purpose flour
- 6 tablespoons sugar
- 4 teaspoons baking powder
- 1 cup milk
- 5 tablespoons butter

For Sprinkling:

- 2 teaspoons sugar
- ¼ teaspoon ground cinnamon

Directions:

1. For filling - in a bowl, add all the filling ingredients and mix until well combined.

2. For topping - in another large bowl, mix together the flour, baking powder, and sugar.

3. Add the milk and butter and mix until a crumply mixture forms.

4. For sprinkling - in a small bowl mix together the sugar and cinnamon.

5. In the bottom of the greased SearPlate, place the blueberries mixture and top with the flour mixture evenly.

6. Sprinkle the cinnamon sugar on top evenly.

7. Press AIR OVEN MODE button of Ninja Foodi Digital Air Fryer Oven and turn the dial to select "Air Fry" mode.

8. Press TIME/SLICES button and again turn the dial to set the cooking time to 20 minutes.

9. Now push TEMP/SHADE button and rotate the dial to set the temperature at 320 °F.

10. Press "Start/Stop" button to start.

11. When the unit beeps to show that it is preheated, open the oven door.

12. Insert the SearPlate in the oven.

13. When cooking time is complete, open the oven door and place the SearPlate onto a wire rack to cool for about minutes before serving.

Honeyed Banana

Servings: 2
Cooking Time: 10 Minutes
Ingredients:
- 1 ripe banana, peeled and sliced lengthwise
- ½ teaspoon fresh lemon juice
- 2 teaspoons honey
- ⅛ teaspoon ground cinnamon

Directions:
1. Coat each banana half with lemon juice.
2. Arrange the banana halves onto the greased SearPlate cut sides up.
3. Drizzle the banana halves with honey and sprinkle with cinnamon.
4. Press AIR OVEN MODE button of Ninja Foodi Digital Air Fryer Oven and turn the dial to select "Air Fry" mode.
5. Press TIME/SLICES button and again turn the dial to set the cooking time to 10 minutes.
6. Now push TEMP/SHADE button and rotate the dial to set the temperature at 350 °F.
7. Press "Start/Stop" button to start.
8. When the unit beeps to show that it is preheated, open the oven door.
9. Insert the SearPlate in oven.
10. When cooking time is completed, open the oven door and transfer the banana slices onto a platter.
11. Serve immediately.

Pineapple Crisp

Servings: 2
Cooking Time: 60 Minutes
Ingredients:
- 2 cups of pineapple rings
- 2 tablespoons of sugar, granulated
- ¼ teaspoon nutmeg
- A pinch of paprika
- Cooking Oil spray for greasing

Directions:
1. In a bowl, mix pineapples, salt, paprika, brown sugar, and nutmeg.
2. Grease the mesh basket with oil spray.
3. Put the pineapple slices in the basket. Put the basket inside the oven.
4. Set a timer to 60 minutes at 320 °F at "AIR FRY" mode.
5. Once it crisp, take out the pineapples and serve.

Cookie Cake

Servings: 2
Cooking Time: 10 Minutes
Ingredients:
- 1 stick butter, softened
- ½ cup brown sugar, packed
- ¼ cup sugar
- 1 egg
- 1 teaspoon vanilla extract
- 1½ cups all-purpose flour
- ½ teaspoon baking soda
- 1 cup semi-sweet chocolate chips

Directions:
1. Mix the cream, butter, brown sugar, and sugar in a large mixing bowl.
2. Mix in the vanilla and eggs until everything is well mixed.
3. Slowly stir in the flour, baking soda, and salt until combined, then stir in the chocolate chips.
4. Spray a 6-inch pan with oil, pour half of the batter into the pan, and press it down to evenly fill it. Refrigerate the other half for later use.
5. Place on wire rack inside the oven.
6. Turn on Ninja Foodi Digital Air Fryer Oven and rotate the knob to select "Air Fry".
7. Select the timer for 5 minutes and the temperature for 370 °F.
8. Remove it from the oven and set it aside for 5 minutes to cool.

Shortbread Fingers

Servings: 10
Cooking Time: 12 Minutes
Ingredients:
- ⅓ cup caster sugar
- 1⅔ cups plain flour
- ¾ cup butter

Directions:
1. In a large bowl, mix together the sugar and flour.
2. Add the butter and mix until a smooth dough forms.
3. Cut the dough into 10 equal-sized fingers.
4. With a fork, lightly prick the fingers.
5. Place the fingers into the lightly greased SearPlate.
6. Press AIR OVEN MODE button of Ninja Foodi Digital Air Fryer Oven and turn the dial to select "Air Fry" mode.
7. Press TIME/SLICES button and again turn the dial to set the cooking time to 12 minutes.
8. Now push TEMP/SHADE button and rotate the dial to set the temperature at 355 °F.
9. Press "Start/Stop" button to start.
10. When the unit beeps to show that it is preheated, open the oven door.
11. Insert the SearPlate in the oven.
12. When cooking time is completed, open the oven door and place the SearPlate onto a wire rack to cool for about 5-10 minutes.
13. Now, invert the shortbread fingers onto the wire rack to completely cool before serving.

Carrot Mug Cake

Servings: 1
Cooking Time: 20 Minutes
Ingredients:
- ¼ cup whole-wheat pastry flour
- 1 tablespoon coconut sugar
- ¼ teaspoon baking powder
- ⅛ teaspoon ground cinnamon
- ⅛ teaspoon ground ginger
- Pinch of ground cloves
- Pinch of ground allspice
- Pinch of salt
- 2 tablespoons plus 2 teaspoons unsweetened almond milk
- 2 tablespoons carrot, peeled and grated
- 2 tablespoons walnuts, chopped
- 1 tablespoon raisins
- 2 teaspoons applesauce

Directions:
1. In a bowl, mix together the flour, sugar, baking powder, spices and salt.
2. Add the remaining ingredients and mix until well combined.
3. Place the mixture into a lightly greased ramekin.
4. Press AIR OVEN MODE button of Ninja Foodi Digital Air Fryer Oven and turn the dial to select the "Bake" mode.
5. Press TIME/SLICES button and again turn the dial to set the cooking time to 20 minutes.
6. Now push TEMP/SHADE button and rotate the dial to set the temperature at 350 °F.
7. Press "Start/Stop" button to start.
8. When the unit beeps to show that it is preheated, open the oven door.
9. Arrange the ramekin over the wire rack and insert in the oven.
10. When cooking time is completed, open the oven door and place the ramekin onto a wire rack to cool slightly before serving.

Chocolate Soufflé

Servings: 2
Cooking Time: 16 Minutes
Ingredients:
- 3 ounces semi-sweet chocolate, chopped
- ¼ cup butter
- 2 eggs, yolks and whites separated
- 3 tablespoons sugar
- ½ teaspoon pure vanilla extract
- 2 tablespoons all-purpose flour
- 1 teaspoon powdered sugar plus extra for dusting

Directions:
1. In a microwave-safe bowl, place the butter and chocolate. Microwave on high heat for about 2 minutes or until melted completely, stirring after every 30 seconds.
2. Remove from the microwave and stir the mixture until smooth.
3. In another bowl, add the egg yolks and whisk well.
4. Add the sugar and vanilla extract and whisk well.
5. Add the chocolate mixture and mix until well combined.
6. Add the flour and mix well.
7. In a clean glass bowl, add the egg whites and whisk until soft peaks form.
8. Fold the whipped egg whites in 3 portions into the chocolate mixture.
9. Grease 2 ramekins and sprinkle each with a pinch of sugar.
10. Place mixture into the prepared ramekins and with the back of a spoon, smooth the top surface.
11. Press AIR OVEN MODE button of Ninja Foodi Digital Air Fryer Oven and turn the dial to select "Air Fry" mode.
12. Press TIME/SLICES button and again turn the dial to set the cooking time to 14 minutes.
13. Now push TEMP/SHADE button and rotate the dial to set the temperature at 330 °F.
14. Press "Start/Stop" button to start.
15. When the unit beeps to show that it is preheated, open the oven door.
16. Arrange the ramekins into the air fry basket and insert in the oven.
17. When cooking time is completed, open the oven door and place the ramekins onto a wire rack to cool slightly.
18. Sprinkle with the powdered sugar and serve warm.

Scalloped Pineapple

Servings: 6
Cooking Time: 30 Minutes
Ingredients:
- 3 eggs, lightly beaten
- 1/2 cup butter, melted
- 8 oz can pineapple, crushed
- 1 1/2 cups sugar
- 1/2 cup brown sugar
- 4 cups of bread cubes
- 1/4 cup milk

Directions:
1. In a large bowl, combine together eggs, milk, butter, brown sugar, pineapple, and sugar.
2. Add bread cubes and stir until well coated.
3. Pour mixture into the greased baking dish.
4. Select bake mode then set the temperature to 350 °F and time for 30 minutes. Press start.
5. Once the Ninja Foodi Digital Air Fryer Oven preheated then place the baking dish into the oven.
6. Serve and enjoy.

Ricotta Cake

Servings: 8
Cooking Time: 55 Minutes
Ingredients:

- 4 eggs
- 18 oz ricotta cheese
- 1 fresh lemon zest
- 2 tablespoon stevia
- 1 fresh lemon juice

Directions:

1. In a large bowl, whisk the ricotta with an electric mixer until smooth.
2. Add egg one by one and whisk well. Add lemon juice, lemon zest, and stevia and mix well. Transfer mixture into the prepared cake pan.
3. Place the wire rack inside.
4. Select "BAKE" mode, set the temperature to 350 °F, and set time to 55 minutes.
5. Press "START/PAUSE" to begin preheating. Once the Ninja Foodi Digital Air Fryer Oven is preheated, place the cake pan on a wire rack and close the oven door to start cooking. Cook for 55 minutes.
6. Place cake in the refrigerator for 1-2 hours.
7. Cut into the slices and serve.

Delicious Cashew Blondies

Servings: 16
Cooking Time: 40 Minutes
Ingredients:

- 2 eggs
- 1 1/2 cups all-purpose flour
- 1 cup cashews, roasted & chopped
- 1 tbsp vanilla
- 2 cups brown sugar
- 1 cup butter, softened
- 1 tsp baking powder
- 1 tsp salt

Directions:

1. In a bowl, mix together flour, baking powder, and salt and set aside.
2. In a separate bowl, beat butter and sugar until light. Add eggs and vanilla and beat until well combined.
3. Add flour mixture and mix well.
4. Add cashews and stir well.
5. Pour mixture into the greased baking pan.
6. Select bake mode then set the temperature to 350 °F and time for 40 minutes. Press start.
7. Once the Ninja Foodi Digital Air Fryer Oven is preheated then place the baking dish into the oven.
8. Slice and serve.

Healthy Cranberry Muffins

Servings: 6
Cooking Time: 30 Minutes
Ingredients:

- 2 eggs
- 1/4 cup Swerve
- 1 1/2 cups almond flour
- 1 tsp vanilla
- 1/4 cup sour cream
- 1/2 cup cranberries
- 1 tsp baking powder
- Pinch of salt

Directions:

1. In a bowl, beat sour cream, vanilla, and eggs.
2. Add Swerve, almond flour, baking powder, and salt and beat until smooth.
3. Add cranberries and fold well.
4. Pour batter into the greased muffin pan.
5. Select bake mode then set the temperature to 325 °F and time for 30 minutes. Press start.
6. Once the Ninja Foodi Digital Air Fryer Oven is preheated then place the muffin pan into the oven.
7. Serve and enjoy.

INDEX

Printed in Great Britain
by Amazon

78934128R00084